Also by Martin Zagler

ENDOGENOUS GROWTH, MARKET FAILURES, AND ECONOMIC POLICY

Growth and Employment in Europe

Martin Zagler
Vienna University of Economics and Business Administration
Austria

palgrave
macmillan

First published 2004 by
PALGRAVE MACMILLAN
Houndmills, Basingstoke, Hampshire RG21 6XS and
175 Fifth Avenue, New York, N.Y. 10010
Companies and representatives throughout the world

PALGRAVE MACMILLAN is the global academic imprint of the Palgrave Macmillan division of St. Martin's Press, LLC and of Palgrave Macmillan Ltd. Macmillan® is a registered trademark in the United States, United Kingdom and other countries. Palgrave is a registered trademark in the European Union and other countries.

ISBN 0–333–77761–1

This book is printed on paper suitable for recycling and made from fully managed and sustained forest sources.

A catalogue record for this book is available from the British Library.

Library of Congress Cataloging-in-Publication Data
Zagler, Martin, 1968–
Growth and employment in Europe / Martin Zagler.
p. cm.
Includes bibliographical references and index.
ISBN 0–333–77761–1 (cloth)
1. Unemployment – Europe. 2. Employment (Economic theory)
3. Europe – Economic conditions. I. Title.

HD5764.A6Z34 2004
331.12′5′094—dc22 2003065487

10 9 8 7 6 5 4 3 2 1
13 12 11 10 09 08 07 06 05 04

Printed and bound in Great Britain by
Antony Rowe Ltd, Chippenham and Eastbourne

Per nana, sempre

Contents

List of Figures and Tables

Figures

Tables

Acknowledgements

This book was initiated and completed at the Vienna University of Economics and Business Administration, and I am grateful to my home institution for the opportunity to pursue scientific work. The project has additionally benefited from two years of research at the European University Institute, Firenze, under the Jean Monnet Fellowship program and an Erwin Schrödinger grant of the Fonds zur Förderung wissenschaftlicher Forschung. Further support has come from research visits to the University College London, the European Center for Applied Social Sciences at the University of Essex and the British Library of Political and Economic Sciences at the London School of Economics and Political Sciences – the latter two under European Union grants.

A number of people deserve special mentions for their support, critical comments, suggestions, advice and guidance. These are, in alphabetical order, Steve Ambler, Giuseppe Bertola, Rene Böheim, Guy Clausse, Thomas Grandner, Harald Hagemann, Andrea Ichino, Marcel Jensen, Dale Jorgenson, Christian Keuschnigg, Julian Messina, Ulrike Mühlberger, Giuliano Mussati, Ewald Nowotny, Silvia Pasqua, Christian Ragacs, Fabio Rumler, Alfred Steinherr, Engelbert Stockhammer, Hank Thomassen, Brigitte Unger, Gianluca Violante, Klaus Vondra and Herbert Walther.

MARTIN ZAGLER

[T]he economy may be away from any full-equilibrium path for a long time. [...] The economy may eventually return to an equilibrium path, [...]: If and when it does, it will not return to the continuation of the equilibrium path it was on before it slipped of. The new equilibrium path will depend on the amount of capital accumulation that has taken place during the period of disequilibrium, and probably also on the amount of unemployment, especially long-term unemployment, that has been experienced. Even the level of technology may be different, if technological change is endogenous rather than arbitrary.

ROBERT M. SOLOW, *Growth Theory and After*, 1988, p. 312

1
Introduction and Overview

This book is not about economic growth. Nor is it about unemployment. Rather, this book investigates the interaction between changes in the level of unemployment and changes in the rate of economic growth. It asks, in both theoretical and empirical terms, whether a change in the growth rate of the economy will affect the level of unemployment which the economy experiences, and whether a decline in the level of unemployment will promote or retard the growth performance of the economy.[1] Unemployment is, first and foremost, a social issue. But it also deprives the economy of part of its resource base. If and when it does, it will also reduce potentially productivity-enhancing activities, thus reducing the engine of economic growth. The presence of unemployment will alter the motivation and incentives of economic agents in many ways. It may induce agents to work harder in order not to lose their jobs, but it is equally likely to lead to a shift away from innovative towards routine tasks, thus either increasing or reducing the level of economic growth. Furthermore, it may lead agents to revise their wage claims, thus potentially influencing the sectoral composition of the economy, which may or may not foster economic growth.

Economic growth is, by definition, an increase in the amount of economic resources available. The prospect of higher future income may induce agents to rethink their behavior in markets, and if this includes the labor market, it may also alter the level of unemployment in the economy. Economic growth is driven by structural change. Structural change implies a higher rate of job creation and job destruction, and in that respect higher rates of growth may lead to higher levels of unemployment.

Therefore, this book does not consider economic growth and unemployment to be unrelated issues, and empirical evidence suggests that this is an appropriate observation. Unemployment and economic growth are systematically negatively correlated over time and countries. However, this pattern has not evolved uniformly over time. In Europe, we can distinguish three phases. During the years of the *Wirtschaftswunder* – a period which could roughly be dated as being from 1955 to 1972 – Europe simultaneously exhibited both high rates of economic growth and low levels of unemployment. Growth stagnated in the 1970s, and at the same time unemployment rates increased dramatically – a phenomenon which became known as Eurosclerosis. Growth rates have improved since this time, but unemployment remained high during a period of jobless growth between the mid-1980s and the mid-1990s. Both the first and the second phase could easily be explained by conventional theories of the business cycle, which typically predict a negative correlation between the level of unemployment and the level of output. The period of jobless growth, however, poses an empirical puzzle. By focusing on the determinants of changes in the long-run rate of growth and changes in the equilibrium rate of unemployment, the analysis contained in this book can overcome the linear relation between the level of unemployment and the level of output.

Economic growth and unemployment have been key issues in the European policy debate in recent years. In two strategy papers, the White Paper on Growth, Competitiveness, Employment (European Commission, 1993), and the Green Paper on Innovation (European Commission, 1995), the European Union has decided to address the two issues jointly. And they have allowed action to follow their words. In the Amsterdam Special Action Programme, the European Union decided to invest ten billion euro on an initiative on Growth and Employment between 1997 and 2000. From an analysis of the strategy papers and a consideration of the specific investment plan, it is evident that this initiative was not aimed at providing a business cycle stimulus, but at changing the underlying determinants of the growth process, with a vague hope (European Commission, 1995, p. 12) of job creation.

The following section of this introduction will review the predictions of the conventional textbook model of growth and unemployment. According to this analysis, growth will ultimately be determined by technological progress, and unemployment by its natural rate, implying that there should be no correlation at all between economic growth and unemployment. As already noted above, there are many potential links between economic growth and unemployment. Some are novel, others have already been raised in the literature, and the introduction will proceed by surveying this stream of literature and setting it in relation to the subsequent analysis. The introduction will end with an overview of the book.

1.1 The orthodox view of unemployment and economic growth

Every day, some people lose their jobs, and others accept new job offers. Many economic forces can influence the process of job creation and job destruction. Amongst them, efficiency considerations may induce firms to pay wages that are above the marginal product of labor at full employment, thus leading to a lower rate of job creation. Unions with market power in the labor market may ask for higher wages, thus leading to job destruction. And we may even consider an increase in aggregate demand to foster job creation. The reason why firms refrain from the lucrative activity to replace their workforce with currently unemployed workers at lower wages is attributed to search costs. Apart from direct costs of recruitment and training, we may also think of efficiency wages as being part of the search costs. In that respect, the search theory of unemployment can be viewed as a unifying framework to think about unemployment.

The equilibrium approach to unemployment states that unemployment is at its natural rate – or in equilibrium – when the flow of people into unemployment equals the flow of people into employment (Mortensen, 1986; Pissarides, 1990). Assuming that every period a fraction δ of all employed workers E_t leave employment, and a fraction η of all unemployed U_t accept a job offer, the change in unemployment equals by definition,

$$\dot{U}_t = \delta E_t - \eta U_t. \tag{1.1}$$

As mentioned above, both the firing rate δ and the hiring rate η may depend on a number of economic factors. Apart from union wage claims and efficiency wages, they may depend on voluntary exits from the labor market because of retirement or outside job offers. The hiring rate will certainly depend on the presence of search costs. Otherwise, firms would have an incentive to hire all of the unemployed, be it only to replace existing workers at lower wages. But then, they would also wish to hire those workers who have just been laid off, to replace another share of their employed workforce, until no unemployed workers are left. Indeed, given an absence of search costs, the hiring rate would converge to infinity and the labor market would clear at the full employment level.

Note that both the hiring and firing rate may vary over the business cycle, as the number of outside job offers would increase, and the number of forced layoffs will decline. As mentioned above, our primary interests are not aspects of the business cycle, so we may ignore these issues for the ease of exposition. It is important to note, however, that the presence of constant returns to scale in production implies that neither the hiring rate nor the firing rate depend systematically on economic growth, as neither the firm size nor the firm's employment level will depend on changes in the level of output.

The flow dynamics of the labor market are defined by equation (1.1), based on two variables, the number of employed and the number of unemployed. In order to analyse whether unemployment will explode over time, decline to full employment, or converge to a positive equilibrium level, we need to reduce the number of variables in the differential equation (1.1) by introducing three definitions. First, assume that the total labor force L_t grows at a constant rate n over time. Second, the employment rate is defined as employment over the labor force, $e_t = E_t/L_t$. Third, the unemployment rate is defined as the number of unemployed divided by the total labor force, $u_t = U_t/L_t$. Dividing both sides of equation (1.1) by the number of unemployment, and making use of the above definitions, we find that the percentage change of the unemployment rate over time equals,

$$\hat{u}_t = \delta(1 - u_t)/u_t - \eta - n. \tag{1.2}$$

At very high levels of unemployment, the unemployment rate will decline. With no unemployment, however, unemployment will increase over time. The unemployment rate will not endogenously change if and only if,

$$u_t = \delta/(\delta + \eta + n) = \mu, \tag{1.3}$$

and we shall define the equilibrium rate of unemployment by μ. Note that in the absence of search costs, the hiring rate goes to infinity, implying an equilibrium unemployment rate of zero. Note also that in the absence of firing or people leaving the labor market, the unemployment rate will also be zero, as firms operating under constant returns to scale have no incentive to lay off workers, even if the economic growth rate changes over time.

The search model of the labor market presents the conventional view of the emergence of unemployment. To an even greater extent, the Solow model (1956) dominates the conventional view on the growth process of the economy. It starts out from a constant return to scale production function, which we assume to be Cobb–Douglas for convenience,

$$Y_t = (A_t E_t)^\alpha K_t^{1-\alpha}, \tag{1.4}$$

where output Y_t is produced using labor and capital inputs, E_t and K_t respectively. Technical progress A_t is labor-augmenting, and it can be shown that the share of labor in income equals α. Dividing both sides by the labor force L_t and taking time derivatives, we arrive at the growth accounting equation for per capita output,

$$\hat{y}_t = \alpha \left(a - \frac{u_t}{1-u_t} \hat{u}_t \right) + (1-\alpha)\hat{k}_t, \tag{1.5}$$

where $y_t = Y_t/L_t$, $k_t = K_t/L_t$ and the growth rate of technical progress is given by a. The growth accounting equation (1.5) states that economic growth is driven by changes in technical progress, changes in employment, evaluated at the share of labor, and changes in the capital stock per worker, evaluated at the share of capital. The growth accounting equation clearly specifies that a change in the unemployment rate may induce a change in the economic rate of growth. This is clearly the essence of many business cycle theories, and represents a version of Okun's law.[2] As noted above, the unemployment rate is constant in equilibrium (1.3), implying that the effect of unemployment on economic growth vanishes in the long run,

$$\hat{y}_t = \alpha a + (1-\alpha)\hat{k}_t, \tag{1.5'}$$

which is the conventional growth accounting equation. We already note that, just as economic growth has no implication for unemployment, unemployment does not influence the long-run rate of economic growth. As the per capita capital stock may evolve over time, equation (1.5) does not present an equilibrium growth path of the economy yet. In order to derive the equilibrium growth rate of the economy, we need to check whether the accumulation process eventually comes to a halt. For this purpose, assume that people save a constant fraction of their income, hence $S_t = sY_t$. A perfect capital market ensures that all savings get reinvested,[3] and in the absence of capital depreciation, this implies that the change in the capital stock is proportional to output. The growth rate of the capital stock then equals

$$\hat{K}_t = s(1-\mu)^\alpha (A_t L_t / K_t)^\alpha. \tag{1.6}$$

Given that both the total labor force and technical progress are determined exogenously, equation (1.6) defines a differential equation in the capital stock. We observe that the aggregate capital stock, and even the per capita capital stock k_t, will exhibit positive growth rates. However, we already realize that the capital stock will grow at a faster rate when technical progress and the labor force increase, but will grow at a slower pace when the rate of technical progress or the labor force decline. We can formalize this observation by taking second derivatives of the capital stock, or evaluating changes in the growth rate of the capital stock,

$$\hat{\hat{K}}_t = \hat{K}_t[a + n - \hat{K}_t]. \tag{1.6'}$$

If the capital stock grows less than labor supply, n, and technical progress, a, the growth rate of the capital stock will accelerate, whereas if the capital stock grows faster than $a + n$, the growth rate will decelerate. The capital stock is therefore on a balanced growth path if the growth rate of the capital stock is equal to $a + n$. Substituting these findings into the growth accounting equation (1.5′), we obtain the long-run rate of economic growth of the economy,

$$\hat{y}_t = a. \tag{1.7}$$

In the long run the per capita growth rate of the economy is determined solely by exogenous labor-augmenting technical progress.

Summarizing, we find that the conventional model of the long-run behavior of the economy states that factors which drive the growth rate leave the unemployment rate unchanged, whereas factors which influence the unemployment rate have no impact on the level of economic growth. Only in transition does the growth accounting equation (1.5) reveal a conventional negatively sloped relation between economic growth and unemployment, as shown in Figure 1.1.

1.2 Stylized facts of economic growth and unemployment

Both the stylized facts on unemployment and the stylized facts on economic growth have been studied intensively in the literature. Even common facts on growth and unemployment have received some attention. The aim of this section is to challenge the conventional model of economic growth and equilibrium unemployment with these facts. Whilst the conventional model can account for a large number of the stylized facts, it fails to account for all of them.

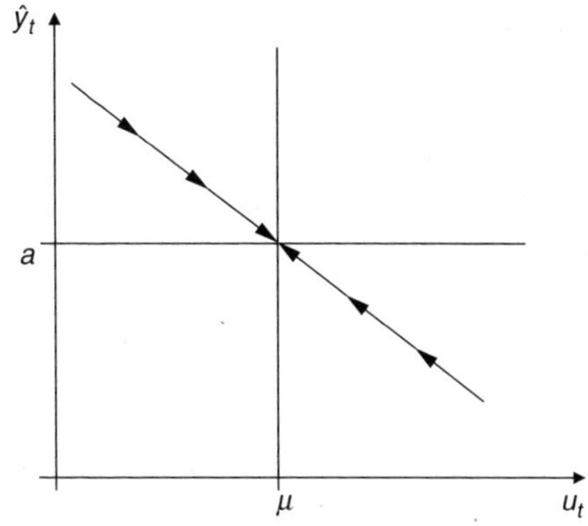

Figure 1.1 The orthodox model of equilibrium unemployment and economic growth: short-run dynamics and long-run neutrality

The stylized facts on economic growth have become known as Kaldor facts (after Kaldor, 1961), and have recently been reviewed by Barro and Sala-i-Martin (1995). The first Kaldor fact is that output per capita grows over time, and that the growth rate does not seem to diminish. The previous model also exhibits positive economic growth, with a long-run equilibrium level of a.

The second and third stylized facts state that physical capital per worker grows over time, whilst the capital to output ratio remains roughly constant. We can easily observe a positive growth rate of the per capita capital stock in the model from equation (1.6), and substituting equation (1.6) into the production function (1.4), we find that the capital to output ratio is indeed constant and equal to $s/(a+n)$.

The fourth stylized fact states that the rate of return to capital remains fairly constant over time. From the production function (1.4), we observe that the marginal product of capital is equal to $(1-\alpha)Y_t/K_t$. The expression outside the parenthesis is the inverse of the capital per output ratio, which has already been proven to be constant, hence the model can also account for this fact. Kaldor's fifth fact states that the shares of capital and labor in national income remain nearly constant. Multiplying the return to physical capital from above by the amount of physical capital and dividing by output, we find that the share of capital in output equals $(1-\alpha)$, which is constant. By the same logic, we can prove that the share of labor is α and constant as well.

Finally, Kaldor states that the growth rate of output differs substantially across countries. This point has always been the most controversial one.

While one may attribute the differences to changes along the transition path, where economic growth may exceed or fall below the rate of exogenous technical progress a, recent evidence on convergence regressions points in a different direction. Moreover, as pointed out by Romer (1994), investment into product and process innovations is positive across time, implying that the rate of technological change may be endogenous rather than exogenous. In that respect, it may also in part be private knowledge, thus explaining persistent international differences in economic rates of growth.

The stylized facts on unemployment have recently been summarized by Layard, Nickell and Jackman (1991). Their first fact on unemployment is the fact that unemployment fluctuates over both the short run and the long run. Looking at Figure 1.1, we note that any change in the fundamental determinants of unemployment – the hiring and the firing rate – changes the unemployment rate in the short run, and even changes in the equilibrium growth rate will induce medium-run changes of unemployment along the convergence path to a new equilibrium. Despite the fluctuations, they find that unemployment is untrended over the long run, which is one of the predictions of the search model, equation (1.3).

Thirdly, they find that unemployment varies much more between business cycles than it does within business cycles. In the search model, the unemployment rate is interpreted as a stock variable, which is driven by two flow variables – job creation and job destruction (1.1). In that respect, even dramatic changes in the flow variables may initially only have minor effects on the unemployment rate, but will subsequently lead to changes in equilibrium unemployment.

Fourthly, they find that the rise in European unemployment has been associated with an increase in long-term unemployment. In the orthodox model, the average duration of unemployment is equal to the inverse of the hiring rate. An increase in the average duration of unemployment therefore leads to an increase in equilibrium unemployment, which is consistent with the observed facts.

Just as is the case with economic growth, unemployment differs greatly between countries. We may continue to ascribe this fact to transitional dynamics. In the case of unemployment, however, a better alternative is available. Whilst different countries should have access to the same exogenously given technology, and hence exhibit identical growth rates, they do not necessarily have the same social institutions. As the institutional setting will certainly influence both job creation and destruction, different countries may therefore exhibit different equilibrium unemployment rates.

Finally, Layard, Nickell and Jackman find that few people deliberately choose to become unemployed. In our model, however, constant returns to scale induce firms to keep their labor force constant. Given positive search costs, this implies that firms will never wish to lay off workers, and apart from retirement all exits from the labor market would be voluntary. The model therefore needs to be adopted in one of three ways. First, firms which pay efficiency wages would need to fire shirking workers in order to induce motivation amongst their remaining workforce. Secondly, unions may demand wages above the market clearing equilibrium level, leading to layoffs. Therefore, despite the fact that we may interpret efficiency wage models and insider–outsider models as particular variants of the search model, there is good reason to study these models in detail. Thirdly, structural change may reduce demand for one firm while increasing demand for another, thus resulting in permanent hiring and firing activities. With a homogenous product as specified in the production function (1.4), structural change is ruled out by definition. Therefore, models which can account for structural change are required to explain the large amount of involuntary exits from the labor market.

Finally, we need to consider whether or not the model can account for common facts of unemployment and economic growth. The most well-known stylized fact on growth and unemployment was Okun's law. In his seminal paper, first published in 1961, Okun (1970) argued that unemployment and economic growth are negatively correlated. Recent evidence, however, suggests that whilst we can observe a negative correlation over time and countries, this correlation is far from being a stable one. Daveri and Tabellini (2000) recently found a negative correlation of 0.43 for a sample of 14 countries over the period from 1965 to 1995. However, the coefficient was very high in some cases and very low in others, and even negative for one country and one time span. When controlling for other variables, the coefficient became insignificant. The transition path of Figure 1.1 indicates a clear-cut negative correlation between unemployment and economic growth, and whilst this is consistent with this aspect of Okun's law, it is inconsistent with recent evidence on the breakdown of this correlation.

Okun's law is also very specific on the magnitude of the effect. Okun originally predicted that a one percentage point decline in unemployment would lead to a 4 per cent increase in output. More recent estimates indicate a coefficient between two and three. The model, however, predicts a coefficient equal to $u_t/(1-u_t)$. For the above parameter values, this would imply that equilibrium unemployment rates would be between 67 per cent and 80 per cent, which is certainly unrealistic.

Finally, the relation between unemployment and economic growth varies over time. We have already noted that there is more fluctuation in unemployment between business cycles than within cycles. As noted in the introductory quote from Robert Solow's Nobel Address, cycles are different from each other due to 'the amount of capital accumulation that has taken place during the period of disequilibrium, and [...] the level of technology may be different' (Solow, 1988). In short, two business cycles are distinct because of the growth process in between. And indeed, whilst the 1960s showed a negative relation between growth and unemployment, the phase of jobless growth (Caballero and Hammour, 1997; Blanchard, 1998b) clearly contradicts the notion of a stable relation. The model, however, predicts a clear relation – and that is that there is no correlation between unemployment and economic growth in the long run. To overcome this major shortcoming will be the task of the following sections. Before, we will review related literature and acknowledge advances made in this direction.

1.3 A survey of the related literature

Labor is an input in the production process, hence a change in employment will, ceteris paribus, change the level of output. This effect depends crucially on the potential that the economy has to intensify its use of resources (labor in particular). When the economy reaches its capacity frontier – or if rigidities impede full utilization of factors – this extensive growth process will cease. At this point, the performance of the economy can only be enhanced intensively through a change in the capacity frontier itself.

Labor economics has delivered a set of mutually complementary theories about why the economy would employ less resources than are available. They all agree that there is a wedge between the maximum wage paid by employers and the minimum wage accepted by workers. The most compelling are the insider–outsider hypothesis, the efficiency wage model, and the search model (Layard, Nickell and Jackman, 1991). Endogenous growth theory has delivered two hypotheses that explain changes in the capacity frontier itself. The first is based on economy-wide non-decreasing returns to reproducible factors. The second is based on a non-declining incentive to invest into innovative products and production processes, leading to a permanent positive growth rate of output, despite limited resources. Both growth models heavily depend on externalities, and it can be shown (see for instance Pelloni, 1997, or Zagler, 1995) that rigidities or externalities outside the market for goods and innovations (blueprints) can alter the growth rate in either direction. This brings us back to Solow's introductory quote, which stated that periods of unemployment can alter the growth process of the economy. But the structure of the growth process may itself change the workings of the labor market and alter employment in the economy.

1.3.1 Endogenous growth theory

Before 1986, economists considered economic growth to originate outside the economic system, resulting from research and major developments that happen in laboratories or scientific institutions, summarized by the rate of technical progress a in the model of section 1.1. Paul Romer's seminal article challenged this view. Romer found that given non-decreasing returns to scale with respect to reproducible factors of production, the capital accumulation process need not cease, hence an economy may grow without bounds (Romer, 1986).

Several authors have contributed specific examples for technologies that enable a growth process as described by Romer. The simplest version is due to Rebelo (1991), who simply postulated a production function linear in capital. Evidently, as more capital enters the production process, the marginal product of capital does not decline, and given a real rate of interest below, the economy will pursue a constant long-run growth path. The model exhibits a major shortcoming, however. In a competitive economy, the owner of the capital stock can extract all revenues from the firm (else she would rent out her capital somewhere else), hence even if labor were necessary for production purposes, workers would receive a zero wage. Hence, the model is inappropriate to discuss employment questions.

Lucas (1988) then proposed a production function with three arguments, human capital, labor, and the economy's (or at least the industry's) average stock of human capital. This technology exhibits constant returns to scale with respect to private (or firm-specific) factors of production, namely human capital and labor, and with respect to reproducible factors of production, namely human capital and the average stock of human capital. As firms have an incentive to invest in human capital, they also augment the economy wide stock of human capital, thus they induce a non-declining marginal product of human capital for any level of economic activity.

Analogous to Rebelo, given an interest rate below the marginal product of human capital, the economy may grow without bound. Similarly, Barro (1990) proposes a model where the public capital stock, as provided by government, plays the role of human capital in the Lucas model. Whilst the firm will pay both capital and labor its private marginal product, this solution is inefficient. Economywide, the technology as proposed by both Lucas and Barro reduces to the Rebelo Ak-type, where labor is socially unproductive, and hence workers should receive a zero wage. Once again, these models are still inadequate to analyze employment issues.

This evidently unpleasant characteristic of the above mentioned growth models triggered a second wave of endogenous growth models, characterized by the writings of Romer (1990), Grossman and Helpman (1991a), and Aghion and Howitt (1992). Basically, all three variants operate through the same channel. Splitting the labor force into two groups, labeled workers and innovators for convenience, one group can produce an ever-improved consumption good, whilst the other can permanently innovate new or better products or production processes, thus triggering a long-run permanent growth process.

These models differ in several respects from the first class of models. First, instead of human capital, they focus on research and development as the engine of growth. Second, instead of perfect competition, they are based on monopolistic competition, which enables providers of innovations and inventions with a possibility of receiving a rent for the research and development efforts. Third, they no longer build upon non-decreasing returns with respect to reproducible factors. Therefore, long-run growth is no longer a knife's-edge property, as argued by Solow (1994).

Empirical support for the endogenous growth theories comes from several directions. If growth is endogenous, temporary shocks to output may exhibit a permanent effect. Campbell and Mankiw (1989) propose a direct test for output persistence, and show that the US data seem to fit the endogenous growth model quite well. Ragacs and Zagler (2002) elaborate the Campbell and Mankiw test strategy to show that the evolution of Austrian GDP is best described by a monopolistic competition endogenous growth model.

Tests of the convergence hypothesis fail after the mid-1970s (Barro, 1992), indicating that different countries do not converge to the same long-run rate of economic growth, and hence that country-specific factors must influence economic performance. Given that the growth rate of output is endogenously determined within the model, there must be a nonzero set of explanatory variables significant in any growth regression. Adopting a less restrictive variant of Leamer's extreme bounds test

(Leamer, 1983), Sala-i-Martin (1997) finds that, amongst others, the investment ratio, the degree of democracy, and the 'Confucius' variable (a dummy variable for countries such as China, Singapore, Taiwan, etc.) fosters economic growth. Similarly, Zagler (2000) finds that in Austria total factor productivity, the part of growth not explained by capital deepening or higher labor participation, is driven by gross investment, the degree of openness and inversely by the average duration of unemployment.

In the second class of endogenous growth models discussed above, innovators are referred to as Schumpeterian entrepreneurs, as they derive their role through a process of creative invention or innovation. The labor market is populated by simple manual labor, which leaves little scope for the analysis of the relation between growth and employment. Indeed, additional employment would be bad for growth, because it reduces the share of innovators, and hence the rate at which additional innovations hit the economy.

The common feature of both classes of models is the necessity of externalities. Whilst human capital externalities positively influence the production and accumulation process, the negative monopolistic competition externality allows innovators to accrue rents and thus enables the growth process. Externalities, however, create a gap between private market demand and supply, and the socially optimal demand or supply. In these models, there is either social excess demand for innovation, or social excess demand for human capital. Given a Walrasian economy, the social excess demand in one market must be matched with social excess supply in yet another. In endogenous growth models, this market is typically the capital market (due to the fact that the demand for credit is derived from the decision to invest), which socially provides too little capital, in other words, private saving is too low.

Under certain circumstances, the excess supply may also appear in other markets. Zagler (1998 and 1999b) introduces market imperfections in the goods and money market, showing that the social excess demand intrinsic in endogenous growth models can be at least partially offset outside the capital market. There is virtually no reason not to apply this analysis to labor markets as well. In the case of the labor market, of course, the term excess supply is conventionally addressed as unemployment. Given plausible frictions in the labor market, which will be discussed in the following section, a (causal) relation between unemployment and growth can be established.

1.3.2 Labor market imperfections

The quantity of labor exchanged, and the price of labor (the real wage rate) are determined in the labor market. A stylized version of the labor market contains a demand schedule for labor, where the quantity of labor demanded by firms and others depends (in general) inversely on its price, and a supply schedule for labor, where workers offer their labor services according to their reservation wage.

Typically, whenever there is excess supply of labor, or unemployment, as introduced above, market forces drive the wage down until demand exactly offsets supply. A theory of persistent unemployment must therefore explain what prevents wages from falling. As Layard, Nickell and Jackman (1991) state, 'Either firms are not free to choose the wage, and wage bargaining forces them to pay more than they wish; or, if firms are free to choose and still pay more than the supply price of labor it must be in their interest to do so.'

The insider–outsider hypothesis (McDonald and Solow, 1985) basically states that a real wage above the full-employment equivalent may be actually in the interest of trade unions. Typically, a centralized union is a monopsonist supplier, whilst a decentralized union acts as an oligopsonistic supplier of labor. In either case, setting the price above its equilibrium, or full employment level, will increase the wage sum received by the entire work force, voluntarily causing unemployment. Note that the unemployed will be involuntarily unemployed, as they are willing to work for the current wage. Unless the union adheres to a Rawlsian welfare concept, valuing only its very weakest members – that is, the unemployed workers – it is in the interest of trade unions to raise wages beyond their equilibrium level and cause unemployment.

As oligopsonistic unions can raise wages less than fully centralized unions, one should observe a positive correlation between the degree of centralization and unemployment. However, Calmfors and Driffill (1988) have shown that this relation follows a hump shape, with both very decentralized and very centralized unions achieving the lowest rates of unemployment. The authors themselves suggest that one reason for the surprisingly good performance of centralized unions may be the fact that they manage to internalize macroeconomic externalities. It therefore appears empirically very promising to consider whether unions internalize the human capital or the monopolistic competition and innovation externalities discussed in the previous section of this survey.

However, if the insider–outsider hypothesis were the only explanation of persistent unemployment, firms would not be willing to pay above the negotiated wage. Voluntary overpayment of workers by firms can be motivated by efficiency wage models. Given that working provides disutility at the margin (i.e. workers may wish to work, but ceteris paribus prefer to work marginally less), firms may use high real wages to motivate workers to contribute effort, and to prevent them from shirking. The efficiency-inducing channel of high real wages may operate either through fairness considerations (Akerlof and Yellen, 1990), that is if workers are paid at least what similar workers are paid, they will be more willing not to shirk, or through monitoring costs on behalf of the firm (Shapiro and Stiglitz, 1984), that is instead of incurring high monitoring costs to induce effort, firms may simply prefer to pay workers more. Empirical support for these models comes from Flabbi and Ichino (1998).

In both cases, wages would increase without bound, creating unemployment. An increase in the unemployment rate increases the risk of an individual worker being laid off, thus potentially increasing her effort for a given wage. This second effect may become large enough to induce full effort on behalf of the workers without raising wages any more (Bowles, 1985).

1.3.3 Endogenous growth and unemployment

For a decade, labor markets have not been a major concern of endogenous growth literature. The labor market was typically assumed to be in equilibrium, with constant labor supply setting quantities and labor demand setting prices. The resulting wage, however, is not a welfare optimum, as the private marginal product differs from the social marginal product (Bertola, 1993). A more precise formulation of the labor market can therefore shed light on our understanding of the growth model.

The literature on endogenous growth and unemployment has flourished over recent years, with a rich diversity of approaches to both the sources of economic growth and the causes of unemployment. We find both equilibrium and disequilibrium approaches to explain unemployment, and both (human) capital externality as well as innovation-driven models of endogenous growth, where there is a clear bias towards the latter, despite the evidence presented in section 1.2.

Charles Bean and Christopher Pissarides (1993) were the first to introduce frictional unemployment into a very stylized endogenous growth model. They proposed a generational model with a simple Rebelo-type production function, where new members of the labor force had to be matched to a job vacancy, according to the matching approach (Pissarides, 1985). Evidently, an increase in the exogenous rate of factor productivity-fostered economic growth, but it also increased the rate of job creation, thus driving the unemployment rate down along the Beveridge curve (Beveridge, 1942). Whilst Bean and Pissarides can explain long-run youth unemployment, they fail to give theoretical foundations for intragenerational layoffs, which account for most of the current level of unemployment.

Several extensions of the Bean and Pissarides models have been suggested in the literature. Hoon (1998) was able to show that the general conclusions of Bean and Pissarides (1993) hold under less stringent assumptions of the generational setup. Both of these models share the idea that unemployment can be an impediment to economic growth, because it reduces savings and thus capital accumulation. The changes introduced by Bean and Pissarides exhibit two effects. First, the assumption of constant returns to scale with respect to reproducible factors of production, private and aggregate capital, and with respect to private factors of production, private capital and labor, implies that the capital to labor ratio remains constant for all levels of capital. Hence equation (1.6) already presents the balanced growth rate of the capital stock, altering the long-run growth rate of the economy (1.7) to $s[(1-u_t)ak]^{\alpha}$, where k now represents the constant capital to labor ratio. Clearly, the savings rate now has an impact on economic growth, and as unemployment reduces savings, unemployment exhibits a negative impact on economic growth.

Two types of deviation from the Bean and Pissarides model have been analysed in the literature. On the one hand, authors have deviated from the assumption of capital externality-driven growth models, and on the other hand, authors have introduced different assumptions on labor market frictions. We shall discuss the later deviation first.

Schaik and DeGroot (1998) present an efficiency wage model with a given number of differentiated products, in which growth is driven by human capital accumulation. Evidently, efficiency wages increase unemployment, thus causing lower rates of accumulation of human capital, and thereby reducing economic growth. Whilst efficiency wage models claim that wages are higher than the market clearing level because firms wish to set wages higher in order to promote efficiency, insider–outsider models start by claiming that unions set wages above market clearing in order to increase the welfare of their members. The simplest model of trade unions and growth has recently been presented by Daveri and Tabellini (2000), who show that in an overlapping generations model with human-capital-driven endogenous growth, union wage claims will cause higher unemployment and lower economic rates of growth. By contrast, Irmen and Wigger (2000) show that in an OLG model where only the young work and save, higher wages will foster savings, thus causing both unemployment and higher economic rates of growth.

Whilst the last two models described here fall into the broad class of human-capital-driven endogenous growth models, Palokangas (1996) and Peretto (1998) have recently suggested two innovation-driven models of unions and endogenous growth. Palokangas finds that higher wages for the unskilled lead to an increase in employment in the innovation sector, thus promoting economic growth. Peretto finds the opposite effect, because he models the labor market as homogenous. Both models have in common that they analyse the different motives of workers to work in either the innovation sector or the production sector. The direction of causality in these models is from unemployment to economic growth.

The institutional setting has always been considered to be a major impediment to full employment in Europe (Blanchard, 1998a). As institutions typically drive a wedge between labor supply and labor demand, and thus represent disequilibrium approaches to unemployment, the only type of labor market institutions which has been analysed are minimum wages. Cahuc and Michel (1996) recently introduced minimum wages into an endogenous growth model, showing that the economy may benefit from minimum wages as it forces individuals to invest more in training, thereby internalizing part of the human capital accumulation externality typical for the first wave of growth models. However, their model remains unsound, as agents fail to realize their work effort and consumption plans, but are not rational enough to realize this (Ragacs, 2000).

We have argued in the previous section that innovation-driven endogenous growth models offer the only possible explanation of the stylized fact of positive investment into the development of new products and production processes. Their scarce application in theoretical models is therefore rather surprising, given that Aghion and Howitt (1991) have already realized that the second type of endogenous growth models introduced in section 1.3.1 of this survey are indeed models of structural change as well. In that respect endogenous growth will affect unemployment in three distinct ways. First, there is the job creation effect, with new industries opening and hiring new workers. Then, there is the job destruction effect, as old firms leave the labor market. Then there is a scale effect, which is due to the fact that as the number of industries increases, firms can benefit less from scale effects, and production gets more labor-intense – a familiar phenomenon in the service sector (Aghion and Howitt, 1998).

The Aghion and Howitt model differs from other models of growth and unemployment models in two important ways. First, it claims that growth is the cause of unemployment, and not vice versa. Secondly, it claims that growth affects unemployment by changing the incentives of workers to search and accept new job offers, and by firms to post a vacancy. Hence, changes in the engine of growth will alter the equilibrium rate of unemployment.

Apart from the search model (Aghion and Howitt, 1994), no model of unemployment and economic growth adopts the empirically more sound imperfect competition models, so that we are at present far from having a consensus model of equilibrium unemployment, as requested by Solow (1988). The next section of this research proposal attempts to investigate the missing elements in the discussion of economic growth and unemployment, and to explore and specify means of filling in these gaps.

1.4 Overview of the book

This introduction has focused on elaborating the theoretical, empirical, and policy significance of the subject, reviewed the literature, presented the conventional model and then confronted it with the facts. We have seen that the conventional model does fairly well empirically, but fails to explain at least three important stylized facts of economic growth and unemployment.

The following theoretical part is divided into five chapters. They separately discuss four sources of unemployment in an innovation-driven endogenous growth framework. Chapter 2 shows that in a model with a monopolistically competitive manufacturing sector and a competitive innovation sector, which both pay efficiency wages, the equilibrium unemployment rate exhibits an unambiguously negative impact on the long-run growth performance, as it reduces the innovative capacity of the economy. The model clearly establishes this resource constraint, which generates a long-run correlation between unemployment and economic growth. In terms of Figure 1.1, it turns the $\hat{y}_t = a -$ line clockwise, thus establishing a causal relation from unemployment to economic growth. Only if efficiency considerations are different across sectors can a causal relation from the growth rate to the level of unemployment be established, since a lower level of innovation shifts the burden of inducing efficiency towards the manufacturing sector, thus fostering unemployment.

The driving force of economic growth in chapter 2 and throughout this book is structural change. In contrast to growth models that build on constant returns with respect to reproducible factors of production, structural change here implies that workers permanently leave existing jobs and search for new work. This is the very reason why this book advocates innovation-driven endogenous growth models. Unemployment in chapter 2, however, is not a result of structural change, as search is assumed to be infinitely fast, but the result of the firm's decision not to undercut current wages due to efficiency considerations.

Chapter 3 develops a model of intersectoral and intrasectoral structural change. It describes the force which induces a shift from a fordist manufacturing sector, as described by the Solow model in section 1.1 of this introduction, towards a service sector with heterogeneous products. It continues to assume frictionless search, and can therefore not account for unemployment. However, the model is capable of describing several other features of modern economies, such as the sectoral shift towards services, international differences in economic development, new forms of flexible work contracts, the emergence of innovation networks, an inflation rate below its fundamentals, and low productivity rates coupled with high rates of economic growth. Most importantly, the model finds that higher growth rates in the service sector and lower growth rates in the manufacturing sector foster structural change.

Chapter 4 then introduces search frictions similar to those introduced in the search model of section 1.1, into the structural change model of chapter 5. Unemployment will result from two factors. First, the intersectoral shift generates structural unemployment, as manufacturing workers will get laid off and only slowly find jobs in other emerging sectors. Secondly, new service innovations permanently reduce the labor demand in existing service firms. This means that employees within the service sector will experience a permanent destruction of their jobs and the creation of new jobs within the sector due to intersectoral structural change. The labor market will be more flexible, resulting in frictional unemployment. The main finding is that the level of unemployment is different between the initial period and the long-run equilibrium growth path, and that along the transition path, the level of unemployment will overshoot its equilibrium level. This could explain the long-run pattern of unemployment observed in most industrialized countries.

Chapter 4 retains the resource constraint from chapter 2, but now introduces an incentive condition, which summarizes both the workers' incentives to accept a job offer and the firms' incentives to establish a vacancy for a given level of unemployment. A change in unemployment alters the firms' decision to hire, and hence changes the rate of economic growth. The incentive condition therefore establishes a relation from unemployment to economic growth, and corresponds to a counterclockwise turn of the $u_t = \mu$ – line in Figure 1.1.

A successful search produces an economic rent, as the employer will certainly prefer to deal with the current worker rather than engaging in costly activities to search for a replacement. Chapter 4 has assumed that the division of these rents is negotiated individually. This is, however, not the case in most modern economies, where unions represent workers in wage negotiations. Chapter 5 introduces unions into the growth model, and finds that the degree of centralization of the bargaining structure plays a crucial rule for economic growth. Central bargaining, which incorporates the leapfrogging externality from firm-level bargaining, will yield lower rates of unemployment for a given rate of economic growth. The increase in labor resources will in turn also yield faster growth rates in a corporatist economy. Indeed, when unions focus on issues other than short-term wage increases, they may even outperform the non-unionized economy, as they can internalize the knowledge externality through long-term wage moderation accords.

Chapters 2 to 5 develop models of economic growth and unemployment with labor market frictions. However, unemployment is not only the consequence of rigidities in the labor market. Chapter 6 argues that in a growing economy unemployment can be the cause of goods markets failures – even if these are purely transitory. The intuition is the following. As the economy grows, new firms wish to enter product markets. It may take some time, however, until their products are accepted on the market. Firms who fail early entry will renege on the job offers, causing some unemployment. Thus, a transitory demand shock will lead to a persistent level of unemployment, which increases with the rate of economic growth.

The empirical part of this book focuses on testing the theoretical aspects of the interaction between economic growth and unemployment discussed in the theoretical section. Chapter 7 will present microeconometric evidence for the search model presented in chapter 4. There, we have established a relation between economic growth and unemployment, but have shown that it will differ across sectors and time. Applying microeconometric time series methods for panel data, we will test the relation between unemployment, structural change, and economic growth. We find that slow economic growth may indeed cause unemployment and, more importantly, that the impact of economic growth on job creation differs from the impact of destruction on economic growth, leading to technological unemployment (Hagemann, 1993).

In section 1.3.3, we demonstrated that in an endogenous growth model with search externalities, economic growth causes unemployment, while the inverse does not hold. In chapter 2, by contrast, that unemployment will cause economic growth to decline, but, opposed to all other models, denied the inverse causality. All other models in the theoretical part of this book claim a dual causality. Chapter 8 will therefore apply Granger causality tests for the four largest European countries – France, Italy, Germany and the United Kingdom – to test causal relationships between unemployment and economic growth, and will assess which model fits the data of each country best.

In the theoretical part, we have been able to summarize the evolution of the economy in two possibly dynamic equations. A resource constraint describes the evolution of output growth for a given rate of unemployment, and an incentive condition identifies the equilibrium unemployment rate – possibly as a function of output. In econometric terms, we can interpret the incentive condition as a cointegrating relationship, and then estimate the system, and in particular the dynamic adjustment path, using vector error correction methods. This will be the aim of chapter 9, once again for the four major European countries.

Finally, chapter 10 outlines a unifying framework for the analysis of economic growth and unemployment, and draws policy conclusions from both the theoretical and empirical parts of this book.

Part I

Theory

2
Efficiency Wages

This chapter establishes a theoretical relation between the level of unemployment and the economic rate of growth. It is posited that in a model with a monopolistically competitive manufacturing sector and a competitive innovation sector, both of which pay efficiency wages, the equilibrium unemployment rate – the Nawru – exhibits an unambiguously negative impact on the long-run growth performance, because it reduces the innovative capacity of the economy. Only if efficiency levels are different across sectors can a causal relation from the growth rate to the level of unemployment be established, since a lower level of innovation shifts the burden of inducing efficiency towards the manufacturing sector, thus fostering unemployment.

2.1 Motivation

This chapter investigates the common correlations and causalities between the level of unemployment and the economic growth rate. Some 30 years since Arthur Okun (1970) postulated a relation between the change in the rate of unemployment and the change in the level of output, little theoretical and empirical work on the joint determinants of the level of unemployment and the rate of growth has been published. Evidence therefore has to be collected from two distinct fields of research.

First, growth theory claims that changes in total factor productivity (TFP) are a key determinant of the level of long-run growth rate in an economy. Whether TFP is exogenous, in the sense of a Solow-residual, or endogenously determined by economic incentives to invest into human capital or research and development remains contested, but there is a great deal of evidence that changes in TFP drive the economic growth rate (e.g., Mankiw, Romer and Weil, 1992).

Second, labor market theory claims that wages are set above the marginal product of labor in order to induce efficiency, thereby creating unemployment (Akerlof and Yellen, 1990). Shapiro and Stiglitz (1984) present a dynamic efficiency model, but choose not to develop its growth implications. Wadhwani and Wall (1990) provide evidence that firms apply efficiency considerations when setting wages.

By contrast, effects from TFP on unemployment, as well as from efficiency on economic growth, are rejected within the consensus of the theoretical literature. Layard, Nickell and Jackman (1991, p. 207) argue that unless there is complete insider power, changes in TFP do not alter the real wage, hence unemployment should remain unaffected. Salter (1966) and Nickell and Kong (1988) present weak favorable evidence for this hypothesis.

Theory also suggests that the growth rate should be independent of changes in labor efficiency. This is a result of the Solow condition, which states that at the margin the cost of an additional unit of efficiency is equal to the cost of an additional unit of labor. Hence changes in efficiency would be offset by a reduction in employment, leaving output unaffected. This postulate is in stark contrast to a vast literature that comes from the field of business administration, as for instance by Caves and Barton (1990) for US manufacturing, Oum and Yu (1998) for the airline industry, and Sudit (1996) for telecommunications. These studies find that firms that adopted methods to foster efficiency would not only see their stock market value increase, but would also achieve significantly higher rates of growth.

The evidence, therefore, seems to offer some support for the idea that the level of unemployment and the rate of economic growth share a common source. Several theoretical papers have already investigated channels which may produce this result. In their seminal paper, Aghion and Howitt (1994) find that changes in the rate of growth may alter the unemployment rate. Realizing that innovation-driven growth models are models of structural change, where a proportion of the labor force has to seek new employment every period, the time-consuming search for work may cause persistent unemployment. In that respect endogenous growth will affect unemployment in three distinct ways. First, there is the job creation effect, with new industries opening and hiring new workers. Then, there is the job destruction effect, as old firms leave the labor market. Then there is an effect, which Aghion and Howitt loosely label the indirect effect. This is the result of the fact that as the number of industries increases, firms can benefit less from scale effects, and production becomes more labor-intensive.

However, the motive for searching is the possibility of finding a better-paid job at some later point in time (Pissarides, 1984, 1985, 1987). In Aghion and Howitt, all wages are identical, hence unemployment is not thoroughly argued. Schaik and de Groot (1998) use efficiency wages to motivate wage differences. However, they motivate unemployment from searching, too, therefore obtaining a result similar to Aghion and Howitt, finding that growth may cause unemployment, but not vice versa.

This chapter, which is complementary to the above, finds an inverse relation – namely that unemployment causes lower growth rates. The model economy is populated by representative households, a monopolistically competitive manufacturing sector and a perfectly competitive innovation sector. Households maximize utility, whilst firms in both sectors maximize profits. Both manufacturers and innovators pay efficiency wages, although not necessarily at the same level. Increasing internal efficiency – for instance, as a result of organizational changes, motivation, or changes in monitoring – implies less use of incentives to motivate the workforce, hence the unemployment rate may decline. This leads to lower wage premia in manufacturing, thereby reducing unemployment, reducing marginal costs in the innovation sector, and increasing profit perspectives in manufacturing, which increases marginal revenues in the innovation sector. This will lead to more intense research and development, thereby fostering the rate of growth. A reduction in the long-run rate of unemployment may therefore foster economic growth.

2.2 The household problem

The model consists of households, firms and innovators. Households maximize intertemporal lifetime utility, which under the assumption of log-linear felicity equals,

$$U_0 = \int_0^\infty e^{-\theta t} \ln c_t \, dt, \tag{2.1}$$

where c_t is consumption, and θ is the individual rate of time preference, subject to an intertemporal budget constraint, which uses the consumption good as a numeraire,

$$\dot{a}_t = r_t a_t + w_t(1 - u_t) - c_t, \tag{2.2}$$

stating that the change in wealth a_t must equal the difference between consumption, interest income $r_t a_t$, and labor income, that is wages

w_t times employment $(1 - u_t)$. It is assumed that unemployment is equally distributed across the workforce, hence we may abstract from unemployment insurance. Given that the unemployment rate is exogenous to the household decision problem, Hamiltonian optimization with respect to consumption and wealth holdings yields the Keynes–Ramsey-Rule,

$$\frac{\dot{c}_t}{c_t} = r_t - \theta. \tag{2.3}$$

Consumption is assumed to consist of a bundle of specific consumption goods $x_{i,t}$, according to the following constant elasticity of substitution felicity function,

$$c_t = \left[\int_0^{n_t} x_{i,t}^{\frac{\varepsilon-1}{\varepsilon}} \, di \right]^{\frac{\varepsilon}{\varepsilon-1}}. \tag{2.4}$$

Households maximize this felicity subject to the following budget constraint,

$$\int_0^{n_t} p_{i,t} x_{i,t} \, di \leq c_t. \tag{2.5}$$

Optimization yields the demand function for a particular consumption good,

$$x_{i,t} = p_{i,t}^{-\varepsilon} c_t, \tag{2.6}$$

where ε is the price elasticity of demand, and a definition for the aggregate price index, which reads due to the normalization,

$$\left[\int_0^{n_t} p_{i,t}^{1-\varepsilon} \, di \right]^{\frac{1}{1-\varepsilon}} = 1. \tag{2.7}$$

2.3 Manufacturing

A particular consumption good is produced by a single firm, which exercises monopoly power in this particular market. Technology is given by,

$$x_{i,t} = e_{i,t} \, l_{i,t}, \tag{2.8}$$

where $l_{i,t}$ is the labor force employed in a particular firm, and $e_{i,t}$ is the efficiency of this workforce. Assume, in accordance with Akerlof and

Yellen (1990), that both an increase in wages relative to those paid by other firms, $w_{i,t}/w_t$, and an increase in the unemployment rate u_t increase efficiency in the following specific form,

$$e_{i,t} = e^{1-\frac{\mu}{u_t}\Big/\frac{w_{i,t}}{w_t}}. \tag{2.9}$$

where $l_{i,t}$ is the labor force employed in a particular firm at the wage rate $w_{i,t}$, and the exponential term is the efficiency of this workforce. In accordance with Akerlof and Yellen (1990), both an increase in the relative wage vis-à-vis the economy-wide average wage, $w_{i,t}/w_t$, and an increase in the unemployment rate u_t increase efficiency. In this chapter, μ has three distinct interpretations. The first interpretation of μ is that it represents the degree to which a firm relies on firing to induce efficiency, or the degree to which workers perceive the threat of becoming unemployed. Assume for a moment that the exponent were equal to minus unity, which will be proven in equation (2.13), then workers will be willing to accept lower than average wages if and only if unemployment exceeds μ. As both the relative wage and the unemployment rate depend on economic conditions outside the firm, they shall be labeled 'external efficiency'.

There is ample evidence that manufacturers can induce efficiency other than with a carrot (a high relative wage) and a stick (a high unemployment rate). Then μ may be a function of the organizational structure (e.g. introducing internal controlling), or the motivation of the workforce (e.g. internal training, promotions, or seniority premia) within a manufacturing firm. As an increase in μ reduces efficiency, $\partial x_{i,t}/\partial \mu < 0$, 'internal efficiency' may be measured by the index $1/\mu$.

In this second interpretation of μ, it may reflect the extent to which the firm needs to rely on external efficiency, and $1/\mu$ the extent of internal efficiency. Whilst one can hardly verify the degree of motivation or the quality of organization, the firing rate is readily accessible, hence firm owners (shareholders) may prefer efficiency-inducing mechanisms that operate through wage premia, requesting high external efficiency, that is a high μ, and thus indirectly foster unemployment.

Profit maximization in manufacturing implies that firms will increase their wage until the increase in effort is just offset by an alternative increase in employment, that is until the output elasticity of employment is equal to the output elasticity of the wage rate,

$$\frac{\partial e_{i,t}}{\partial w_{i,t}} \frac{w_{i,t}}{e_{i,t}} = 1, \tag{2.10}$$

Any firm will increase (reduce) its wage relative to the average wage, whenever unemployment exceeds (lies below) μ. This will equiproportionally increase (reduce) the average wage, thus inducing another round of relative wage increases (declines), implying ultimately that wages will increase without bound (decline to a zero rate). Hence a third interpretation of μ is the manufacturing non-accelerating wage rate of unemployment (Nawru), as the specific functional form of the efficiency function reduces equation (2.10) to,

$$\mu = \frac{w_{i,t}}{w_t} u_t, \tag{2.11}$$

The efficiency condition (2.10) implies that productivity in manufacturing will equal unity,

$$e_{i,t} = 1. \tag{2.12}$$

When setting prices, firms maximize profits subject to demand (2.6) and technology (2.9), which yields the following first-order condition,

$$p_{i,t} = \frac{\varepsilon}{\varepsilon - 1} \frac{w_{i,t}}{e_{i,t}}, \tag{2.13}$$

stating that the price the firm charges equals the mark-up over costs, the wage in efficiency terms. Note that the manufacturing sector is completely symmetrical, as every firm will choose identical efficiency levels because of equation (2.12), set identical wages because of equation (2.9), and identical prices because of equation (2.13). The demand function (2.6) then implies that output will be identical for all manufacturers, and therefore also employment, due to the production function (2.8). This allows us to identify economic profits of the manufacturing sector, d_t, by simple aggregation over all individual profits,

$$d_t = n_t \pi_{i,t} = n_t (p_{i,t} x_{i,t} - w_{i,t} l_{i,t}) = \frac{1}{\varepsilon - 1} n_t w_{i,t} l_{i,t}, \tag{2.14}$$

where i now represents any representative manufacturer.

2.4 The innovation sector

The innovation sector is assumed to produce new varieties under perfect competition according to the following aggregate technology,

$$\dot{n}_t = \phi n_t e_t l_t, \tag{2.15}$$

where ϕ is productivity in innovation, l_t is the labor force employed in the R&D sector, and n_t is an externality, stating that it is easier to innovate when the stock of knowledge, that is the existing number of innovations, is large. Efficiency is defined according to equation (2.9), where we assume a rather plausible difference in internal efficiency between the two sectors,

$$e_t = e^{1-\frac{\delta\mu}{u_t}\Big/\frac{s_t}{w_t}}. \tag{2.16}$$

This condition differs from manufacturing efficiency (2.9) by δ. If δ is less than unity, then ceteris paribus employees in the innovation sector are less productive than workers in manufacturing. This is equivalent to stating that the exogenous firing probability of standard efficiency wage models is lower in the innovation sector, which seems to be borne out of the facts. Nonetheless, we shall consider all potential cases of $\delta > 0$ in the following.

In the innovation sector, the efficiency relation may of course be labeled creativity. An increase in unemployment need not unambiguously raise creativity. Whilst an initial increase in unemployment will raise creativity here as well, very high rates of unemployment may result in the opposite effect. Given risk-averse researchers, they may engage in less risky, short-sighted projects with a lower yield, thus reducing the value of output of the innovation sector, or measured efficiency (2.16). Approximating efficiency (2.16) by a quadratic efficiency equation of the form $exp\{1 - \mu w_t/s_t\,(\delta - u_t)^2\}$, the qualitative results as presented in the following sections will not change for peaks δ in the efficiency function between zero and unity. Equation (2.16) therefore represents a good linear approximation to the more general case.

In line with most endogenous growth models (Romer, 1990; Grossman and Helpman, 1991a), it is assumed that the search for profit fosters innovations. Maximizing profits of an innovator subject to technology (2.15) and efficiency (2.16), we find that the salaries set by research institutions will be above market clearing, following the Solow condition,

$$\frac{s_t}{e_t}\frac{\partial e_t}{\partial s_t} = 1 = \frac{\delta\mu}{u_t}\Big/\frac{s_t}{w_t}. \tag{2.17}$$

Competitive firms in the innovation sector will invest into the development of new products until the marginal revenues exactly offset marginal costs. Assuming that labor is the only input in R&D, marginal costs equal salaries s_t. Assuming perfect competition in the innovation sector, the price of a new innovation q_t will equal,

$$q_t = \frac{s_t}{\phi e_t n_t}. \tag{2.18}$$

The maximum price that potential manufacturers will pay for a novel innovation is equal to the discounted stream of profits. No arbitrage on capital markets implies that an investor should be indifferent between a risk-free investment of the amount q_t, yielding interest payments of $r_t q_t$, or the purchase of a manufacturer's stock. From the latter, she may benefit from changes in the stock's value over time, and profits distributed to shareholders,

$$\dot{q}_t + \pi_{i,t} = r_t q_t. \tag{2.19}$$

Because of the symmetry of the model, the value of all firms in manufacturing, or the stock market capitalization v_t, will equal $n_t q_t$. Aggregation over all firms, and substitution of dividends d_t from equation (2.14), the firm value from the innovator's first-order condition (2.18), and the interest rate from the intertemporal Euler equation (2.3), yields,

$$\frac{\dot{v}_t}{v_t} - \frac{\dot{n}_t}{n_t} + \frac{\phi n_t l_{i,t}}{\delta(\varepsilon - 1)} = \frac{\dot{c}_t}{c_t} + \theta. \tag{2.20}$$

2.5 The labor market

Normalizing the labor force to unity, we find that employees will work either in manufacturing or in research, hence the labor market clearing condition reads,

$$\int_0^{n_t} l_{i,t} di + l_t = 1 - u_t. \tag{2.21}$$

Note that average wages w_t are defined as wages paid by firm i to its workers $l_{i,t}$, and salaries s_t by research institutions to its employees l_t divided by the total labor force,

$$w_t = \left[s_t l_t + \int_0^{n_t} w_{i,t} l_{i,t}\, di \right] \Big/ \left[l_t + \int_0^{n_t} l_{i,t}\, di + u_t \right], \tag{2.22}$$

The average wage includes income from employment and unemployment, where the later has been set to zero. Moreover, as leisure does not enter the utility function, opportunity costs of unemployment are simply wages foregone. Hence unemployed appears in the denominator, but not in the numerator.

2.6 Equilibrium unemployment

The wage equation (2.22) may be simplified, applying the two Solow conditions (2.11) and (2.17), and the labor market clearing condition (2.21), to reduce equation (2.22) to,

$$\mu(\delta - 1)l_t = (1 + \mu)u_t - \mu. \tag{2.23}$$

Assuming for an instant that both manufacturers and innovators share the same degree of internal efficiency, or, equivalently, that $\delta = 1$, then equation (2.23) reduces to

$$u_t = \frac{\mu}{1 + \mu}. \tag{2.24}$$

Given identical degrees of internal efficiency, the unemployment rate is independent of any other economic parameters, and in particular independent of the economic growth rate. Note that the average rate of unemployment u_t is lower than the non-accelerating wage rate of unemployment, μ, or the median rate of unemployment, due to the concavity of the wage index. Integrating the budget constraint (2.2), we find that stock market capitalization and consumption grow at the same rate, reducing the no-arbitrage condition (2.20) by substitution of the labor market clearing condition (2.21) and innovation technology (2.15) to,

$$(\delta\varepsilon + 1 - \delta)l_t = 1 - u_t + \frac{\theta}{\phi}(1 - \delta). \tag{2.25}$$

Eliminating innovation sector employment by equations (2.23) and (2.25), the equilibrium rate of unemployment in the model emerges as,

$$u_t = \frac{\delta\varepsilon\mu + \delta\mu(1 - \delta)(\varepsilon - 1)\theta/\phi}{\delta(\varepsilon - 1) + \delta\varepsilon\mu + 1}. \tag{2.26}$$

Whilst the denominator of this expression is strictly positive by definition, the numerator is greater than zero if and only if $\varepsilon/(\varepsilon - 1) \geq (\delta - 1)\theta/\phi$. Given the fact that the rate of time preference θ is typically small, and productivity in the innovation sector, ϕ, is not too different from manufacturing, where it equals unity by definition, this condition is likely to hold.

Equation (2.26) implies that an increase in patience reduces unemployment if and only if $\delta < 1$, or that the exogenous firing probability is higher in manufacturing. The intuition is that more patient societies are more willing to defer consumption and invest into innovations that yield higher welfare later on. This leads to an increase in the innovation sector labor force, reducing average wages and thus leading to higher aggregate employment. Similarly, an increase in research productivity reduces unemployment, as the lower relative wage in the innovation sector will enable innovators to hire a larger share of the labor force.

An increase in the price elasticity of product demand, ε, will unambiguously reduce unemployment. Here, the reason is that a reduction of the imperfect market externality will lead to higher levels of output and production. Evidently, an increase in the non-accelerating-wage rate of unemployment will reduce the unemployment rate, for evident reasons. Finally, an increase in the firing probability in innovation, δ, will reduce unemployment if and only if $\phi\varepsilon/((\varepsilon - 1)\theta) < \delta^2(\varepsilon + \varepsilon\mu - 1) - 1$. Given that unemployment is bound to be nonnegative, a sufficient condition for a negative effect of innovation sector firing on unemployment is $\varepsilon + \varepsilon\mu - 1 > 1/\delta$.

Summarizing, we find that patience, high research productivity, product substitutability, and high internal efficiency, $1/\mu$, are beneficial for employment, whilst the effect of the firing probability in innovation remains ambiguous.

2.7 Equilibrium growth

Equations (2.23) and (2.25) may also be solved for innovation sector employment, which will be constant. Given a constant unemployment rate from equation (2.26), we find from the definition of the consumption basket (2.4), manufacturing technology (2.8), and the labor market clearing condition (2.21), that consumption growth is $1/(\varepsilon - 1)$ times the growth rate of innovations. Hence, the growth rate of the economy can be derived to give,

$$\frac{\dot{c}_t}{c_t} = \frac{\phi - (1 + \mu)\theta}{\delta\varepsilon(\varepsilon - 1)(1 + \mu) + (\varepsilon - 1)(1 - \delta)}, \tag{2.27}$$

which is positive if and only if $\phi > (1 + \mu)\theta$. This condition is met when innovation productivity does not fall too far behind manufacturing productivity. The economy will grow faster if consumers become more patient, as they will allocate more funds to the innovation sector, leading to a higher output of innovations and a higher output growth rate. Similarly, higher productivity in the innovation sector will also foster economic growth, whilst a higher firing probability in the innovation sector, δ, will reduce the rate of growth, as it reduces innovation sector productivity. Whilst an increase in product substitutability reduced unemployment, it will be detrimental to economic growth, unless $(1 + \mu)(2\varepsilon - 1) > (\delta - 1)/\delta$, which certainly holds for $\delta < 1$, but for most realistically positive values of δ as well. The intuition is that a high degree of substitutability reduces monopoly rents, thus reducing the incentive to engage in innovations, leading to a decline in output growth.

Finally, an increase in the non-accelerating wage rate of unemployment, μ, will reduce economic growth if and only if $\theta(\delta - 1) < \delta\varepsilon\phi$. This condition will hold whenever δ is less than unity, which is the more plausible case. Even if δ exceeds unity, a sufficient condition for a negative impact of the level of unemployment on the rate of economic growth is $\delta > 1/(\varepsilon - 1)$. This is also equivalent to stating that the firing probability in innovation has a negative impact on unemployment.

Summarizing, we find that patience, high innovation productivity, a low firing probability in the innovation sector, low product substitutability, and high internal efficiency or a low Nawru, all foster economic growth. Most importantly, we have established a typically negative tradeoff between the level of unemployment – or, to be more specific, the unemployment rate – and the change in output, or the economic rate of growth.

2.8 Conclusions

This chapter has established a relation between the unemployment rate and the long-run rate of economic growth. The main result is that an increase in the unemployment rate, caused by a greater pressure towards outside efficiency, will also reduce the growth rate of the economy, because employment will be reduced in both the manufacturing and the innovation sectors, the latter leading to a decline in the innovation rate, and hence to a slower rate of economic growth.

Only if internal efficiency considerations are different between the manufacturing and the innovation sectors, which may be due to differences in the ease to monitor workers' efforts, will there also be a channel that leads from the growth rate to unemployment. If patience in the economy declines, if manufacturing products get more homogenous, or simply if innovation productivity declines, the economy will accumulate fewer innovations, thereby reducing the rate of economic growth.

This will also lead to a shift away from innovation sector employees towards manufacturing workers. Since the manufacturing sector now receives a greater weight in average wages, wage increases in manufacturing must increase to induce the desired level of efficiency, thereby fostering unemployment.

3
A Model of Economic Growth and Structural Change

Several distinguished stylized facts form the new economy – an information technology service sector organized in network forms of organization, an inflation rate below its fundamentals, a stock market boom, low productivity rates but high rates of economic growth. This chapter presents a model in which new varieties of services are introduced to generate rents, and offers an explanation of the stock market boom of the late 1990s. Whilst a particular service provider is assumed to realize no productivity gains at all, the increase in variety increases value-added per employee, thus explaining high growth rates despite low productivity rates. This unmeasured productivity gain is the implicit reason for the intrinsic inertia in the consumer price index.

3.1 Motivation

> The deeper question is whether there has been a profound and fundamental alteration in the way our economy works that creates discontinuity from the past and promises a significantly higher path of growth than we have experienced in recent decades. (Greenspan, 1998)

A set of distinguished stylized facts of the American economy form the key elements of the 'new economy'. First, there is an innovative information technology service sector, which is organized in network firms of organization, rather than traditional firms or markets. Secondly, despite high rates of economic growth, a level of GDP above potential output, and unemployment figures below the natural rate, there appears to be an intrinsic inertia in the rate of price inflation. Thirdly, in the late 1990s the American economy experienced one of the longest continuing booms on stock markets. This appeared to be particularly true for companies in emerging markets, with internet service providers amongst the companies with the largest increases in stock market capitalization. Finally, there is a productivity puzzle in the new economy. Despite low rates of total factor productivity, manifested in the productivity slowdown of recent decades, the American economy grew rapidly from the mid-1990s to the start of the twenty-first century.

Whilst most economists still attribute low price inflation and high stock price inflation to conventional, may be prolonged, reactions of the business cycle, the productivity puzzle has received closer attention in recent literature. In a seminal article, David (1990) supplied a first explanation of the phenomenon. He suggests that the implementation of information technology, which is a special case of a general purpose technology (Bresnahan and Trajtenberg, 1995), exhibits long lags that may last for decades before they show up in productivity statistics. The reason is that general purpose technologies render parts of the existing capital obsolete, even though it will continue to remain in the data. Indeed, in a recent article, Gordon (1999) shows that some 99 per cent of the recent productivity gains have been realized in the manufacturing of computers, but not in sectors applying computers – a phenomenon known as the Solow paradox.

By contrast, Griliches (1994) provides empirical evidence that the driving force behind the growth process are sectors where performance, and therefore productivity, is hard to measure – notably mining, transportation, utilities, construction and most of the services. Given the fact that services represent a major share in national income, this chapter considers whether a shift towards a service economy alone can explain several distinct features of the new economy.

The service sector exhibits a series of empirical peculiarities that distinguish it from other sectors, in particular manufacturing. First, there is a larger heterogeneity in the provision of services. Whilst manufacturing goods are typically procured by tayloristic production schemes, services are provided individually at the point of sale. Evidently, the service sector exhibits lower rates of productivity gains, but higher economic profits, since specialization leads to a certain market power (Hage, 1998). With lower rates of productivity growth, the question arises where the growth dynamics that have reached the American economy are coming from.

This chapter draws on the fact that the increase in the service sector is due to an increase in the variety of services provided. As consumers shift their spending towards services, productivity as conventionally measured will decline. However, a greater choice will be reflected in the valuation of service consumption, which gives an explanation for the increase in rates of economic growth. The presence of a networking externality in the innovation process of new services produces a constant flow of innovations in the service sector, which finally leads to a permanent decline in the price index, which is the basis for the intrinsic inertia of inflation.

3.2 The demand side

Households are assumed to provide one unit of labor inelastically, and to face an intertemporal tradeoff between consumption and savings on the one hand, and an intratemporal tradeoff between the consumption of a single manufacturing product and an ever-expanding variety of services on the other. Households are assumed to maximize intertemporal utility. The intertemporal tradeoff is modeled according to the conventional logarithmic utility function,

$$U_s = \int_s^{\infty} e^{-\theta(t-s)} \ln c_t dt, \tag{3.1}$$

where θ is the individual rate of time preference, and c_t is aggregate consumption over time t. Households maximize utility subject to an intertemporal budget constraint,

$$\dot{b}_t = r_t b_t + w_t - c_t, \tag{3.2}$$

which states that a household saves that part of interest income $r_t b_t$, and labor income w_t, that is not spent on consumption c_t. Hamiltonian optimization of the utility function subject to the budget constraint with respect to consumption, asset accumulation, and a shadow price of income yields the well-known Keynes–Ramsey rule,

$$\frac{\dot{c}_t}{c_t} = r_t - \theta. \tag{3.3}$$

stating that households will delay consumption into the future when the interest rate exceeds their individual rate of time preference. Consumption is devoted to services and manufacturing products according to the following Cobb–Douglas felicity (or subutility) function,

$$c_t = x_t^{\frac{n_t-1}{n_t}} y_t^{\frac{1}{n_t}}, \tag{3.4}$$

where y_t is the amount of manufacturing products, x_t is the amount of services, and n_t is the increasing number of services in the society. The motivation for this specific functional form is twofold. The economic interpretation is that as the number of available services increases, agents devote an increasing proportion of their expenditure to purchasing services. The sociological argument follows from the fact that n_t reflects knowledge in the society (see Zagler, 1999b). It states that agents will shift their consumption towards services as they become more educated (Hage, 1998, p. 7f). Given that households will spend an amount c_t on services and manufacturing products, the intratemporal budget constraint yields,

$$p_t x_t + q_t y_t \leq c_t, \tag{3.5}$$

where q_t is the price of manufacturing products, and p_t is the price index for services.[1] Upon Lagrange optimization of the subutility function subject to the budget constraints with respect to manufacturing and service consumption, one finds that the relative price must equal the marginal rate of substitution,

$$(n_t - 1)\frac{y_t}{x_t} = \frac{p_t}{q_t}. \tag{3.6}$$

Finally, we assume that services are heterogeneous and are supplied in an increasing number of varieties. Households demand differentiated services according to the following constant elasticities of substitution subfelicity function,

$$x_t = \left[\int_0^{n_t} x_{i,t}^{\frac{\varepsilon-1}{\varepsilon}} di\right]^{\frac{\varepsilon}{\varepsilon-1}}, \tag{3.7}$$

where $x_{i,t}$ is a specific variety of service. Households will only spend $p_t x_t$ on services, hence the budget constraint for optimization reads,

$$\int_0^{n_t} p_{i,t} x_{i,t} di \leq p_t x_t, \tag{3.8}$$

where $p_{i,t}$ is the price of a specific service i. The final stage in the household problem yields after optimization a demand function for a specific service,

$$x_{i,t} = \left(\frac{p_{i,t}}{p_t}\right)^{-\varepsilon} x_t, \tag{3.9}$$

and we find that ε is the demand elasticity for any particular service. Moreover, we obtain a definition for the price index of services,

$$p_t = \left[\int_0^{n_t} p_{i,t}^{1-\varepsilon} di\right]^{\frac{1}{1-\varepsilon}} \tag{3.10}$$

To complete the discussion of the household sector, note that the intratemporal maximization implies that the spending share on manufacturing products $q_t y_t / c_t$ will equal $1/n_t$, whilst the spending share on services $p_t x_t / c_t$ will equal $(n_t - 1)/n_t$.

3.3 Manufacturing

For the sake of simplicity, let us assume that competitive manufacturers face a constant returns to scale production function[2] with labor as the only input,

$$y_t = A_t l_t, \tag{3.11}$$

where A_t measures productivity in manufacturing. It is assumed that productivity augments continuously by a factor a. Assuming that the producer price of labor equals the real wage w_t, profit maximization yields,

$$w_t = A_t q_t, \tag{3.12}$$

implying that each worker must earn its marginal product.

3.4 The service sector

As argued, services are provided in many different forms. Moreover, it is assumed that the provision of services earns economic rents. The market setting is assumed to be monopolistically competitive. A firm in the service sector therefore operates along the demand function introduced above, and sets prices in order to maximize profits. However, service suppliers consider their individual influence on aggregate variables, such as the total amount of services x_t and the price index p_t thereof, to be negligible. We simply assume that inputs in the service sector equal output, or $x_{i,t} = e_{i,t}$, where $e_{i,t}$ is service sector employment. Profit maximization yields the mark-up of prices over costs,

$$p_{i,t} = \frac{\varepsilon}{\varepsilon - 1} w_t. \tag{3.13}$$

Service sector firms therefore obtain rents equal to,

$$d_{i,t} = \frac{1}{\varepsilon - 1} w_t e_{i,t}, \tag{3.14}$$

which implies that aggregate profits, d_t, equal,

$$d_t = \int_0^{n_t} d_{i,t} di = \frac{1}{\varepsilon - 1} \int_0^{n_t} w_t e_{i,t} di = \frac{1}{\varepsilon} p_t x_t. \tag{3.15}$$

The mark-up equation implies that prices, and according to the demand function also quantities, in the service sector are independent of the specific variety. The price index (3.10) therefore equals,

$$p_t = \frac{\varepsilon}{\varepsilon - 1} w_t n_t^{\frac{1}{1-\varepsilon}}. \tag{3.16}$$

Ceteris paribus, as the number of varieties increases, the price index declines, implying that for a given spending share on services, there may be an increase in quantity. However, market shares of a particular service will decline as new services are provided,

$$x_{i,t} = n_t^{\frac{\varepsilon}{1-\varepsilon}} x_t. \tag{3.17}$$

Due to the mark-up equation (3.13), all service sector firms will charge the same price, and sell the same quantity due to equation (3.17). The model therefore is completely symmetrical. Hence we may set the labor force of a particular service sector firm i as equal to the average employment in the service sector, $e_{i,t} = e_t$ for all i. Substitution of manufacturing technology (3.11), service sector quantities (3.17), aggregate service sector prices (3.16), and manufacturing supply (3.12) into the optimality condition (3.6) yields,

$$n_t e_t / l_t = (n_t - 1)(\varepsilon - 1)/\varepsilon. \tag{3.18}$$

Aggregate service sector employment is proportional to manufacturing employment for a given number of varieties, but increases relatively, as variety increases.

3.5 The innovation sector

The innovation sector is populated by perfectly competitive R&D firms, which sell innovations to emerging service sector firms in order maximize profits. The stock of knowledge, or the level of innovations, does not enter the innovation technology without cost. By contrast, innovators engage in costly activity to acquire knowledge, by forming internal or external networks. We hence assume that new varieties are created according to,

$$\dot{n}_t = \varphi s_{n,t}^{\alpha} \eta_t. \tag{3.19}$$

Given that it is uncertain whether a single innovation will be successful, φ measures the probability of success in innovation, when the number of attempts to innovate is large, or productivity in innovation. If not all innovations are marketable, φ may also measure the share of innovations that reach the implementation stage at the product market, or the degree of diffusion of innovations. η_t represents networking capital, $s_{n,t}$ is either the amount of time that a particular researcher devotes to the innovation of new products, or the number of scientists (or science managers) engaged in networking activities, with diminishing marginal product of innovative activities. Network capital is acquired according to the following process,

$$\eta_t = \psi n_t s_{\eta,t}^{1-\alpha}. \tag{3.20}$$

Koput and Powell (2000) provide evidence that an increase of the number of nodes in a network, equivalent to the number of n_t's, indeed fosters innovation, irrespective of the number of ties held by each individual firm. The time spent in networking activities, $s_{\eta,t} = s_t - s_{n,t}$, exhibits a diminishing marginal product as well. Note that firms in the innovation sector will maximize their output by setting $s_{\eta,t} = (1 - \alpha)s_t$. Productivity in networking is assumed to equal ψ. Finally, we assume that the number of existing innovations facilitates networking, as the number of coalitions increases with n_t, which is therefore a true networking externality, instead of an innovation externality, where the positive correlation between new and existing innovations was rather ad hoc. The arrival rate of new innovations (3.19) can therefore be reduced to,

$$\dot{n}_t = \varphi\psi(\alpha s_t)^{\alpha}((1 - \alpha)s_t)^{1-\alpha} n_t = \phi s_t n_t, \tag{3.21}$$

where ϕ is a measure of productivity in the innovation sector. Given that it is uncertain whether a single innovation will be successful, ϕ measures the probability of success in innovation, when the number of attempts to innovate is large.

The model is closed with a condition for labor market clearing. A fully flexible wage and perfect sectoral mobility ensures that the entire labor force is employed. Assuming that households supply one unit of labor inelastically, and the number of households is normalized to unity, and manufacturers, service firms and innovators demand labor according to its relative marginal product, the labor market clearing condition reads,

$$l_t + s_t + n_t e_t = 1. \tag{3.22}$$

Competitive firms in the innovation sector maximize profits. The highest price a potential service provider can pay to an innovator will equal the service firm i's value, $v_{i,t}$. The only costs for an innovator are wages w_t, paid to scientists, s_t. Hence, given technology as stated in (3.18), the marginal cost for the provision of a new variety will equal its price,

$$v_{i,t} = \frac{w_t}{\phi n_t}. \tag{3.23}$$

By the symmetry of the model, the total value of all service sector firms will equal $v_t = n_t v_{i,t}$. No arbitrage on the stock market implies that changes in the value of a bond plus the profits the company earns must equal the return on a risk-free asset, or for the aggregate service sector,

$$\frac{\dot{v}_t}{v_t} - \frac{\dot{n}_t}{n_t} + \frac{d_t}{v_t} = \frac{\dot{c}_t}{c_t} + \theta. \tag{3.24}$$

The growth rate of stock market capitalization will equal the growth rate of real wages, because of equation (3.23). Assuming that initial household wealth is zero, wages will equal consumption from integration of the budget constraint (3.2). Substitution of aggregate profits (3.15), the Keynes–Ramsey rule (3.3), innovation technology (3.19), the labor market clearing condition (3.22), the ratio of service to manufacturing workers (3.18) and the optimality condition for the innovation sector implies, that the growth rate of innovations equals,

$$\frac{\dot{n}_t}{n_t} = \frac{\phi - \theta(\varepsilon - 1)}{\varepsilon} - \frac{\phi + \theta}{\varepsilon n_t}, \tag{3.25}$$

where the second term on the right-hand side vanishes as n_t goes to infinity.

3.6 The new economy

3.6.1 An expansion of the service sector

The fundamental change in the economy is the shift towards the service sector. However, not every economy will develop a sufficiently large service sector. Substituting equations (3.16) and (3.12) into (3.6), the ratio of service to manufacturing products (SMR) can be determined,

$$\frac{x_t}{y_t} = \frac{\varepsilon - 1}{\varepsilon} A_t^{-1}(n_t - 1)n_t^{\frac{1}{\varepsilon-1}}. \tag{3.26}$$

Whilst an increase in manufacturing productivity unambiguously lowers the ratio of service to manufacturing products, the effect of an increase in service varieties raises the ratio for two reasons. First, there is the direct substitution effect. Secondly, an increase in the number of varieties reduces the price, enabling a larger quantity of services to be consumed for a given share of spending. This is represented by the second n_t in the preceding equation. Taking time derivatives, we can identify a development threshold, as we find that the service sector grows relative to manufacturing if and only if

$$\frac{\dot{n}_t}{n_t} = \frac{\phi - \theta(\varepsilon - 1)}{\varepsilon} - \frac{\phi + \theta}{\varepsilon n_t} > \frac{n_t - 1}{\varepsilon n_t - 1}(\varepsilon - 1)a. \tag{3.27}$$

As diversity in the service sector increases, the right-hand side of this condition reduces to $a(\varepsilon - 1)/\varepsilon$, whilst the left-hand side converges to $\phi/\varepsilon - \theta(\varepsilon - 1)/\varepsilon$. Hence, an increase in the mark-up on services makes the sector more attractive, thereby reinforcing the shift.[3] Moreover, note that the condition may either hold permanently, never, or only initially. In the latter case, we may find an initial increase in the service sector, followed by a subsequent decline. This will separate postindustrialist countries from manufacturing economies.

3.6.2 The intrinsic inertia in the inflation rate

The model now enables us to explain the three stylized facts of the new economy, as postulated in the introduction. The inflation rate of an economy is conventionally measured as the consumption share weighted sum of product price changes,

$$\pi_t = \frac{p_t x_t}{c_t}\frac{\dot{p}_t}{p_t} + \frac{q_t y_t}{c_t}\frac{\dot{q}_t}{q_t}. \tag{3.28}$$

Note that by definition, the inflation rate in the model is zero, hence (3.28) presents the difference between measured inflation and the fundamental inflation rate – in other words, the bias in the inflation rate. As stated earlier, the consumption shares depend solely on the number of varieties. Moreover, both the rate of price changes in manufacturing and in the service sector can be derived from equations (3.9) and (3.13), respectively, to yield, after some rearrangement,

$$\pi_t = \frac{\dot{w}_t}{w_t} - \frac{a}{n_t} - \frac{\phi}{(\varepsilon - 1)\varepsilon}\left(\frac{n_t - 1}{n_t}\right)^2 + \frac{\theta}{\varepsilon - 1}\frac{n_t - 1}{n_t}. \tag{3.29}$$

The first term on the right-hand side is the conventional cost-push element in inflation. If wages rise, inflation will pick up as well. The second part, of course, corrects for productivity gains. Note, however, that it depends inversely on the number of varieties in services. If the service sector expands, this element is of less and less importance, which may be the reason why inflation hasn't increased despite low rates of productivity growth in the recent past. The third term now is the reason for the intrinsic inertia in the new economy. It states that inflationary pressure declines, if productivity in the innovative sector increases. Hence productivity gains in small innovative sectors, such as the computer service industry, are sufficient to keep inflation low. The square term implies that this term gains importance as the new economy develops. This implies that there is a substantial bias in the measurement of the consumer price index, even after the conventional substitution bias has been accounted for (Boskin et al., 1997). Finally, impatience has an accelerating impact on inflation. Considering the low rates of saving in the American economy, this is the only inflationary aspect that should deserve some attention. Overall, one may conclude that there is an heterogeneity bias in the consumer price index.

3.6.3 The emerging stock markets boom

By substituting the growth rate (3.25) into the stock market capitalization growth rate (3.24), we find that stock market capitalization growth will equal consumption growth. Changes in stock market values will therefore initially depend upon the growth rate of manufacturing, a, but converge to the growth rate of the service sector, $\phi/\varepsilon - \theta$, given a service sector will emerge. Given constant returns to scale and perfect competition, profits in the old economy – the manufacturing sector – are zero, and so are discounted profits, and therefore the stock market value of these firms. If they do in reality exhibit a positive listing, it should be mainly due to the value of their capital stock (Brainard and Tobin, 1968). Since the manufacturing firms, which produce under conditions of perfect competition without the use of physical capital, do not exhibit any value, the entire stock market capitalization will initially be divided upon a few service firms.

3.6.4 The productivity puzzle

Note that productivity differs across sectors. First, productivity in manufacturing equals output per worker, which, considering the production function, equals $y_t/l_t = A_t$. Note that manufacturing productivity increases continuously by a. Secondly, productivity in a particular service firm equals $x_{i,t}/e_{i,t} = 1$. This is due to our normalization, but also accounts for the fact that services are known to have lower rates of productivity growth than other sectors of the economy (Baumol, 1967). Given that service provision may realize some productivity gains, productivity growth a should be considered to represent relative productivity changes in manufacturing. Finally, the service sector as a whole does exhibit productivity gains as a result of increases in variety. Due to the symmetry of the model, total service production equals,

$$x_t = \left[\int_0^{n_t} e_t^{\frac{\varepsilon-1}{\varepsilon}}\right]^{\frac{\varepsilon}{\varepsilon-1}} = e_t n_t^{\frac{\varepsilon}{\varepsilon-1}}. \tag{3.30}$$

As the total labor force employed in the service sector equals $n_t e_t$ workers, productivity in the service sector equals $x_t/n_t e_t = n_t^{1/(\varepsilon-1)}$. Productivity growth within the service sector is therefore proportional to the growth in variety, and equals $(\phi/\varepsilon - \theta)/(\varepsilon - 1)$. Depending on the parameter values, this may well exceed the rate of manufacturing growth, a, which would lead to an increase in the growth rate of real GDP. However, as productivity remains to be measured at the plant level, these sectoral productivity gains will hardly find their way into the total factor productivity statistics, which is an explanation of the productivity puzzle.

3.6.5 High economic rates of growth

Equations (3.25) and (3.21) imply that the number of scientists will equal,

$$s_t = \frac{1}{\varepsilon} - \frac{\theta}{\phi}\frac{\varepsilon-1}{\varepsilon} - \frac{\phi+\theta}{\phi\varepsilon n_t}, \tag{3.31}$$

which converges to $(1 - \theta(\varepsilon - 1)/\phi)/\varepsilon$, as the number of varieties goes to infinity. The last element ensures that the labor force in the innovative sector is declining in the economy, roughly at the rate of product innovation. Whilst employment in the innovative sector is proportional to employment in the service sector, they are both declining with respect to the workforce in manufacturing, given (3.18). Thus, this model is consistent with the Jones critique. Jones (1995) found that the share of employees working in the innovation of new products has tripled from the 1960s to the 1990s, with little effect on the growth rate of output. In this model, the growth in the share of workers in innovative activities increases as the service sector expands at the cost manufacturing, with an ambiguous effect on output growth. The labor market clearing condition (3.22), together with (3.32) and (3.18), and the service to manufacturing ratio (3.26) imply that

$$l_t = \frac{y_t}{A_t} = \left(1 + \frac{\theta}{\phi}\right)\frac{1}{n_t}, \tag{3.32}$$

which converges to zero as n_t goes to infinity. Note that a high rate of time preference increases the labor force in manufacturing at any point in time, or, quite plausibly, that it reduces the speed of structural adjustment. Hence the growth rate of the manufacturing sector equals,

$$\frac{\dot{y}_t}{y_t} = a - \frac{\dot{n}_t}{n_t}, \tag{3.33}$$

where the growth rate of variety is described by equation (3.25). Manufacturing growth will slow down as innovation in the service sector draws more and more personnel from manufacturing. Given the labor force in manufacturing from (3.32) and the innovation sector from (3.31), the labor market clearing condition (3.22) implies,

$$n_t e_t = x_t n_t^{\frac{1}{1-\varepsilon}} = \frac{\varepsilon - 1}{\varepsilon}\left(1 + \frac{\theta}{\phi}\right)\frac{n_t - 1}{n_t}, \tag{3.34}$$

which converges to $(1 + \theta/\phi)(\varepsilon - 1)/\varepsilon$ as n_t goes to infinity. The growth rate of diversity therefore equals,

$$\frac{\dot{x}_t}{x_t} = \frac{\dot{n}_t}{n_t}\left[\frac{1}{\varepsilon - 1} + \frac{1}{n_t - 1}\right], \tag{3.35}$$

where the square parenthesis converges to $1/(\varepsilon - 1)$ as n_t goes to infinity. It is much lower initially, implying that the growth rate of the service sector will increase as the economy evolves. Note that subtraction of manufacturing sector growth (3.33) from service sector growth (3.34) yields, after some algebraic transformation, the condition for the emergence of a 'new' service economy, condition (3.27). Economic growth of the model economy may be approximated by a conventional consumption weighted average over sectoral growth rates, where the weights for the spending share in manufacturing and services are $1/n_t$ and $(n_t - 1)/n_t$, respectively,

$$\frac{\dot{c}_t}{c_t} = \frac{a}{n_t} + \frac{\varepsilon}{\varepsilon - 1}\frac{n_t - 1}{n_t}\frac{\dot{n}_t}{n_t}. \tag{3.36}$$

The rate of growth of a 'new economy' will exceed the rate of growth of a manufacturing economy if and only if the growth rate of services (3.35) remains above the rate of manufacturing productivity growth (3.33),

$$\frac{\phi - \theta(\varepsilon - 1)}{\varepsilon} - \frac{\phi + \theta}{\varepsilon n_t} > a. \tag{3.37}$$

Whilst condition (3.27) on the development of a services sector reduces to $\phi > (\varepsilon - 1)/(a + \theta)$ as n_t goes to infinity, condition (3.37) reduces to $\phi > (\varepsilon - 1)/(\varepsilon a + \theta)$. Note the latter condition, which defines whether the service economy will grow faster than the manufacturing economy is strictly stronger since $\varepsilon > 1$, and therefore summarizes the conditions for the emergence of a new economy. Hence, the new economy requires high rates of productivity growth in the innovation sector, high mark-ups in the service sector, and patience on behalf of individual agents to exploit its full growth potential.

3.7 Conclusions

This chapter develops an economy with an endogenously expanding service sector, in order to provide a theoretical framework for most of the stylized facts that form the 'new economy'. An increase in the heterogeneity of services provided makes consumers shift their spending towards services. Innovative services are provided by a small segment of the economy, which here is labeled the innovative sector, but may well correspond to information technology providers, in their search for market openings that yield economic rents. First, the increase in variety reduces the impact of productivity gains on the inflation rate. Secondly, it fosters competition amongst service providers, leading to a permanent decline in service prices. Both factors can account for the new intrinsic inertia in the inflation rate. There is a heterogeneity bias in the consumer price index.

As service sector firms exhibit some market power, they will obtain a stream of monopoly rents. A shift from a manufacturing economy towards a service society will therefore inevitably go alongside a boom in stock market capitalization, provided service companies are able to access outside finance.

The model economy described in the previous chapters is assumed to exhibit constant rates of productivity growth in manufacturing and no productivity gains in a single service firm. Hence, as the economy shifts towards a service sector, total factor productivity growth rates are bound to decline. However, since the service sector as a whole will produce an ever-increasing value-added per employee, due to the fact that consumers value variety, the growth rate of the economy may well increase as it turns into a new service economy, resolving the productivity puzzle. One novel contribution of this chapter is that a model based on the above features is able to explain most of the stylized facts of the new economy. In that sense, the new economy is not so new after all (Jorgenson and Stiroh, 2000).

With the emergence of a large service sector, the economy is being transformed, and it may be appropriate to talk of a 'new economy'. The changes in the service sector go beyond the aspects described in this chapter. Whilst this chapter has only considered consumer services, industry services deserve an equal amount of attention. Industry services are distinct from consumer services in two ways. First, they are more likely to be complements in production than substitutes in consumption, as modeled here. Secondly, unless the service provision and the innovation process are integrated into a single enterprise, the public aspect of innovations limits the scope to realize economic rents.

Finally, services substantially alter the production process. Whilst manufacturers could easily disconnect production from purchase, it is in the nature of the service sectors to produce at the point of sale. This, of course, has significant implications for the stability of the service production function. The efficiency of service provision will depend upon the stability of consumer demand, unless firms manage to transfer the risk of low turnover to the discretion of its employees, which forms the basis for the emergence of atypical employment relations in the service sector (Mühlberger, 1999).

4
Structural Change and Search Frictions

Economic growth is driven by structural change. Structural change does not come without a cost, the most evident social cost being high and persistent unemployment. This chapter develops a model of an economy with an endogenously expanding service sector, in which the constant flow of workers in and out of the employment relation leads to structural unemployment. The main finding is that the level of unemployment is different between the initial period and the long-run equilibrium growth path, and that along the transition path, the level of unemployment will overshoot its equilibrium level, which can explain the long-run pattern of unemployment in most industrialized countries.

4.1 Motivation

As stated earlier, economic growth is driven by structural change. The introduction of new modes of production, which allow for a more efficient allocation of resources, or the innovation of a new product line itself, which augments the value of a product, form the essence of the growth process, but necessitate the decline of existing product or production techniques alongside.

Structural change, however, comes at a cost. The most evident social cost of structural change is a high and persistent level of unemployment. Firms producing a product in a declining market will lay off workers. Workers specializing in a particular mode of production will lose their jobs when new modes of production render their qualifications redundant. Until these workers requalify and are matched to a new job in an expanding product segment or in a new technology, they will experience periods of unemployment.

The first aspect has been extensively studied in the literature on endogenous growth. In his seminal paper, Paul Romer (1990) shows that when technology changes to take account of new inputs into production, an economy may grow without bounds. Although not explicitly formulated, the model implies that the labor force employed in the production of a specific factor input will permanently decline. The first to emphasize this aspect were Phillippe Aghion and Peter Howitt (1992), who claimed that growth is a permanent process of creative destruction.

Aghion and Howitt (1994) have also noted that this process of creative destruction can produce persistent unemployment in an imperfect labor market. They argue that the introduction of new products will render part of the workforce unemployed. If it takes time until the unemployed are matched to a job in the emerging sectors, persistent unemployment arises. Whilst their paper contributes to an understanding of structural unemployment, it exhibits scope for extensions. First, the unemployment rate is procyclical and entirely driven by the growth rate. Secondly, along the balanced growth path, unemployment rates will not change. The model, in particular, does not allow for long waves in the pattern of the unemployment rate. However, the evolution of unemployment rates in the OECD has not been that straightforward. In OECD countries selected for Table 4.1, the initially low rates of unemployment have increased until they have reached a peak between 1982 (USA) and 1997 (Switzerland), as shown in the second column. Then, it seems that unemployment rates have been fairly stable in the initial period of the sample, from 1960 onwards. Unemployment rates have stabilized well below their maximum level recently, at least for those countries that experienced an early peak, notably the United States and the Netherlands. Table 4.1 tries to capture this element by identifying two bliss points, that is the maximum increase of the unemployment rate and the maximum decrease of the unemployment rate, presented in columns three and four respectively. Note that we have selected all of those OECD countries where a second bliss point could be identified. Finally, it appears that equilibrium unemployment rates are higher now than they were in the initial period of the sample. This implies that the time path is asymmetric, which we try to capture by presenting the ratio of the downward bliss point over the upward bliss point in column five. Should it exceed unity, which it does in all cases, chances are that the ultimate level of unemployment exceeds the initial level.

These stylized facts lead to the conclusion that the economy has undergone substantial changes, and has shifted from a regime of low unemployment to a regime with high unemployment. Along the transition path, unemployment has increased beyond the equilibrium

Table 4.1 The unemployment experience in selected OECD countries

	*Maximum rate of unemployment**	*Upward bliss point**	*Downward bliss point**	*Ratio of downward to upward bliss point***
Australia	10.9 (1993)	7.1 (1982)	10.9 (1993)	1.54 (0)
Belgium	13.2 (1983)	7.9 (1980)	11.3 (1987)	1.43 (4)
Denmark	12.1 (1993)	2.3 (1974)	12.0 (1994)	5.22 (1)
Finland	16.6 (1994)	6.6 (1991)	14.6 (1996)	2.21 (2)
Ireland	17.1 (1986)	7.0 (1980)	14.8 (1994)	2.11 (8)
Netherlands	11.0 (1983)	2.1 (1981)	3.8 (1984)	1.81 (1)
New Zealand	10.3 (1991)	7.8 (1990)	8.1 (1994)	1.04 (3)
Norway	6.0 (1993)	3.2 (1988)	4.1 (1997)	1.28 (4)
Sweden	8.2 (1993)	5.3 (1992)	8.0 (1997)	1.51 (4)
Switzerland	5.2 (1997)	2.5 (1992)	5.2 (1997)	2.08 (0)
UK	11.8 (1986)	6.1 (1980)	10.2 (1987)	1.67 (1)
USA	9.7 (1982)	5.6 (1974)	9.6 (1983)	1.71 (1)

Notes: The table only presents those countries that have already experienced the second bliss point.

* Numbers in parenthesis are years of occurrence.

** Numbers in parenthesis is the time elapsed since the maximum rate of unemployment.

Source: OECD, *Economic Outlook, 1960–2000* (forecast), and my own calculations.

level. We try to capture these elements by assuming an economy with a manufacturing sector that exhibits exogenous technological progress and service sector with endogenous innovation of new services, where the latter expands at the cost of the prior.

4.2 The demand side

Households are assumed to provide one unit of labor inelastically, and face an intertemporal tradeoff between consumption and savings on the one hand, and an intratemporal tradeoff between the consumption of a single manufacturing product and an ever-expanding variety of services on the other hand. Households are assumed to maximize intertemporal utility. The intertemporal tradeoff is modeled according to the conventional logarithmic utility function,

$$U_s = \int_s^\infty e^{-\rho(t-s)} \ln c_t dt, \tag{4.1}$$

where ρ is the individual rate of time preference, and c_t is aggregate consumption over time t. Households maximize utility subject to an intertemporal budget constraint,

$$\dot{a}_t = r_t a_t + w_t E_t(1 - u_t) - c_t, \tag{4.2}$$

which states that a household saves that part of interest income $r_t a_t$, and labor income w_t for those who expect not to be unemployed u_t, that is not spent on consumption c_t. Unemployed workers receive no benefits. This, however, has no consequences for the macroeconomic outcome, as will be shown later. Hamiltonian optimization of the utility function subject to the budget constraint with respect to consumption, asset accumulation, and a shadow price of income yield the well-known Keynes–Ramsey rule,

$$\hat{c}_t = r_t - \rho, \tag{4.3}$$

where the hat (^) denotes the growth rate of consumption. This intertemporal Euler condition states that households will delay their consumption into the future when the interest rate exceeds their individual rate of time preference. Integrating the budget constraint (4.2), we find that lifetime consumption depends on initial wealth and the expected level of human capital, defined as the discounted stream of future labor income,

$$\begin{aligned} \int_s^\infty c_t e^{-\int_s^t r_\tau d\tau} dt &= a_t + E_t h_t \\ &= a_t + E_t \int_s^\infty w_t(1 - u_t) e^{-\int_s^t r_\tau d\tau} dt. \end{aligned} \tag{4.4}$$

The only uncertainty in the preceding expression is whether, at a given point in time, someone is unemployed or not. As every single household can have a different record of employment and unemployment situations, a multitude of different consumption paths may arise. However, the change in human capital at each point in time will only be bivariate, and will be of great interest later on. Taking time derivatives of expected human capital yields,

$$E_t\dot{h}_t = r_t E_t h_t - w_t E_t(1 - u_t). \tag{4.5}$$

Consumption is devoted to services and manufacturing products according to the following Cobb–Douglas felicity (or subutility) function,

$$c_t = x_t^{\frac{n_t-1}{n_t}} y_t^{\frac{1}{n_t}}, \tag{4.6}$$

where y_t is the amount of manufacturing products, x_t is the amount of services, and n_t is the increasing number of services in the society. The motivation for this specific functional form is twofold. The economic interpretation is that as the number of available services increases, agents devote an increasing proportion of their expenditures on services. The sociological argument follows from the fact that n_t reflects knowledge in the society (see Zagler, 1999a). It states that agents will shift their consumption towards services as they become more educated (Hage, 1998, p. 7f). Given that households will spend an amount c_t on services and manufacturing products, the intratemporal budget constraint yields,

$$p_t x_t + q_t y_t \le c_t, \tag{4.7}$$

where q_t is the price of manufacturing products, and p_t is the price index for services.[1] Upon Lagrange optimization of the subutility function subject to the budget constraints with respect to manufacturing and service consumption, one finds that the relative price must equal the marginal rate of substitution,

$$(n_t - 1)\frac{y_t}{x_t} = \frac{p_t}{q_t}. \tag{4.8}$$

Finally, we assume that services are heterogeneous and are supplied in an increasing number of varieties. Households demand differentiated services according to the following constant elasticities of substitution subfelicity function,

$$x_t = \left[\int_0^{n_t} x_{i,t}^{\frac{\varepsilon-1}{\varepsilon}} di\right]^{\frac{\varepsilon}{\varepsilon-1}}, \tag{4.9}$$

where $x_{i,t}$ is a specific service variety. Households will only spend $p_t x_t$ on services, hence the budget constraint for optimization reads,

$$\int_0^{n_t} p_{i,t} x_{i,t} di \leq p_t x_t, \tag{4.10}$$

where $p_{i,t}$ is the price of a specific service i. The final stage in the household problem yields after optimization a demand function for a specific service,

$$x_{i,t} = \left(\frac{p_{i,t}}{p_t} \right)^{-\varepsilon} x_t, \tag{4.11}$$

and we find that ε is the demand elasticity for any particular service. Moreover, we obtain a definition for the price index of services,

$$p_t = \left[\int_0^{n_t} p_{i,t}^{1-\varepsilon} di \right]^{\frac{1}{1-\varepsilon}}. \tag{4.12}$$

To complete our discussion of the household sector, note that the intratemporal maximization implies that the spending share on manufacturing products $q_t y_t / c_t$ will equal $1/n_t$, whilst the spending share on services $p_t x_t / c_t$ will equal $(n_t - 1)/n_t$.

4.3 Manufacturing

For the sake of simplicity, let us assume that competitive manufacturers face a constant return to scale production function[2] with labor as the only input,

$$y_t = A_t l_t, \tag{4.13}$$

where A_t measures productivity in manufacturing. It is further assumed that productivity augments continuously by a factor α. In chapter 3 of this book, we have demonstrated that manufacturers will permanently reduce their labor force. Assuming that they incur a cost of firing workers equal to δw_t, profit maximization yields,

$$q_t A_t = w_t (1 + \delta\alpha - \delta\hat{y}_t), \tag{4.14}$$

implying that each worker must earn its marginal product and his potential future firing costs.

4.4 The service sector

As argued, services are provided in many different forms. Moreover, it is assumed that the provision of services earns economic rents. The market setting is assumed to be monopolistically competitive. A firm in the service sector therefore operates along the demand function introduced above, and sets prices in order to maximize profits. However, service suppliers consider their individual influence on aggregate variables, such as the total amount of services x_t and the price index p_t thereof, to be negligible. We simply assume that inputs in the service sector equal output, or $x_{i,t} = e_{i,t}$, where $e_{i,t}$ is service sector employment. It has been shown in chapter 3 that service firms hire workers initially, and then continuously reduce their workforce. Without loss of generality, we may assume that an emerging service sector firm not only receives the blueprint for a novel type of service, but also the already recruited workforce, from the innovation sector. Hence, we defer the matching problem to the innovation sector, a matter that will be discussed below. Service sector firms do incur firing costs, however, which we assume to be identical to those incurred in the manufacturing sector. Therefore, δ corresponds to the firing rate of the firm or the firing probability facing the individual. Hence profit maximization yields the mark-up of prices over costs,

$$p_{i,t} = \frac{\varepsilon}{\varepsilon - 1} w_t (1 - \delta \hat{x}_{i,t}), \tag{4.15}$$

where it should be noted that the quantity of a particular service is declining, hence the mark-up is greater than in the absence of firing costs. The mark-up equation implies that prices – and according to the demand function also quantities – in the service sector are independent of the specific variety, given identical growth rates. Market shares of a particular service will decline as new services are provided,

$$x_{i,t} = n_t^{\frac{\varepsilon}{1-\varepsilon}} x_t. \tag{4.16}$$

The price index (4.12) therefore equals,

$$p_t = \frac{\varepsilon}{\varepsilon - 1} w_t n_t^{\frac{1}{1-\varepsilon}} \left(1 - \delta \hat{x}_t + \frac{\varepsilon}{\varepsilon - 1} \delta \hat{n}_t\right), \tag{4.17}$$

making use of the time derivative of equation (4.16). Ceteris paribus, as the number of varieties increases, the price index declines, implying that for every given spending share on services, there will be an increase in quantity. Due to the mark-up equation (4.15), all service sector firms will charge the same price, and sell the same quantity due to equation (4.16). The model therefore is completely symmetric. Hence we may set the labor force of a particular service sector firm i equal to average employment in the service sector, $e_{i,t} = e_t/n_t$ for all i. Substitution of manufacturing technology (4.13), service sector quantities (4.16) aggregate service sector prices (4.17), and manufacturing supply (4.14) into the optimality condition (4.8) yields,

$$e_t/l_t = \Gamma(n_t - 1)(\varepsilon - 1)/\varepsilon, \tag{4.18}$$

with

$$\Gamma = (1 + \delta a - \delta \hat{y}_t) \Big/ \left(1 - \delta \hat{x}_t + \frac{\varepsilon}{\varepsilon - 1}\delta \hat{n}_t\right),$$

hence aggregate service sector employment is proportional to manufacturing employment for a given number of varieties, but increases relatively, as variety increases. Taking logarithms and derivatives of the service to manufacturing employment ratio (4.18) for a constant fraction Γ, we find that the numerator and the denominator in Γ are equal, implying indeed $\Gamma = 1$ to be constant. Service sector firms therefore obtain rents equal to,

$$d_{i,t} = \frac{1}{\varepsilon - 1} w_t e_{i,t}(1 - \delta \hat{x}_{i,t}), \tag{4.19}$$

which implies that aggregate profits, d_t, equal,

$$\begin{aligned} d_t = \int_0^{n_t} d_{i,t} di &= \frac{1}{\varepsilon - 1} \int_0^{n_t} w_t e_{i,t}(1 - \delta \hat{x}_{i,t}) di \\ &= \frac{1}{\varepsilon - 1} w_t e_t \left(1 - \delta \hat{x}_t + \frac{\varepsilon}{\varepsilon - 1}\delta \hat{n}_t\right). \end{aligned} \tag{4.20}$$

4.5 The innovation sector

The innovation sector is populated by perfectly competitive R&D firms, which sell innovations to emerging service sector firms in order maximize profits. The existing stock of knowledge, captured here by the index n_t, is assumed to exhibit a positive – and for the sake of simplicity linear – impact on the creation of new varieties (Romer, 1990). Moreover, labor enters linearly in this relation as well, where s_t are scientists in the innovative sector. The arrival rate of new innovations therefore equals,

$$\dot{n}_t = \phi s_t n_t, \tag{4.21}$$

where ϕ is a measure of productivity in the innovation sector. Given that it is uncertain whether a single innovation will be successful, ϕ measures the probability of success in innovation, when the number of attempts to innovate is large. As successful workers in innovating firms leave the sector to join a newly created service sector firm at rate $\hat{n}_t e_t$, exogenous to the firm, innovation sector firms need to permanently hire new workers. For this purpose, they advertise vacancies v_t at a cost of κw_t, which yields a new worker with probability $m(\theta_t)$, where θ_t is the ratio of unemployed workers u_t to vacancies v_t. $m(\theta_t)$ is a conventional matching function as described by Pissarides (1990), stating that the probability that the matching process returns a worker for a particular firm increases when unemployment goes up, and declines when the aggregate number vacancies rises, hence $m'(\theta_t) > 0$. The dynamics of the innovation sector labor force therefore reads,

$$\dot{s}_t = m(\theta_t)v_t - \hat{n}_t e_t. \tag{4.22}$$

Competitive firms in the innovation sector maximize profits. The highest price a potential service provider can pay to an innovator will equal the value of a particular service firm, b_t/n_t, normalized by the number of observations for reasons which will become apparent.

The only costs for an innovator are wages w_t, paid to scientists, s_t, and costs for vacancies, $\kappa w_t v_t$. Assuming that Hamiltonian multiplier λ_t is the shadow price of an additionally filled vacancy, the first-order conditions are,

$$\lambda_t m(\theta_t) = \kappa w_t. \tag{4.23}$$

and the equation of motion,

$$b_t \phi - w_t = r_t \lambda_t - \dot{\lambda}_t. \tag{4.24}$$

Taking time derivatives of equation (4.23) and eliminating λ_t from the equation of motion, we find that the marginal cost for the provision of a new variety will equal its market price b_t,

$$b_t = \frac{w_t}{\phi}\left[1 + \frac{\kappa}{m(\theta_t)}\left(r_t + \frac{\theta_t m(\theta_t)}{m'(\theta_t)}\hat{\theta}_t - \hat{w}_t\right)\right], \tag{4.25}$$

where $\theta_t m(\theta_t)/m'(\theta_t)$ is the elasticity of the matching function with respect to the unemployment to vacancy ratio.

4.6 Search unemployment

When a firm is able to find a worker to fill its vacancy, there is a rent created, equal to the shadow value of an additionally filled vacancy, λ_t. If the firm and the worker bargain over the division of this rent, we need to derive the potential gain of the worker from accepting the offer. Noting from the integration of the budget constraint (4.6), that for a given initial wealth the worker's consumption path, and hence her utility is only affected from changes in human wealth, the potential gain for the worker depends only on the difference in her human wealth. Denoting the human wealth of a person currently unemployed ($u_t = 1$) with h_t^u, and the human capital of a person currently employed ($u_t = 0$) with h_t^e, the Nash bargaining problem reads,

$$Max(h_t^e - h_t^u)^\beta \lambda_t^{1-\beta}, \tag{4.26}$$

where β is the relative bargaining power of the individual worker. Given the simple structure of the model, the worker receives a share β of total rents, or after rearrangement,

$$(1-\beta)(h_t^e - h_t^u) = \beta\lambda_t. \tag{4.27}$$

As we have noted above, an employed worker keeps her job at rate $(1-\delta)$, gets fired at rate δ, hence her change in human capital equals,

$$\dot{h}_t^e = \delta h_t^u + (1-\delta)h_t^e - h_t^e = \delta(h_t^u - h_t^e). \tag{4.28}$$

Substituting h_t^e for $E_t h_t$ in equation (4.5), setting $u_t = 0$, solving for h_t^e, and substituting the result into the bargaining outcome (4.27), yields

$$(1-\beta)(w_t - r_t h_t^u) = \beta(r_t + \delta)\lambda_t. \tag{4.29}$$

By a similar reasoning, an unemployed worker will find a job with probability $\theta_t m(\theta_t)$, implying that the change in human capital of the currently unemployed workers equals,

$$\dot{h}_t^u u = \theta_t m(\theta_t) h_t^e + (1 - \theta_t m(\theta_t))h_t^u - h_t^u = \theta_t m(\theta_t)(h_t^e - h_t^u), \tag{4.30}$$

which will equal to $r_t h_t^u$, according to equation (4.5). This equation now allows us to eliminate human capital from the bargaining outcome altogether, leading to a bargaining outcome of

$$(1 - \beta)w_t - \beta\theta_t\kappa w_t = \beta(r_t + \delta)\lambda_t. \tag{4.31}$$

Eliminating the shadow value an additionally filled vacancy from the innovation sector first-order condition, the interest rate from the intertemporal Euler condition (4.3), and rearranging terms yields,

$$\hat{c}_t = \frac{1 - \beta}{\beta\kappa} m(\theta_t) - \theta_t m(\theta_t) - (\rho + \delta). \tag{4.32}$$

If the number of matches on the labor market, $m(\theta_t)$ will be zero when there is no unemployment, this expression reduces to $-(\delta - \rho)$, implying a negative rate of growth in this case. As θ_t is defined as the number of unemployed to the number of vacancies, this expression defines a first relation between the growth rate of the economy and the unemployment rate. We can simplify this expression further by eliminating the number of vacancies, v_t. Note that in this model vacancies are posted by innovators, who are assumed to only sell staffed innovations. But this implies that innovators maximize their output, the number of targeted innovations, with respect to the number of vacancies posted. Hence at the margin the number of vacancies should be independent of the rate of innovation, as any potential gains have already been accounted for in the optimization process of innovators. By contrast, the number of vacancies posted may well turn out to depend upon the number of unemployed, $v_t = v(u_t)$. This vacancy function, together with the Beveridge curve, $v_t = u_t/\theta_t$, implies that we can express labor market tightness as a function of unemployment only, $\theta_t = u_t/v(u_t)$. Moreover, as has been shown by Pissarides (1990, p. 23), the unemployment function will exhibit the same properties as the matching function, hence we may reformulate equation (4.32),

$$\hat{c}_t = \frac{1 - \beta}{\beta\kappa} \eta(u_t) - u_t \eta(u_t) - (\rho + \delta). \tag{4.33}$$

Equation (4.33) is the matching tradeoff between unemployment and economic growth. As it summarizes the worker's incentives to accept a job offer, and the firm's incentives to hire that particular applicant, we may refer to equation (4.33) as the incentive condition. The probability that a firm finds an employee in the absence of unemployment is zero, and this property carries over to $\eta(u_t)$. The incentive condition (4.33) therefore takes the value $-(\delta - \rho)$ twice, namely at $\eta(u_t) = 0$, and at $u_t = (1 - \beta)/\beta\kappa$. The derivative of the growth rate with respect to unemployment along the incentive condition equals,

$$\frac{\partial \hat{c}_t}{\partial u_t} = \frac{1 - \beta - \beta\kappa u_t}{\beta\kappa}\eta'(u_t) - \eta(u_t). \tag{4.34}$$

First, the derivative of $\eta(u_t)$ is positive, as this property carries over from the matching probability as $m(\theta_t)$ well. This implies that the slope of the incentive condition is initially positive, and reaches a maximum rate of economic growth at

$$\frac{u_t\eta'(u_t)}{\eta(u_t)} = \frac{\beta\kappa u_t}{1 - \beta - \beta\kappa u_t}. \tag{4.35}$$

where $u_t\eta(u_t)/\eta'(u_t)$ is the elasticity of the matching probability with respect to unemployment.

4.7 Endogenous growth

No arbitrage on the stock market implies that changes in the value of a bond plus the profits the company earns must equal the return on a risk-free asset, or for the aggregate service sector,

$$\hat{b}_t - \hat{n}_t + \frac{d_t}{b_t} = r_t = \hat{c}_t + \rho. \tag{4.36}$$

Noting that the integrated budget constraint (4.4) implies that consumption growth must equal the change in private wealth a_t, and by the capital market clearing condition, the change in aggregate stock market evaluation, eliminating dividends d_t from equation (4.20) and stock market capitalization from equation (4.25), the growth rate of the economy equals,

$$\hat{n}_t = \frac{\phi}{\varepsilon - 1}\Omega e_t - \rho, \tag{4.37}$$

with

$$\Omega = \frac{1 - \kappa\hat{x}_t + \dfrac{\varepsilon\kappa}{\varepsilon - 1}\hat{n}_t}{1 + (\delta + \eta(\theta_t)\hat{\theta}_t)\kappa/m(\theta_t)}.$$

Assuming that households, if not unemployed, supply one unit of labor inelastically, and the number of households is normalized to unity, and manufacturers, service firms, and innovators demand labor according to its relative marginal product, the labor market clearing condition reads,

$$l_t + s_t + e_t = 1 - u_t. \tag{4.38}$$

We can eliminate manufacturing labor from the service to manufacturing employment ratio (4.18), and innovation sector employment from the innovation sector employment (4.21). This allows us to solve for service sector employment as a function of the deep parameters of the model and the rate of innovation only. Substituting this back into equation (4.37), we may solve for the innovation rate, noting in passing that Ω will be roughly equal to unity if innovation productivity does not deviate much from the productivity of a service firm. The innovation rate of the economy therefore equals,

$$\hat{n}_t = \frac{n_t - 1}{\varepsilon n_t}\phi(1 - u_t) - \frac{(\varepsilon - 1)n_t + 1}{\varepsilon n_t}\rho, \tag{4.39}$$

which is equivalent to the result in chapter 3 of this book, augmented for the possibility of unemployment.

4.8 Unemployment and growth dynamics

In order for the innovation locus (4.39) to be comparable to the matching locus (4.33), we first substitute manufacturing production (4.13) and aggregate service sector production (4.16) into the definition of the consumption bundle, and then take time derivatives, noting in passing that all employment growth rates will cancel out due to the service to manufacturing employment ratio (4.18), hence

$$\hat{c}_t = \frac{1}{\varepsilon - 1}\frac{n_t - 1}{n_t}\hat{n}_t + \frac{\alpha}{n_t}, \tag{4.40}$$

which yields the innovation locus in the unemployment to economic growth space, namely

$$\hat{c}_t = \left(\frac{n_t - 1}{n_t}\right)^2 \frac{\phi(1 - u_t)}{\varepsilon(\varepsilon - 1)} - \frac{n_t - 1}{n_t}\frac{(\varepsilon - 1)n_t + 1}{\varepsilon n_t(\varepsilon - 1)}\rho + \alpha. \tag{4.41}$$

This innovation locus is downward sloping and linear in the unemployment rate, because an increase in unemployment reduces the available labor resources for all economic activities, including innovatory activities. Therefore, we may refer to equation (4.41) as the resource constraint.

Apart from the evident results that higher productivity in innovation and more patience encourage economic growth, we find that an increase in the elasticity of substitution reduces the growth rate for two reasons. First, high substitutability reduces the magnitude of an innovation, which is equivalent to a decline in research productivity, as indicated by the first ε in the previous equation. Secondly, it reduces the mark-up, as the potential stream of profit from an innovation declines, which is indicated by the $(\varepsilon - 1)$ term in the above expression. Finally, we find that in contrast to Aghion and Howitt (1994), unemployment exhibits a direct and negative impact on the rate of economic growth, as a reduction in the employed workforce will reduce labor in all sectors, and here in particular in the innovation sector.

As the number of innovations changes through time, the resource constraint shifts systematically. We can evaluate the impact of an increase in the number of innovations on the economic rate of growth by taking the derivative of equation (4.41) with respect to n_t,

$$\frac{\partial \hat{c}_t}{\partial n_t} = \frac{\partial \hat{c}_t}{\partial n_t} + \frac{\partial \hat{c}_t}{\partial u_t}\frac{\partial u_t}{\partial \hat{c}_t}\frac{\partial \hat{c}_t}{\partial n_t}.$$

The first part is the direct effect of increasing variety on economic growth, and the second is the indirect effect of an increase in the number of varieties on economic growth through the impact on unemployment. We can directly compute the direct effect and the first part of the indirect effect from the resource constraint (4.41). We can use the fact that the incentive condition is independent of the level of innovations by evaluating the second part of the indirect effect along the incentive condition (4.33).

Finally, the last part of the indirect effect is equivalent to the right-hand side, so that we can calculate the compound effect to equal after some rearrangement,

$$\frac{\partial \hat{c}_t}{\partial n_t} = 2(1 - u_t)\frac{\partial \hat{c}_t}{\partial u_t}\left[\frac{n_t - 1}{n_t} + \frac{\varepsilon(\varepsilon - 1)n_t}{\phi(n_t - 1)}\frac{\partial \hat{c}_t}{\partial u_t}\right]^{-1}, \tag{4.42}$$

where the derivative of output growth with respect to unemployment has been defined in equation (4.34). The incentive condition, equation (4.33), and the resource constraint, equation (4.39), completely define a dynamic system in the unemployment to economic growth

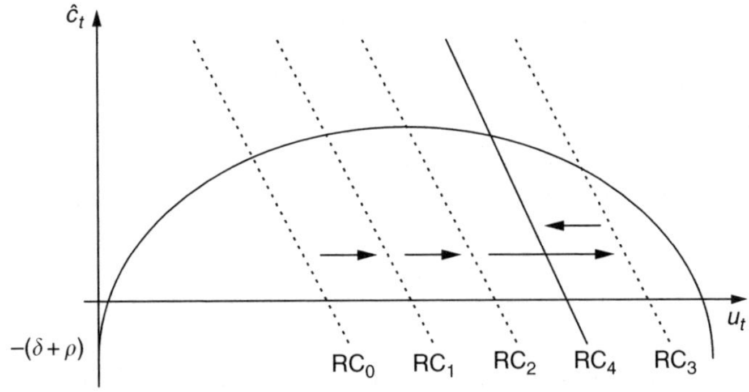

Figure 4.1 The resource constraint (RC) and the incentive condition (IC)

space. Whilst the resource constraint will shift through time as the number of innovations goes to infinity, the matching locus is time-invariant, hence describing the saddlepath of the system. In Figure 4.1, we describe the solution graphically.

As the resource constraint shifts with an increase in the number of varieties, the economy goes through three distinct phases. Initially, a manufacturing regime prevails, characterized by low rates of unemployment and low rates of economic growth. In the absence of large changes in the resource base, the service sector can only expand if it exhibits faster growth rates than the manufacturing sector, leading to an increase in aggregate growth. As the service sector expands in the economy, unemployment rises for two distinct reasons. First, there is sectoral unemployment, mainly experienced by recently fired manufacturing workers seeking job opportunities in the emerging service sector. Secondly, structural unemployment – that is, employees fired in declining service firms and attempting to find a job elsewhere in the new service economy – increases as the service sector as a whole expands in size.

Formally, for low rates of unemployment, which prevail in a pure manufacturing economy, the derivative of the incentive condition is positive, hence all terms in the derivative of the resource constraint (4.42) will be positive, implying that economic growth will increase as the number of varieties increases. Graphically, this is represented by an outwards shift of the resource constraint, from RC_0 to RC_1. Over time, both unemployment and economic growth will increase. As soon as the resource condition reaches the maximal growth rate, for the resource constraint RC_2, given by (4.35), the numerator in equation (4.42) turns negative, implying that from now on an increase in variety will reduce economic growth. The reason is that employment will continue to decline, reducing the number of available resources for innovative activities strong enough so that the overall impact on economic growth is negative. Graphically, this is represented by a further outward shift of the resource constraint, beyond the maximal growth rate, from RC_2 to RC_3.

When most of the sectoral unemployment has been digested as the new service economy emerges, unemployment rates will decline again, but will never return to previous levels, as the new economy is defined by a continuous flow of people into unemployment and out of unemployment, which is the novel feature of the emerging flexible labor market. Note that this result is capable of explaining the stylized facts as described in the introduction, in particular the increase of unemployment rates, reaching a peak and then declining to a level above the initial unemployment rate, as shown in Table 4.1.

Formally, we note that the maximal rate of growth the derivative of the incentive condition (4.34) is small, but will gain momentum as the resource constraint shifts further outwards. For certain parameter values, the second part of the denominator of equation (4.42) may exceed the first part, thus rendering the denominator negative. At that point, the impact of an increase in variety on economic growth will turn positive again, which we can graphically represent by an inward shift of the resource constraint, from RC_3 to RC_4. The shift of the resource constraint will cease, however, in the long run, and as the number of innovations goes to infinity, the resource constraint (4.41) converges to,

$$\lim_{n_t \to \infty} \hat{c}_t = \frac{\phi(1 - u_t)}{\varepsilon(\varepsilon - 1)} - \frac{\rho}{\varepsilon}. \tag{4.43}$$

4.9 Comparative dynamics

In the previous sections, we have been able to completely describe the evolution of the economy by two equations, the incentive condition (4.33) and the resource constraint (4.41), both represented graphically in Figure 4.1. Within this framework, we can analyse the impact of parameter changes. It has become conventional to refer to the immediate impact of a parameter change on the endogenous variables as the short run, the equilibrium impact as the long run, and the transitional dynamics from the short run to the long run as the medium run, and we will follow this classification in the following discussion.

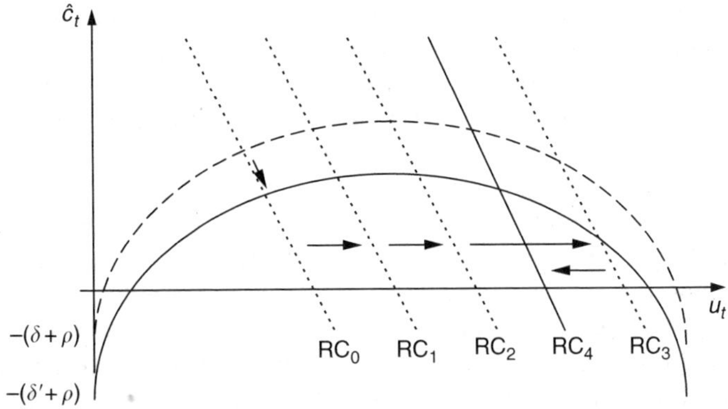

Figure 4.2 The comparative dynamics of an increase in the firing rate δ

First, an increase in the firing rate of the economy, δ, will shift the matching locus downward, but leave the resource constraint unaffected, as shown in Figure 4.2. In the short run, an increase in the firing rate will evidently encourage layoffs and thus increase unemployment. Unemployment rises much less than in the case of a horizontal resource constraint, which would be observed in an orthodox growth model, as presented in section 1.1 of this book. We can capture the intuition by realizing that in this model the firing rate works in much the same way as a depreciation rate. Indeed, δ is the depreciation rate for jobs, which in this setting is similar to a minimum capital requirement. When the rate of job destruction increases, the shadow value of an existing job will increase, and existing firms in the service sector will observe their profits rise as well. Given the monopolistic market structure, service firms can extract higher current profits than the higher discounted costs for layoffs, which fits empirical evidence recently produced by Walther (1999). As this makes entry in service markets more attractive, the rate of job creation will increase as well, reducing the impact of the increase in the firing rate. The evolution of the economy will be similar to that seen before. However, the long-run equilibrium will be characterized by a higher rate of unemployment and consequently a lower rate of growth, because of the lower availability of innovative workers.

Secondly, an increase in the individual rate of time preference, ρ, will also lead to a downward shift in the matching locus. At the same time, however, the resource constraint will also shift downwards by a factor of $1/\varepsilon$, which exceeds the shift of the matching locus. We therefore observe a reduction in both the growth rate and the unemployment rate in the economy. The growth effect is evident. As agents become less patient, they refrain from deferring consumption into the future, thus saving less. This leads to higher interest rates and therefore a decline in innovative investments. The unemployment effect is due to the fact that low rates of innovations expand the average product cycle, hence the number of layoffs declines, and labor market fricitions will become less severe, lowering the unemployment rate.

Thirdly, an increase in hiring costs κ will again only affect the incentive condition. However, it will turn the incentive condition downward through the zero unemployment point, leading to a lower maximum rate of growth (4.35). An increase in hiring costs will therefore unambiguously increase unemployment and reduce economic growth as n_t converges to infinity.

Fourthly, an increase in the individual bargaining power, β, has the same effect as an increase in hiring costs, turning the matching locus upwards. Indeed, higher bargaining power can be directly interpreted as an increase in hiring costs. If every personnel manager faces on average a tougher new employee, he will have to pay higher wages in every period that follows. Instead, we may discount this stream of costs to the present date, in which case they are a perfectly equivalent to an increase in hiring costs.

Fifthly, an increase in the arrival rate of new innovations, ϕ, will promote economic growth for every possible state of the resource constraint, thus pushing the resource constraints narrower together, e.g. from RC_2 to RC_2'. The effect, depicted in Figure 4.3, is an immediate increase in output growth, as a result of the productivity gains. These productivity gains

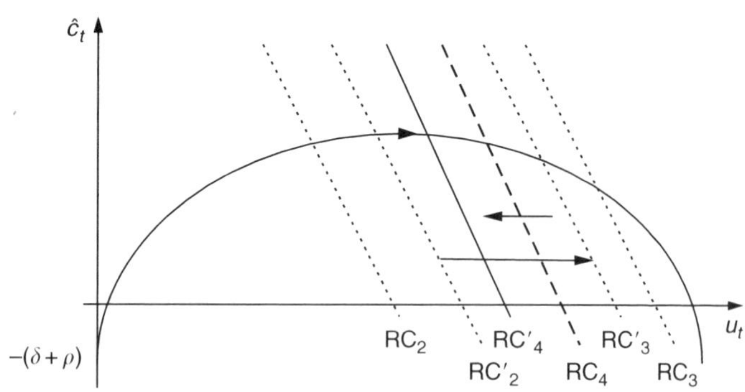

Figure 4.3 The comparative dynamics of an increase in innovation productivity ϕ

translate into faster structural change, thereby leading to an increase in the unemployment rate in the short run. In the long run, we observe the inverse. Whilst economic growth will still be higher than without the positive productivity shock, equilibrium unemployment will decline. The reason is that higher productivity renders a larger number of innovations lucrative, thus creating secure jobs in the innovative sector of the economy.

An increase in the elasticity of substitution, ε, has exactly the opposite effect. As an increase in substitutability decreases the degree of monopoly power for providers of innovative products, monopoly rents will decline for every product, current or future. But this implies that the rate of innovation will decline, reducing economic growth and unemployment in the short run. In the long run, economic growth will still be lower, but unemployment will be higher, due to a larger share of workers being in insecure jobs in the service sector.

4.10 Conclusions

This chapter has developed an economy with an endogenously expanding service sector, in which the constant flow of workers in and out of the employment relation leads to structural unemployment. The main finding is that the level of unemployment is different between the initial period, when everybody is employed in the service sector, and the final period, when a constant share of workers leave existing service firms to search for work in emerging service sector firms. During transition from the initial to the final state, the level of unemployment will overshoot its equilibrium level, the intuition being that in addition to the fluctuation within the service sector, workers from the manufacturing sector have to be allocated to the emerging service sector firms and the innovation sector.

We find that different parameters exhibit a different impact on economic growth and unemployment, and that their short-run impact may differ considerely from their long-run impact. First, we find that an increase in the rate of time preference reduces economic growth and unemployment in both the short and the long run. By contrast, an increase in hiring costs or a increase in the workers' bargaining power will evidently increase unemployment, but still lead to a lower rate of growth, in both the short and the long run. Somewhat surprisingly, the same holds for an increase in firing costs. This is essentially due to the fact that employers are aware today that they will have to lay off workers in the future, and firing costs are therefore simply deferred hiring costs.

Finally, we find that an increase in the innovation sector productivity and an increase in the mark-up will encourage economic growth in both the short and the long run, but will exhibit a negative impact on unemployment in the short run whilst ameliorating the unemployment problem in the long run.

The new economy, which will consist of a range of highly innovative service firms, will therefore alter not only the growth process, as described in chapter 3, but also the labor relations. First, the new economy will exhibit higher rates of unemployment, as the number of fluctuations in the economy increases. Given a more educated and flexible workforce in the new economy, we may assume that additional pressure on the labor market will come from the shift in relative bargaining power towards the workers.

5
Can Long-Term Wage Accords Promote Growth and Employment?

This chapter presents an innovation-driven endogenous growth model, in which firms and unions bargain over wages. We find that the degree of centralization of the bargaining structure plays a crucial rule in economic performance. Central bargaining, which incorporates the leapfrogging externality incorporated in firm-level bargaining, will yield lower rates of unemployment for a given rate of economic growth. The increase in labor resources will in turn also yield faster growth rates in a corporatist economy. Indeed, when unions focus on issues other than short-term wage increases, they may even outperform the non-unionized economy, because they can internalize the knowledge externality through long-term wage moderation accords.

5.1 Introduction

The success of the Dutch Polder model has led to a resurgent interest into the nature of wage accords. It is undoubtedly true that the Dutch model has led to high levels of employment, rapid economic growth, and eventually to a low rate of unemployment. The most significant feature of the Dutch Polder model is the fact that it has been agreed upon by weak unions, but at a centralized level of bargaining, over a longer time horizon, and essentially includes little other than an agreement to moderate wages. Indeed, Muysken (1999) went as far as to argue that the Dutch Polder model is about little else but wage moderation vis-à-vis its main trading partner, Germany.

The Dutch Polder model is only a last element in a row of wage agreements throughout Europe. The first evidence comes from Sweden, where a strong single union for a long period of time pursued long-term goals, in particular full employment (*arbete at alle*), the welfare state and prosperity (Meidner, Rehn et al., 1953; Rehn, 1952). In the Swedish Rehn–Meidner model, a key element has been the solidaristic wage policy, which in many circumstances implied wage moderation, in particular for the highly skilled employees (Agell and Lommerud, 1993).

Another interesting case has been Austria, which – with the possible exception of Sweden – has been historically the most corporatist regime in Europe. During the 1960s and 1970s, when the Austrian economy has characterized by high rates of economic growth, the president of the Austrian trade unions claimed that the process of wage bargaining should yield a productivity and inflation compensation. Needless to say, wages did indeed follow this Benya rule throughout the period, with deviations being largely due to forecasting errors (Nowotny, 1999). Given an initial moderation of wages, the pursuit of the Benya rule perpetuated the initial moderate agreement throughout the period.

Finally, even Germany initiated an attempt to produce a long-term wage agreement, in the Bündnis für Arbeit. The declared goal of this long-term accord between social partners has been to promote employment and growth through wage moderation. Apart from complementing government policies, this agreement has failed, since unions required employers to give job guarantees to compensate for the wage moderation (Heise, 2000).

The common features of these successful wage accords have been a fundamentally unilateral, but long-term agreement to moderate wages, in which firms did not have to commit to any other accompanying policy or concessions. Whilst the bargaining level of the accord has been at the central level, the relative bargaining power of the unions did not seem to matter, with both the strong Swedish Landsorganisationen and the weaker Dutch unions signing long-term wage accords. By contrast, the intervention of unions into firm policy seemed to have had a negative impact on the German agreement, as firms were willing to make any form of concessions.

The question then arises as to why unions would be willing to sign such an agreement, and by the same token why firms, which evidently benefit from wage moderation, seem so reluctant to make concessions in this area. We will agree that the central element which can explain such behavior lies in the internalization of macroeconomic, in particular endogenous growth, externalities, which is beneficial to the union and its members. By contrast, incumbent firms are indifferent to a wage accord, as the entire surplus of the internalization goes to novel firms, leaving incumbents unaffected.

5.2 Related literature

There exists a vast literature on the impact of unions on wage bargaining and economic performance. The debate has essentially focused on two issues – the bargaining power of trade unions, and the level of the bargaining, from firm level to the national and even supranational levels (Strozzi, 2000).

The idea that the degree of centralization of the bargaining structure exhibits a nonlinear relation dates back to the work of Calmfors and Driffill (1988). They have shown that as the bargaining level increases from the firm level to the industry level, wage rates increase, as the lower degree of product substitution allows unions to demand higher wage increases. By contrast, as the level of bargaining increases further to the national level, unions begin to internalize the leapfrogging externality of wage increases which get translated into subsequent price increases, hence wage deals become moderate again, leading to a higher level of economic performance.

The hump-shape hypothesis put forward by Calmfors and Driffill (1988) has been challenged on both theoretical and empirical grounds. The OECD (1994, p. 18ff) notes that the beneficial effect of corporatist, or centralized-bargaining, economies lies in the creation of private sector employment as the result of low wage deals, which contrasts with the evidence. It appears that small variations in the observation period and in the country sample may negate the findings of Calmfors and Driffill. On the other hand, high degrees of centralization are often correlated with high union bargaining power, and we may attribute bad economic performance to the latter factor.

Rowthorn (1992) offers two criticisms of Calmfors and Driffill. First, he notes that different degrees of unionization across sectors, which implicitly assumes different degrees of union bargaining power across sectors, will lead to wage dispersion for given average values of corporatism – thereby weakening the clear-cut correlation as suggested by Calmfors and Driffill. Second, he suggests that the hump shape may break down completely as unions cease to pursue only short-term material gains. Barth and Zweimueller (1995) have demonstrated that one can preserve the hump-shape even in the presence of wage dispersion.

This chapter addresses the second aspect of the Rowthorn critique. It argues that in the presence of a macroeconomic externality, unions may prefer to pursue long-term policies which focus not only on short-term monetary gains in the form of higher wages, as suggested by Calmfors and Driffill, but on long-term economic perspectives, in particular economic growth. This chapter shows that this policy can be unilaterally implemented by unions adopting a commitment to long-term wage moderation. In the presence of macroeconomic externalities, unions have always been considered as an important element to explain economic performance. Bertola (1994) has shown that in the presence of irreversible investment and firing costs, unions can exploit their increased bargaining power to extract a larger share of national income, thus reducing investment and economic growth. Irmen and Wigger (2000) extend the Uhlig and Yanagawa (1996) overlapping generations framework, where workers – the young generation – save and thus a reallocation of income to labour is growth enhancing, to include unions. Whilst Uhlig and Yanagawa make the case for capital taxation, Irmen and Wigger show that unions, which raise wages, have a similar impact on the reallocation of income – they foster savings, and, thus, economic growth. Whilst Irmen and Wigger claim that workers, who engage most in accumulation, are the driving force of growth as opposed to capitalists, and hence increasing wages fosters economic growth, this chapter claims that Schumpeterian innovators are the engine of growth. Raising wages will therefore increase innovation costs and thereby reduce economic growth. If unions, however, engage in wage moderation, innovation and economic growth will increase, inducing faster wage growth and thus potentially higher welfare. In that respect, a long-term wage agreement can be interpreted as a dynamic coalition between workers and firms establishing an efficient equilibrium allocation (Cooley and Smith, 1989; Prescott and Boyd, 1986).

5.3 Households and unions

In this model economy, households face four types of choices. First, they have to choose between whether they wish to consume their labor and non-labor income today or in the future. In other words, they face an intertemporal tradeoff between consumption and savings. Secondly, they have to choose which quantities from a variety of goods they wish to consume today. Given homothetic preferences, we can separate the two problems. Hence, they also face an intratemporal tradeoff between different varieties of consumption goods. Thirdly, they have to choose whether or not to offer labor services. We shall abstract from this choice by assuming that households supply one unit of labor inelastically. This assumption is made for the sake of simplicity, because it allows us to determine all unemployment as involuntary. Fourthly, households have to choose whether or not to join a trade union. Assuming that trade union membership is free but conditioned on employment in an organized sector, this choice is trivial. All households with a job in an organized sector will join the union and will be represented by the union in wage negotiations. Households determine their intertemporal consumption pattern by maximizing an intertemporal utility function, where we assume point-in-time utility (felicity) to be linear,

$$U_s = \int_s^\infty c_t e^{-\rho(t-s)} dt, \tag{5.1}$$

where ρ is the individual rate of time preference, and c_t is aggregate consumption over time t. Households maximize utility subject to an intertemporal budget constraint,

$$\dot{a}_t = r_t a_t + w_t(1 - u_t) - c_t, \tag{5.2}$$

which states that a household saves that part of interest income $r_t a_t$, and labor income w_t for those who expect not to be unemployed u_t, that is not spent on consumption c_t. Unemployed workers receive no benefits. However, this has no consequences for the macroeconomic outcome, as will be shown later on. Hamiltonian optimization of the utility function subject to the budget constraint with respect to consumption, asset accumulation, and a shadow price of income yield an intertemporal Euler condition,

$$r_t = \rho, \tag{5.3}$$

which fixes the rate of interest at the individual rate of time preference. This condition implies that savings are completely elastic. If the interest rate only slightly exceeds the intertemporal rate of time preference, households will completely refrain from consumption, leading to an excess supply of loanable funds that drives the interest back to the rate of time preference. By contrast, if the interest rate falls short of the rate of time preference, households immediately demand infinite amounts of credit for consumption, driving the interest rate back up. The intuition for this result is simple. In the absence of a diminishing marginal product of consumption, given that felicity is linear, households are indifferent about the time of consumption. As they can transfer funds across time at the interest rate, but discount future consumption at the rate of time preference, any difference between the two will lead to either a shift of consumption into the present or the infinite future. In every point in time, households demand differentiated products according to the following constant elasticities of substitution subfelicity function,

$$c_t = \left[\int_0^{n_t} x_{i,t}^{(\varepsilon-1)/\varepsilon}\, di\right]^{\varepsilon/(\varepsilon-1)}, \tag{5.4}$$

where $x_{i,t}$ is a specific product variety. As households spend $p_t c_t$ on consumption products, the budget constraint for optimization reads,

$$\int_0^{n_t} p_{i,t} x_{i,t}\, di \le p_t c_t, \tag{5.5}$$

where $p_{i,t}$ is the price of a specific service i. The final stage in the household problem yields after optimization a demand function for a specific product,

$$x_{i,t} = \left(\frac{p_{i,t}}{p_t}\right)^{-\varepsilon} c_t, \tag{5.6}$$

and we find that ε is the demand elasticity for any particular product. Moreover, we obtain a definition for the price index of consumption products,

$$p_t = \left[\int_0^{n_t} p_{i,t}^{1-\varepsilon}\, di\right]^{1/(1-\varepsilon)}. \tag{5.7}$$

5.4 The product market

We assume that each differentiated product is provided by a single profit-maximizing firm, which uses labor as the sole input. For simplicity, we assume that technology is linear in its labor force $e_{i,t}$,

$$x_{i,t} = e_{i,t}, \tag{5.8}$$

where labor productivity has been normalized to unity. Firms hire workers on an organized labor market for a negotiated wage of $w_{i,t}$. Firms maximize profits, defined as revenues minus costs,

$$\pi_{i,t} = p_{i,t} x_{i,t} - w_{i,t} e_{i,t}, \tag{5.9}$$

subject to demand (5.6), which yields a well-known optimality condition,

$$p_{i,t} = \frac{\varepsilon}{\varepsilon - 1} w_{i,t}, \tag{5.10}$$

namely that the price is equal to the mark-up over costs. Service sector firms therefore obtain rents equal to,

$$\pi_{i,t} = \frac{1}{\varepsilon - 1} w_{i,t} e_{i,t}, \tag{5.11}$$

Firms will, either jointly or separately, have to negotiate over wages with the respective trade union, as will be discussed below.

5.5 Industry unions and employment

Unions organize workers in order to extract rents from employers. In our model we assume that unions are benevolent, and that they will try to maximize welfare for their members. Given the linearity of utility in consumption, this is equivalent to maximizing the income of the union members. For the moment, we shall assume that unions can only negotiate over current wages, hence the union operating in sector *i* has an objective function $\overline{\omega}_{i,t}$ equal to,

$$\overline{\omega}_{i,t} = s_{i,t} w_{i,t} e_{i,t} + (1 - s_{i,t}) o_t e_{i,t}, \tag{5.12}$$

given that workers remain in the sector with probability $s_{i,t}$, leading to earnings of $w_{i,t}e_{i,t}$, and will have to leave the sector with probability $(1 - s_{i,t})$, in which case they will earn the outside option income of $o_{i,t}e_{i,t}$. Evidently, as the union demands a higher wage, the probability of remaining in the sector declines. However, the wage elasticity of survival can be shown to be constant. In order to show this point, we separate the wage elasticity of survival into an employment elasticity of survival and a wage elasticity of employment. Substituting technology (5.8) and the mark-up equation (5.10) into product demand (5.6), we find that the wage elasticity of employment is equal to $-\varepsilon$. Given that there are no voluntary redundancies and that everybody is a union member, everybody will survive on the job if and only if employment does not decline, whereas only a certain proportion of the workforce remains on the job if employment within a firm declines, hence

$$s_{i,t} = P(e_{i,t} > e_{i,t-1}) + e_{i,t}/e_{i,t-1} P(e_{i,t} \leq e_{i,t-1}). \tag{5.13}$$

Noting that employment within a particular firm is bound to decline in a growing economy, as shown in chapter 3, hence equation (5.13) reduces to $s_{i,t} = e_{i,t}/e_{i,t-1}$, implying that the employment elasticity of survival is equal to unity. Hence, the wage elasticity of survival equals,

$$\eta = \frac{\partial s_{i,t}}{\partial w_{i,t}} \frac{w_{i,t}}{s_{i,t}} = -\varepsilon. \tag{5.14}$$

The outside option, which workers – who will have to leave the firm – are facing, depends on their chance of finding another union job, a job in the innovation sector, or whether they will be forced into unemployment, in which case they will not receive any payments,

$$o_t = (1 - \varphi u_t)w_t + \delta\varphi u_t w_t^{RD}. \tag{5.15}$$

Evidently, as unemployment increases, the probability of getting another union job $(1 - \varphi u_t)$ which yields the average wage w_t declines (Layard, Nickell and Jackman, 1991, p. 101), implying that workers either have to look for a job in the innovation sector, which they obtain and accept with probability δ, or become unemployed. Note that the outside option is dramatically reduced in the case of centralized bargaining, where the first term in equation (5.15) vanishes.

Firms and unions engage in bargaining over the wage, and it can be shown that the outcome of this bargaining process will equal the maximum of the following expression, the so-called Nash maximand (Rubinstein, 1982),

$$\Omega_t = [\overline{\omega}_{i,t} - o_t]^{\beta}[\pi_{i,t}] = [s_{i,t}e_{i,t}(w_{i,t} - o_t)]^{\beta}[p_{i,t}x_{i,t} - w_{i,t}e_{i,t}], \tag{5.16}$$

where the first expression equals the union's objective function minus the union's threat point in case of no agreement, in which case all union members would have to refrain to the outside option. The second term equals the firm's objective function, noting that the firm's threat point equals zero, because no agreement implies no production and hence no revenues, but also no costs. β describes the relative bargaining power of unions, and equals zero in the case of no union power, leading to the market solution, and infinity in the case of a monopoly union which can set wages univocally.

Taking logs and derivatives, applying the envelope theorem, and making use of the definition of profits (5.11) and the wage elasticity of survival (5.14), we obtain the following first-order condition for an optimal bargain,

$$\frac{w_{i,t} - o_t}{o_t} = \frac{\beta}{\varepsilon - 1 - \beta(\eta + 1)} = \frac{\beta}{(1 + \beta)(\varepsilon - 1)}, \tag{5.17}$$

stating that the share of the rent the union can extract depends positively on its bargaining power, negatively on the elasticity of substitution on the product market, and positively on the elasticity of survival. The first result is self-explanatory. Noting that higher wages get translated into higher prices due to the mark-up equation (5.10), a higher price elasticity of demand ε exhibits a drastic reduction in demand and hence employment, and thus weakens the bargaining position of unions. Finally, a high wage elasticity of survival allows unions to make tougher settlements, and thus increase the wage mark-up.

The outside option can be straightforwardly referred to as the reservation wage. In the absence of any disutility of labor, households should offer their entire labor services on the labor market if the wage only slightly exceeds the reservation wage, but refrain from offering labor services if the wage falls short of the reservation wage. In the presence of unions, $\beta > 0$, equation (5.17) therefore drives a wage between the labor supply schedule and the labor demand schedule. We may therefore already conclude that as the wage exceeds its marginal product, union activity leads to unemployment.

5.6 Equilibrium

Once we know the value of the outside option, equation (5.17) solves the model straightforwardly. The outside option (5.14) contains five endogenous variables: the average wage in the unionized part of the economy w_t, the wage in the non-unionized innovation sector w_t^{RD}, the probability of obtaining and accepting a job in the unionized sector, φu_t, and the innovation sector, δ, respectively, and the unemployment rate u_t. Given symmetry over technology and preferences in the consumption goods sector, no firm or union can agree to a different wage, without triggering adjustment processes in the negotiations of other – or even their own – firms. This implies that in equilibrium we must have $w_{i,t} = w_t$ for all i, which, in turn, implies that all product market firms set identical prices, according to the mark-up equation (5.10).

Substituting this into the price index (5.7), and then into demand (5.6), yields aggregate consumption as a function of product market employment, $e_t = e_{i,t}n_t$, and the number of available products,

$$c_t = e_t n_t^{1/(\varepsilon-1)}. \tag{5.4'}$$

Along the balanced growth path, employment in the consumption product sector will be constant, implying that the growth rate of consumption depends only upon the growth rate in the number of varieties,

$$\hat{c}_t = \frac{1}{\varepsilon - 1}\hat{n}_t, \tag{5.4''}$$

which is also equal to the growth rate of real wages, as can be seen by differentiating the price index (5.7). Finally, we find that in an equilibrium with positive growth, individual firms will permanently deploy workers, at the same rate as new products, and hence new firms arrive at the market, since $e_{i,t} = e_{i,t} = e_t/n_t$, we have

$$\hat{e}_{i,t} = -\hat{n}_t, \tag{5.8'}$$

This now allows us to determine the probability of obtaining a job in the unionized sector which, following Layard, Nickell and Jackman (1991, p. 145), equals

$$\varphi = 1 - r_t/\hat{e}_{i,t} = 1 + \rho/(\varepsilon - 1)\hat{c}_t, \tag{5.18}$$

where we have made use of the Euler equation (5.3) and the growth rate of aggregate consumption (5.4). In order to determine both the wage in the innovation sector and the probability of obtaining and accepting a job in the unionized sector, we now turn to the determinants of the innovation sector.

5.7 Economic growth and the innovation sector

People engage in activities to introduce new varieties to the goods market. This costly activity takes time and effort. Recently, Unger and Zagler (2003) have made an attempt to estimate arrival functions for new product innovations. They find evidence that the number of employed researchers has a direct positive impact on the arrival rate of new innovations, and that the number of existing product innovations has a positive indirect effect, because the number of differentiated products increases the number of potential research networks, which exhibit a direct effect on the arrival rate of innovations. This leads to the following specification for the arrival rate of new innovations,

$$\dot{n}_t = \phi n_t s_t. \tag{5.19}$$

Competitive firms in the innovation sector maximize profits. The highest price a potential service provider can pay to an innovator will equal the value $v_{i,t}$ of any given firm *i*. The only costs for an innovator are wages w_t^{RD}, paid to scientists, s_t. Hence, given technology as stated in (5.16′), the marginal cost for the provision of a new variety will equal its price,

$$v_{i,t} = \frac{w_t^{RD}}{\phi n_t}. \tag{5.20}$$

As the innovation has to be prefinanced, an innovator has to raise the costs of an innovation on the capital market. No arbitrage on the capital market implies that the change in the sales value of an innovation and the maximal amount of dividends which one can obtain from an innovation must equal the return from a safe investment, $r_t v_{i,t}$,

$$\dot{v}_{i,t} + \pi_{i,t} = r_t v_{i,t}, \tag{5.21}$$

where the maximum amount of dividends evidently equals the running profits $\pi_{i,t}$ of a product market firm applying the innovation. Dividing both sides of equation (5.21) by the capital market value $v_{i,t}$, eliminating the growth rate with the time derivative of (5.20), profits from equation (5.11), and the capital market value from equation (5.20), and the interest rate from the intertemporal Euler equation (5.3), we obtain

$$\hat{w}_t^{RD} - \hat{n}_t + \frac{\phi e_t}{\varepsilon - 1}\frac{w_t}{w_t^{RD}} = \rho. \tag{5.21′}$$

By differentiating equation (5.21′), we find that along the balanced growth path, where employment in the consumption goods sector is constant, the relative consumption goods to innovation sector wage, w_t^{RD}/w_t, is also constant.

We can determine the relative wage by looking at the innovation sector labor market. For the sake of simplicity, assume that not everybody is capable of working in the innovation sector, but only a fraction δ of the workforce, and that the ability is revealed to both the employee and the employer at the job interview. Moreover, as the type of innovation changes over time, we shall assume that any previous ability or inability to work in the innovation sector exerts no impact on whether you are able to work in the sector now – hence jobs in the innovation sector only last for one period. Keeping this in mind, we find that the total potential labor supply in the innovation sector is constant and equal to $\delta(1 - e_t)$.

In order to determine the wage in the innovation sector, note that the innovation sector wage must be equal or below the consumption goods sector wage, otherwise everyone would stream into the innovation sector labor market, leading to a breakdown in the consumption goods sector. Assuming that workers can only have one job interview every instant, or one attempt to match to a vacancy, once the wage in the innovation sector falls below a certain threshold, the innovation sector reservation wage, workers will refrain from looking for a job in the innovation sector, and will only apply for jobs in the unionized consumption goods sector.

Whilst in the absence of unions the influx of workers into the consumption goods sector drives innovation sector wage to their consumption goods sector counterparts, a closed labor market in the consumption goods sector implies that competition in the innovation sector labor market drives innovation sector wages down to the innovation sector reservation wage. As in this case workers choose not to accept jobs in the innovation sector, this reservation wage reduces to the first term in equation (5.15), namely $(1 - \varphi u_t)w_t$.

We can therefore eliminate the relative wage in the no arbitrage condition (5.21). Moreover, because the entire labor force, which we shall normalize to unity, can be either working in the product market sector, e_t, the innovation sector, s_t, or be unemployed, we can eliminate product market employment from equation (5.21′) as well, resulting in a relationship between economic growth and unemployment,

$$\hat{c}_t = \frac{\phi}{\varepsilon - 1}(1 - u_t) - (1 - \varphi u_t)[\rho - (\varepsilon - 2)\hat{c}_t]. \tag{5.22}$$

This equation summarizes in which way the economy allocates resources to the different sectors, and therefore describes a resource constraint. Note in particular that, as unemployment increases, there are less labor resources available for every sector, implying a decline in economic growth. Note that in the market solution, the $(1 - \varphi u_t)$ term vanishes, leading to lower growth rates, as innovation labor becomes more expensive.

5.8 Unemployment and union size

We are now able to determine all elements of the outside option (5.15), and can therefore derive the unemployment rate as a function of growth and the industrial relation regime. Assuming that the level of unemployment is low, so that the square of the unemployment rate is negligible, then the unemployment rate in the case of firm-level bargaining equals,

$$u_t^f = \frac{\beta}{\varphi(1 - \delta)(\beta\varepsilon + \varepsilon - 1)}, \tag{5.23}$$

where the f denotes firm-level bargaining. The unemployment rate depends upon the growth rate through two channels. First, an increase in the growth rate increases labor demand in the innovation sector, raising the incidence of innovation. This pushes the outside option up, leading to higher wage deals in the unionized sector, and making more people unemployed. As the unions push up wages when wages in other sectors increase, we may refer to this effect as the intersectoral leapfrogging effect. Secondly, an increase in the growth rate implies that more new firms open in the unionized sector, increasing the probability of a fired worker obtaining a new unionized job. This, again, increases the outside option, fostering high wage deals and unemployment. As this effect is due to a decline in the value of the job of an employed worker, we may refer to it as a capitalization effect (Aghion and Howitt, 1998). Finally, note that by setting the relative union power to zero, we obtain the market outcome, denoted by m,

$$u_t^m = 0, \tag{5.24}$$

where unemployment equals zero. In contrast to the firm-level bargaining (5.19), centralized bargaining will produce a different outcome. This is essentially because of the leapfrogging externality that is present in firm-level bargaining, but largely absent in centralized bargaining. In the first instance, a firm which reaches a high wage deal will raise the average wage of the unionized sector, and therefore augment the outside option, leading to higher wage deals everywhere, resulting in high unemployment. In centralized bargaining, the outside option widely vanishes, which leads to an unemployment rate equal to,

$$u_t^c = \frac{(1+\beta)(\varepsilon-1)}{\varphi\delta(\beta\varepsilon+\varepsilon-1)}, \tag{5.25}$$

where the c stands for centralization. Evidently, due to a lower value of the outside option, a centralized union will strike a lower wage deal, leading to lower unemployment for every rate of economic growth.

We can represent the equilibria of the different industrial relations regimes on a unifying graph. With the exception of the market outcome, the resource constraint (5.22) is identical for all regimes. It is a downward-sloping plane in a growth-unemployment graph. The second condition differs across regimes due to the specifities of the bargaining situation. Given that it is the different level of the outside option which determines the location of the locus, we may refer to it as an incentive constraint.

With the exception of the market outcome, the slope of the incentive constraint is upward sloping, since

$$\frac{\partial u_t}{\partial \hat{n}_t} = \frac{\rho u_t}{\varphi \hat{n}_t^2}. \tag{5.26}$$

Figure 5.1 summarizes the results. We observe a result rather similar to the findings of Calmfors and Driffill (1988). The market solution leads to the lowest rate of unemployment and to the highest rate of growth. Firm-level bargaining leads to both the highest levels of unemployment and the lowest rates of economic growth. The centralized bargaining situation is somewhere in between these two regimes, resulting in the typical hump-shape curve as presented in Calmfors and Driffill (1988). However, the analysis presents an important extension. The actual level of unemployment depends upon the growth rate experienced within the economy, which has been ignored as a control variable in their analysis.

In any case, the analysis leads to a strong conclusion – that unions are an obstacle to economic growth and foster unemployment. However, the question arises whether unions really pursue the policies as described

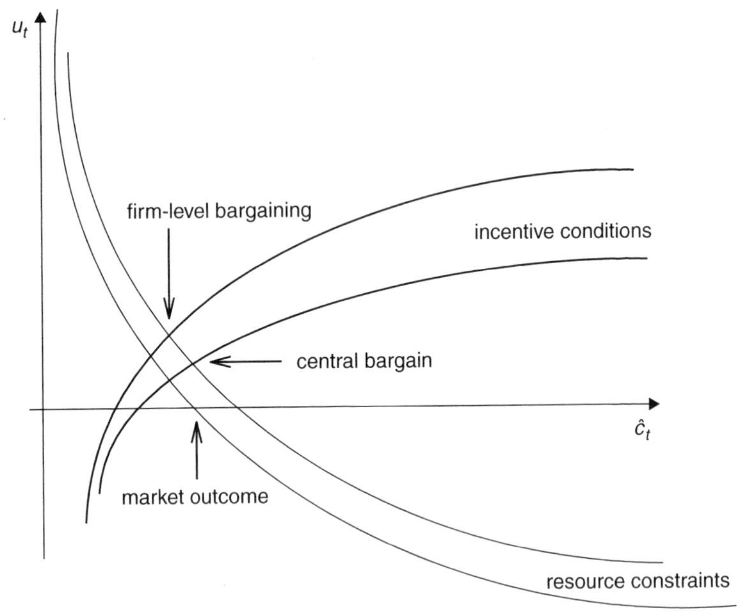

Figure 5.1 The unemployment to economic growth space

in the simple one-period bargaining solution presented in section 5.3. In the following, we will ask whether unions can improve the situation of their members by offering a deal which would find acceptance among firms.

5.9 Externalities, social optimum and long-term union policy

The economy previously described contains three types of externalities. First, there is monopolistic competition in the product markets, leading to product prices that are above their socially optimal level. Secondly, there is a knowledge externality in the growth process. As existing knowledge enters innovation technology (5.19) without cost, innovators tend to produce too few innovations in equilibrium, leading to a suboptimal rate of economic growth. Finally, the industrial organization regime presents the third type of externality. It is therefore by no means clear whether or not the results presented in the previous sections indeed maximize the welfare of union members. In order to answer this question, we would have to compare the social planner solution with the market outcomes, and judge whether union policy could indeed be ameliorated.

First, note that the monopolistic competition externality is due to the fact that firms face a downward-sloping demand schedule (5.6), leading them to reduce quantities in order to increase prices and profits. It is well-known that either a revenue subsidy equal to $1/(\varepsilon - 1)$ or a wage subsidy equal to $1/\varepsilon$ would lead to welfare-optimal prices, and hence eliminate the externality. However, as subsidies have to be raised by non-distortionary taxation, most governments will refrain from undertaking such a policy. As the same result can be generated by wage moderation of $(\varepsilon - 1)/\varepsilon$ below the market wage, unions could in principle internalize the monopolistic competition externality as well, and thus induce the welfare optimum. However, workers will benefit from such a union policy only indirectly – through lower product prices and higher profits. Given that a single firm, and hence a single firm-union only exhibits a negligible influence on the aggregate price level, this policy can only be induced by centralized bargaining. Given that unions will have a hard time to communicate their indirect influence on welfare to union members, and that they will reject the distributional consequences of higher profits, wage moderation – though desirable – appears unlikely.

Secondly, we have to ask how to internalize the knowledge externality. In order to develop this point, consider an institution, or a firm operating under perfect competition, which purchases the exclusive right of all knowledge at a price κ_t, and sells at a market price q_t to innovators, leaving aside the problem of property rights for the moment. Then profits of the knowledge institutions would equal,

$$\Pi_0 = \int_0^\infty \kappa_t n_t e^{-rt} dt - \int_0^\infty q_t \dot{n}_t e^{-rt} dt$$

$$= \int_0^\infty (\kappa_t - q_t/r) n_t e^{-rt} dt - q_0 n_0. \tag{5.27}$$

Maximizing profits implies an optimal pricing rule for the initial period equal to

$$\kappa_0 = q_0(1 + 1/\rho), \tag{5.28}$$

where we have substituted the interest rate from the Euler condition (5.3), and for any subsequent period,

$$\kappa_t = q_t/\rho. \tag{5.28'}$$

Evidently, the knowledge holder immediately makes windfall profits from all existing knowledge which he did not have to purchase at the beginning of the operation, with no consequences for his pricing policy thereafter.

The appropriation of knowledge property rights now alters the decision of innovation sector firms in three ways. First, they have to pay a cost κ_t for all the knowledge they apply when innovating new products, but receive, secondly, a price q_t from the knowledge holder for every new innovation, hence innovation sector firms maximize profits,

$$\pi_t = v_{i,t}\dot{n}_t - w_t^{RD} s_t - \kappa_t n_t + q_t \dot{n}_t, \tag{5.29}$$

subject to technology (5.15). Third, firms now actively choose the amount of knowledge they demand for their innovations, leading to two first-order conditions,

$$\frac{\partial \pi_t}{\partial s_t} = v_{i,t}\phi n_t - w_t^{RD} + q_t \phi n_t, \tag{5.30}$$

and

$$\frac{\partial \pi_t}{\partial n_t} = v_{i,t}\phi s_t - \kappa_t + q_t \phi s_t. \tag{5.30'}$$

Together with equation (5.29′), we can then determine optimal purchasing and sales prices of knowledge, where the sales price will equal

$$\kappa_t = \frac{v_{i,t}\hat{n}_t}{1 - \rho\hat{n}_t}, \tag{5.28''}$$

and the purchasing price follows from (5.28′). Subsequently, we can then also determine the optimal price of an innovation, which equals

$$v_{i,t} = \frac{(1 - \rho\hat{n}_t)w_t^{RD}}{\phi n_t}, \tag{5.29'}$$

Compared with equation (5.20), we find that the optimal price of an innovation is lower by a fraction $1 - \rho\hat{n}_t$ than the market price. Apart from technical difficulties, the optimal price can therefore be achieved by subsidizing the sales price of an innovation (5.20) by an amount τ, implying $v'_{i,t} = v_{i,t} + \tau$, hence $\tau = \rho w_t^{RD}\hat{n}_t/\phi n_t$, which is increasing over time as wages grow faster than innovations. Governments therefore face three difficulties in promoting the welfare optimal solution: first there is a technical difficulty in determining innovation revenues, then there is the problem of raising non-distortionary taxes to finance the subsidy, and finally governments will have to spend ever-increasing amounts of money to sustain the welfare optimal equilibrium. Given that the growth rate of innovation differs from the growth rate of consumption, not even the share of subsidies to output is constant. Only if GDP would include non-tangible investment into new innovations at the hypothetical market price q_t, would the share of government spending to GDP be stationary.

Noting that innovation sector wages are proportional to wages in the organized sector, the alternative possibility for inducing the social optimum would be for unions to negotiate a wage moderation of $1 - \rho\hat{n}_t$. Once again, this wage deal can only be agreed upon by centralized unions, given the fact that small unions have no impact on aggregate wages, but every incentive to deviate from a wage moderation agreement.

Given that wage moderation leads to faster economic growth, real wages will grow faster as well (5.4″), leading in the long run to higher wages, and therefore to a direct increase in the welfare of unionized workers. Given that wage moderation also internalizes the monopolistic competition externality, wage moderation is in any case welfare improving. As opposed to the indirect effects, wage moderation to internalize the knowledge externality exerts direct, however intertemporal, effects on wages.

However, while workers may benefit from wage moderation, incumbent firms do not. Three offsetting effects are the cause of the indifference of firms striking a wage accord or not. First, note that running profits, which for a particular product market firm will equal $c_t/(\varepsilon n_t)$ in equilibrium, decline, as the wage moderation will also induce lower current consumption. Whilst workers will see their wages, and hence utility increase at the growth rate of consumption, profits will only grow at $\hat{c}_t - \hat{n}_t$, with the remaining profits going to emerging firms. Incumbent firms, as opposed to unions, are therefore much less willing to strike a long-term wage accord, hence unions will have a hard time negotiating other forms of compensation from a wage moderation accord, but must more or less unilaterally set the lower wage.

An agreement to moderate wages must be long lasting, and product market and innovation sector firms must be aware of this fact. If they consider the wage moderation to be temporary in nature, product market firms will seize the opportunity to make windfall profits out of lower purchasing prices, and will discount future rents immediately. Innovation sector firms will hold back innovations and sell when the prices have gone up again, actually reducing economic growth.

For this reason, growth pacts between unions and firms will have to contain a long-lasting feature. This can be either in the form of wage formulas, according to which an initial wage moderation is carried over by strict productivity rules – as was the case in both Austria and the Dutch Polder model – or when unions commit to low R&D wage rates due to a solidaristic wage policy, as has been the case in Sweden.

5.10 Conclusions

This chapter has shown that long-term wage accords may indeed improve the performance of an economy in the presence of macroeconomic externalities. The intuition from this result is straightforward. If innovation takes two factors, existing knowledge and effort, but only the latter is remunerated, then equilibrium prices are distorted, with innovation sector labor being paid too much, and the existing stock of knowledge being paid too little. Union policy which accounts for this effect can therefore improve the situation and promote a welfare-improving industrial relations system. Moreover, we have seen that government policy is much less likely to adopt similar policies, both because of the technical difficulties of the required tax and subsidy scheme, and because of the necessity of permanently increasing subsidy rates. The wage accord has to meet certain features. First, it is intertemporal in nature, with forgone income yielding higher wages only in the future, and unions may need to convince their members of the advantages or necessities of such a long-term agreement. We have seen arguments based on solidarity both within a generation and amongst generations as one possible union communication strategy, as has been the case in Sweden, and arguments along the line of competitiveness in the Netherlands, where wage moderation today has been interpreted as an investment into high growth and high future income, which indeed it is.

The wage accord must be settled at the central bargaining level, since leapfrogging would prevent industry-level or firm-level unions from sticking to a wage accord, and it must run over longer time horizons, in order to provide the incentive for innovators to invest into new products and technologies.

Wage accords will be more beneficial to unions and its members than to incumbent firms, which will not see their profits increase greatly. This implies, on the one hand, that the burden of the wage accord must be fully carried by unions, but, on the other, that the unions' bargaining power is irrelevant in determining the outcome of the agreement. Given that unions must unilaterally forgo wages, it is of little relevance whether or not the accord is officially signed, or whether unions unilaterally commit themselves to according wage policy strategy.

Indeed, we have seen both officially signed wage accords – such as the Dutch Wassenaar agreement – and unilateral union commitment to pursue long-term wage policies. Whilst the Austrian Benya rule exhibits the feature to extrapolate a given rate of wage moderation into the indefinite future, hence internalizing the growth externality according to equation (5.29′), the Swedish solidaristic wage policy may be interpreted as a means of reducing the relative wage in equation (5.21′), leading to similar results for economic growth.

In short, we have seen that wage accords may lead to faster economic growth, lower unemployment, and higher welfare, at the cost of lower initial wages, which may explain both the success and failure of these industrial relations agreements.

6
Aggregate Demand and Keynesian Unemployment

This chapter argues that in a growing economy unemployment can be the cause of goods markets failures, even if these are purely transitory. As the economy grows, new firms wish to enter product markets. It may take some time, however, for their products to be accepted in the market, a phenomenon which we model as a purely transitory demand shock. Firms who fail early entry will renege on any job offers, causing unemployment. Anticipating this, workers will ask for a risk premium in insecure contracts, distorting the price and supply decisions of firms, and reducing incentives to invest into novel products. This will reduce, but will not eliminate the number of precarious job offers. Thus, a transitory demand shock will lead to a persistent level of unemployment in a growing economy.

6.1 Motivation

Reading Okun's seminal contribution on the relationship between growth and unemployment carefully (Okun, 1970), we learn that, according to his estimates, a one per cent decline in the unemployment rate will lead to a 3 per cent growth in output, whereas the recent political debate has inverted this relationship to argue that an increase in economic growth will reduce unemployment (European Commission, 1993).

The difference between these two positions lies in the focus of the analysis. A modern version of Okun's law argues that whenever producers wish to extend output beyond productivity growth, they will need to hire workers, thus reducing unemployment. This is essentially a supply-side argument. By contrast, Okun had originally stressed the importance of demand factors in his analysis. He argues that as positive shock hits aggregate demand, firms begin to employ new workers, who contribute to additional aggregate demand, thus supporting a new equilibrium where unemployment has declined whilst output has grown.

However, the argument inverts for a negative shock to aggregate demand. Thus, if we assume that demand shocks are transitory and mean reverting, Okun's law cannot explain persistent unemployment, unless one assumes that labor markets fail to clear even in the long run.

Despite having an interpretation that is quite different from the original Okun article, the renewed interest in the subject has led to a series of interesting empirical results. Starting with the work of Bishop and Haveman (1979), Holloway (1989) and Courtney (1991), and more recently Candelon and Hecq (1998), a number of authors have suggested that there has been a breakdown of Okun's law. However, in recent years cointegration studies have found renewed confidence in a relationship between unemployment and economic growth (Altissimo and Violante, 1999; Attfield and Silverstone, 1998).

Hence, whilst we have seen a breakdown of the relation between growth and unemployment in the short run, we find evidence that there is a relation in the long run. We can only explain this fact if we can identify different shocks in the economy, some of which will cause a unidirectional shift in unemployment and economic growth, while others must have an opposite effect on growth and unemployment. Then, evidence collected in the short run can be distorted enough to eliminate the Okun relationship, whereas in the long run, when the impact of the shocks has passed through the system, the underlying structural relationship between unemployment and economic growth is revealed. Traditional models of economic growth and unemployment are not able to capture this fact. Consider first the Solow model (Solow, 1956). Assume that there is an exogenously given amount of unemployment. In the steady state, the optimal capital stock and GDP per worker will be independent of the level of unemployment. Then, a shock to unemployment will not affect these equilibrium values. However, as an increase in unemployment reduces the labor force, GDP and GDP per capita will decline – although this will still not affect the growth rate of GDP. Therefore, only a permanent decline or increase in the unemployment rate, which is ruled out by definition, may give rise to the above mentioned structural relationship between growth and unemployment.

The endogenous growth literature, by contrast, can motivate a structural relation between growth and unemployment (Aghion and Howitt, 1994). However, we find that the relation between unemployment and growth suggested in this literature is unidirectional, and an increase in unemployment fosters economic growth (de Groot, 2000, p. 25). Therefore, any shock to unemployment should exhibit a qualitatively equal effect on the economic growth rate, hence there is no reason why the structural relationship between unemployment and economic growth should not hold even in the short run. This, however, is refuted by the evidence.

We argue that demand considerations can account both for the breakdown of Okun's law in the short run and for the stability of Okun's law in the long run. As positive demand shocks encourage economic growth and reduce unemployment, whereas supply shocks increase both economic growth and unemployment, we should find little correlation. As demand shocks fade out in the long run, however, we should be able to identify a long-run relationship, an analysis which is supported by the evidence.

This chapter proceeds as follows. The next section presents the demand side of the model. After a discussion of the product variety index in Dixit–Stiglitz utility functions, we argue that impediments to market entry can, apart from availability, determine the number of products in consumer markets. We argue that emerging firms face a transitory risk of failure to enter the product market. We then argue in section 6.3 that the smallest of all possible labor market restrictions, the instantaneous inability to renegotiate labor contracts, can motivate permanent unemployment in this case, as opposed to the persistent rigidities required in the original Okun model. Moreover, as workers demand a risk premium to ensure themselves against unemployment, the optimal decision rules of firms are distorted, leading to lower levels of entry and, hence, lower economic growth. Section 6.4 describes technological determinants of market entry. We propose a model of innovation networks to describe the permanent influx of new innovations on product markets. After giving failures to aggregate demand an externality interpretation in section 6.5, we show in section 6.6 that distorted incentives for both workers and firms lead to unemployment whenever economic growth is positive. Section 6.7 then derives the maximum feasible growth rate due to resource constraints, and section 6.8 finally interprets the equilibrium of the economy.

6.2 Households

Households are assumed to provide one unit of labor inelastically, and to face an intertemporal tradeoff between consumption and savings on the one hand, and an intratemporal tradeoff between differentiated consumption products on the other hand. Given homothetic preferences, we can solve the household problems in two stages. The intertemporal tradeoff is modeled according to the conventional logarithmic utility function,

$$U_s = \int_s^{\infty} e^{-\rho(t-s)} \ln c_t dt \tag{6.1}$$

where ρ is the individual rate of time preference, and c_t is aggregate consumption over time t. Households maximize utility subject to an intertemporal budget constraint,

$$\dot{a}_t = r_t a_t + w_t(1 - u_t) - c_t, \tag{6.2}$$

which states that a household saves that part of interest income $r_t a_t$, and labor income w_t for those who expect not to be unemployed u_t, that is not spent on consumption c_t.

Unemployed workers are assumed to receive no benefits. Hamiltonian optimization of the utility function subject to the budget constraint with respect to consumption, asset accumulation, and a shadow price of income yields the well-known Keynes–Ramsey rule,

$$\hat{c}_t = r_t - \rho, \tag{6.3}$$

where the hat (ˆ) denotes the growth rate of consumption. This intertemporal Euler condition states that households will delay consumption into the future when the interest rate exceeds their individual rate of time preference. At each point of time, households demand differentiated services from an infinite variety according to the following constant elasticities of substitution subutility function,

$$c_t = \left[\int_0^{\infty} x_{i,t}^{(\varepsilon-1)/\varepsilon} di \right]^{\frac{\varepsilon}{\varepsilon-1}}, \tag{6.4}$$

where $x_{i,t}$ is a specific service variety, ranging from zero to infinity. If households have chosen to purchase a total of c_t consumption goods at time t for a price p_t, then spending on all products will be constrained by

$$\int_0^{\infty} p_{i,t} x_{i,t} di \leq p_t c_t, \tag{6.5}$$

where $p_{i,t}$ is the price of a specific service i. The intratemporal household problem yields after optimization of a demand function for a specific service,

$$x_{i,t} = (p_{i,t}/p_t)^{-\varepsilon} c_t, \tag{6.6}$$

and we find that ε is the demand elasticity for any particular service. Moreover, we obtain a definition for the price index of services,

$$p_t = \left[\int_0^{\infty} p_{i,t}^{1-\varepsilon} di \right]^{\frac{1}{1-\varepsilon}}. \tag{6.7}$$

Evidently, not all products will be available at all times. It is conventional to assume that unavailable products have an infinite price.[1] We have found it convenient to split the integral into two parts, where the available products at time t are in the interval $[0, m_t]$, whilst unavailable products range from $(m_t, \infty]$.[2] This leads to several simplifications. First, note that despite the fact that some prices are infinitely high, the price index (6.7) is not, as

$$\lim_{\{p_{i,t}\}_{m_t}^{\infty} \to \infty} p_t = \lim_{\{p_{i,t}\}_{m_t}^{\infty} \to \infty} \left[\int_0^{m_t} p_{i,t}^{1-\varepsilon} di + \int_{m_t}^{\infty} p_{i,t}^{1-\varepsilon} di \right]^{\frac{1}{1-\varepsilon}} = \left[\int_0^{m_t} p_{i,t}^{1-\varepsilon} di \right]^{\frac{1}{1-\varepsilon}}, \tag{6.7'}$$

which implies that we only need to know the prices of available products in order to measure the price index. As the prices of all available products are finite, so is the price index. Then, by multiplying demand (6.6) by the product price, and integrating over all m_t available products, we find that households devote all of their planned spending (6.5) to available products,

$$\lim_{\{p_{i,t}\}_{m_t}^{\infty} \to \infty} \int_0^{m_t} p_{i,t} x_{i,t} di = \lim_{\{p_{i,t}\}_{m_t}^{\infty} \to \infty} p_t c_t \int_0^{m_t} (p_{i,t}/p_t)^{1-\varepsilon} di = p_t c_t. \tag{6.5'}$$

Given non-negativity of demand and prices, the planned spending share for any individual unavailable product is zero, which furthermore implies that individual product demand for an unavailable product must converge to zero as its price converges to infinity,

$$\lim_{p_{i,t} \to \infty} x_{i,t} = 0, \tag{6.6'}$$

which, finally, allows us to derive aggregate demand c_t to equal,

$$\lim_{\{p_{i,t}\}_{m_t}^{\infty} \to \infty} c_t = \lim_{\{p_{i,t}\}_{m_t}^{\infty} \to \infty} \left[\int_0^{m_t} x_{i,t}^{\frac{\varepsilon-1}{\varepsilon}} di + \int_{m_t}^{\infty} x_{i,t}^{\frac{\varepsilon-1}{\varepsilon}} di \right]^{\frac{\varepsilon}{\varepsilon-1}} = \left[\int_0^{m_t} x_{i,t}^{\frac{\varepsilon-1}{\varepsilon}} di \right]^{\frac{\varepsilon}{\varepsilon-1}}. \tag{6.4'}$$

We have thus been able to reformulate the intratemporal consumer problem as a maximization of (6.4′) with respect to (6.5′), where the difference to the original optimization problem is the length of the integral. In the transformed intratemporal problem, households are only required to make choices over all available products, ranging from zero to m_t. It is therefore a crucial question as to what determines the number of available products, m_t. Endogenous growth theory has always stressed technical factors – in particular, the number of researchers developing new products, or productivity in research and development.[3]

However, both demand factors and market failures may be of equal importance. Here, we shall discuss three reasons for this. First, consumers may refrain from consuming certain products, when they cannot judge their immediate usefulness, or because they consider them to be a danger to health. Typical examples of the former are the telephone or the personal home computer, whereas examples for the latter are pharmaceuticals, the microwave, or biotechnology products. Second, and in part as a reaction to the latter, government regulation may prevent or defer entry of some new consumer products, through either health laws or product market regulation (Messina-Granovsky, 2000). Finally, some products may fail to succeed on the market, because of failures of promotion. As an example, several American fast-food chains failed to establish themselves in European markets, when they attempted to implement the same marketing campaign as they had adopted in the United States.

The number of available products will be determined by both technical feasibility and social feasibility. We assume that n_t products are technically feasible, whilst only m_t products are both technically and socially feasible, with $m_t \leq n_t$. Secondly, whilst we assume that products may be forever technically unfeasible, social unfeasibility is only temporary, and will vanish in the next period. In that respect 'supply shocks' to product availability are persistent, whilst 'demand shocks' are purely transitory.

Once a product is invented, it has a specific probability φ_i of failing to gain social acceptance, and therefore a probability of $1 - \varphi_i$ of gaining social acceptance. We assume that the probability of achieving social acceptance is drawn from an exponential distribution,

$$1 - \varphi_i = \frac{1}{1 - \tilde{\varphi}_i} e^{\frac{\epsilon}{\tilde{\varphi}_i - 1}}, \tag{6.8}$$

where ϵ is a positive random number, which is assigned to a particular innovation. ϵ is observable, and therefore $1 - \varphi_i$ is observable as well. This is equivalent to stating that the odds of whether or not an innovation will be successful are known immediately, whereas the actual realization is not. Note that the expected value for a particular firm equals,

$$E(1-\varphi_i) = \int_0^{\infty} \frac{\epsilon}{1-\tilde{\varphi}_i} e^{\frac{\epsilon}{\tilde{\varphi}_i - 1}} \, d\epsilon = 1 - \tilde{\varphi}_i, \tag{6.9}$$

which we assume to be equally distributed over a random sample of innovations.

6.3 Firms, wage contracts and entry

Each particular product variety is provided monopolistically by a single firm. They use labor as the single input, and we normalize output so that one unit of labor input yields one unit of the product. Firms therefore maximize profits, that is revenues $p_{i,t}x_{i,t}$ minus employment costs ω_t,

$$\pi_{i,t} = p_{i,t}x_{i,t} - \omega_{i,t}, \tag{6.10}$$

subject to technology, $x_{i,t} = e_{i,t}$, and demand (6.6). We assume that workers cannot renegotiate their wage or employment level instantaneously, but allow for full flexibility ex-ante. As there is no risk involved with incumbent firms, this does not affect decisions in these firms, and they can simply pay market wages w_t to their workforce $e_{i,t}$, hence $\omega_t = w_t e_{i,t}$.

New firms, however, face the instantaneous risk of social unfeasibility (6.8). As they cannot renegotiate the contract after observing their social acceptability, and as their workers cannot instantaneously be hired by another firm, they offer their potential workers a contract which compensates them for the risk incurred. The risk premium may be either attached to the wage rate of workers in secure jobs, $w_{i,t} = \gamma w_t$, in which case we would observe wages above the marginal product, or by a lump-sum payment to the workers, $\sigma_{i,t}$. The latter is a very common form of payment in start-up enterprises, where workers receive large parts of their income in the form of stock options, profit shares, or bonus schemes. Hence the wage contract equals zero if marketability fails, and

$$\omega_{i,t} = \gamma w_t e_{i,t} + \sigma_{i,t}, \tag{6.11}$$

Profit maximization in incumbent firms therefore yields the first-order condition,

$$p_{i,t} = \frac{\varepsilon}{\varepsilon - 1} w_t, \tag{6.12}$$

hence the price will equal the mark-up over (marginal employment) costs, whilst firms would have to pay marginal employment costs of γw_t.

Therefore, we have at most two different prices, one for the incumbent, and one for emerging firms. Hence, the price index (6.7′) reduces to,

$$p_t = \frac{\varepsilon}{\varepsilon - 1}\left[\int_0^{n_t - \dot{n}_t} w_t^{1-\varepsilon} di + \int_{n_t - \dot{n}_t}^{m_t} (\gamma w_t)^{1-\varepsilon} di\right]^{\frac{1}{1-\varepsilon}},$$

$$= \frac{\varepsilon}{\varepsilon - 1} w_t[n_t - \dot{n}_t + \gamma^{1-\varepsilon}(m_t - n_t + \dot{n}_t)]^{\frac{1}{1-\varepsilon}} \qquad (6.7'')$$

where $\dot{n}_t$ is the change of technically feasible prices from period $t - \tau$ to t, as the time span τ converges to zero.[4] Demand for a particular product line (6.6), making use of the aggregate price index (6.7″), will therefore equal,

$$x_{i,t} = c_t[n_t - \dot{n}_t + \gamma^{1-\varepsilon}(m_t - n_t + \dot{n}_t)]^{\frac{\varepsilon}{1-\varepsilon}}, \qquad (6.6'')$$

which, taken to the power of $\varepsilon/(\varepsilon - 1)$, and integrated over all m_t available product lines, implies that $\gamma = 1$ by definition, or that workers cannot ask for a risk element in their wages, but have to rely on the lump-sum payment $\sigma_{i,t}$ to adjust for changes in risk. This, of course, implies that prices (6.12), quantities supplied (6.6″), and labor demand will be identical across all firms, whether incumbent or emerging. The consumption goods sector is therefore completely symmetric. The intuition behind this argument is simple. Once a firm is in operation, there is no more risk involved in working for this particular firm, and hence the risk premium should not depend on the actual amount of time spent on the job. In other words, if a firm has succeeded in placing a product on the market, its workforce cannot, despite the fact that firms obtain monopoly rents, charge wages above the competitive level. However, workers may very well ask for compensation of the risk to sign with an emerging firm in terms of $\sigma_{i,t}$, reducing profits. Substitution of the wage contract (6.11) and the mark-up (6.12) implies that profits equal

$$\pi_{i,t} = w_{i,t}e_{i,t}/(\varepsilon - 1) - \sigma_{i,t}. \qquad (6.10')$$

This implies that even if profits for incumbent firms are always positive, emerging firms may choose not to proceed to enter the market early, whenever

$$w_t e_{i,t} < (\varepsilon - 1)\sigma_{i,t}. \qquad (6.13)$$

This condition implies that firms are not only deferred from market entry by technical and social unfeasibility, but may also choose themselves to await market entry, if the risk of entry is large enough. Note that if condition (6.12) is binding for all new products, then no firm will try to enter the market early. Therefore, all workers would sign contracts with secure firms, and would not face the risk of unemployment. However, as it would take 'time to build' new innovations, the growth rate would decline as well. A similar argument holds, of course, if condition (6.12) is binding only for some firms.

The minimum risk premium $\sigma_{i,t}$ that emerging firms can offer, must of course make workers indifferent between hiring with an emerging firm or an incumbent firm. Assuming that workers can pool risk across emerging firms with an identical risk of market failure φ_i, instantaneous utility from wage income in risky firms and wealth must equal utility from a certain wage and wealth, or

$$\ln[E_t(1-\varphi_i)(w_t e_{i,t}+\sigma_{i,t})+a_t]=\ln[w_t e_{i,t}+a_t], \tag{6.14}$$

where workers who hire with an emerging firm receive wages and a risk premium only in the case of succeeded market entry at a probability of $1-\varphi_i$, whilst workers in incumbent firms receive wages for sure, but no risk premium.[5] Reformulating (6.14) implies that the risk premium will be proportional to wage payments, or

$$\sigma_{i,t}=\frac{\tilde{\varphi}_i}{1-\tilde{\varphi}_i}w_t e_{i,t}. \tag{6.15}$$

Substituting the risk premium (6.15) into the early-entry condition (6.13), we find that only those firms with a probability of failing market entry below $1/\varepsilon$ will pursue a policy of early entry. In principle, the model allows for two types of firing. First, there is firing because of bad luck. Firms who fail to enter the market early will have no use for labor inputs and will therefore renege on their employment contracts. Secondly, there is firing for profits. If the probability to succeed market entry is sufficiently low, firms will refrain from pursuing early entry, as it would imply losses. Evidently, if the probability to fail is known ex-ante, firms will not even offer job contracts, and hence no firing will take place, In the case of a stochastic probability to fail,[6] wage contracts would be signed on the basis of an expected probability to fail, and firms may be inclined to renege if they find out that the realized probability to succeed early entry falls short of the expected probability.

6.4 Technical determinants of market entry

The innovation sector is populated by perfectly competitive R&D firms, which sell innovations to emerging service sector firms in order to maximize profits. The stock of knowledge, or the level of innovations, does not enter the innovation technology without cost. By contrast, innovators engage in costly activities to acquire knowledge, by forming internal or external networks. We hence assume that new varieties are created according to,

$$\dot{n}_t = \xi s_{n,t}^{\alpha}\eta_t. \tag{6.16}$$

Given that it is uncertain whether a single innovation will be successful, ξ measures the probability of success in innovation, when the number of attempts to innovate is large, or productivity in innovation. $S_{n,t}$ is either the amount of time that a particular researcher devotes to the innovation of new products, or the number of scientists (or science mangers) engaged in innovatory activities, with diminishing marginal product of innovatory activities.

η_t represents networking capital, which increases with the size of the network. We can in general measure the size of a network in different ways. First, we can measure the nodes of a network, or the number of participants. If there are n_t existing products, the potential number of nodes in an innovation network equals n_t, hence $\eta_t = \eta(n_t)$. With n_t nodes, the number of potential ties within the network would equal $(n_t - 1)!$, and if we use potential ties as a measure for the size of the network, we would have $\eta_t = \eta((n_t - 1)!)$. Finally, the number of actual ties within a network lies between n_t and $(n_t - 1)!$, hence the definition of networking capital would have to be attached to this number. All three potential measures of the size of the network depend on the number of existing innovations n_t, and we shall therefore assume for the sake of simplicity that $\eta_t = \eta(n_t)$, and that it is linear in n_t for convenience. As already mentioned, networking capital takes effort, measured in terms of employment in networking activities, $s_{\eta,t}$, with $s_{\eta,t} = s_t - s_{n,t}$, and exhibiting a diminishing marginal product as well. Hence, network capital is acquired according to the following process,

$$\eta_t = \psi n_t s_{\eta,t}^{1-\alpha} \tag{6.17}$$

Productivity in networking is assumed to equal ψ. Note that innovation firms will maximize output by setting $s_{\eta,t} = (1 - \alpha)s_t$. The arrival rate of new innovations (6.16) can therefore be reduced to,

$$\dot{n}_t = \varphi\psi(\alpha s_t)^\alpha((1-\alpha)s_t)^{1-\alpha}n_t = \phi s_t n_t, \tag{6.16'}$$

where ϕ is a measure of productivity in the innovation sector. Given that it is uncertain whether or not a single innovation will be successful, ϕ measures the probability of success in innovation, when the number of attempts to innovate is large. The advantage of the specification of (6.16′) over the traditional specification used in endogenous growth literature (6.16) is twofold. First, whilst endogenous growth theory has lacked a proper justification for the positive impact of existing innovations on current and future innovations[7] the explanation with networking capital gives a sound justification for this assumption. Secondly, whilst the parameter ψ is free in specification (6.16), ranging anywhere between zero and infinity, we can obtain a clearer indication of ϕ in specification (6.16′). If we assume that workers are not much more productive in innovation and networking than in the production of consumption goods, where the benchmark labor productivity is unity, we find that $\phi < 1$, since $\alpha^\alpha(1-\alpha)^{1-\alpha} < 1$.

Competitive firms in the innovation sector maximize profits. The highest price a potential service provider can pay to an innovator will equal the service firm i's value, $v^*_{i,t}$. The only costs for an innovator are wages w_t, paid to scientists, s_t. Hence, given technology as stated in (6.16′), the marginal cost for the provision of a new variety will equal its price,

$$v^*_{i,t} = \frac{w_t}{\phi n_t}. \tag{6.18}$$

6.5 The market for consumer products and aggregate demand failures

There will be four types of potential firms populating this economy at each point in time, and we will line them up systematically on the consumption good interval from zero to n_t. First, there will be $n_t - \dot{n}_t$ incumbent firms. They may have experienced a negative demand shock in the previous period, but whether they have been in the market before has no impact on their supply and demand decision today or in any period in the future. Then, there will be firms which have been refrained from pursuing early entry due to condition (6.13). Given that the probability of failing early market entry is equally distributed over a large number of firms, the early-entry condition implies that exactly $(\varepsilon - 1)/\varepsilon$

of all emerging firms will refrain from pursuing early entry, and we will group these firms towards the end of the consumption goods index interval, from $n_t - \dot{n}_t(\varepsilon - 1)/\varepsilon$ to n_t.

Finally, there will be two types of incumbent firms, which pursue early entry – those which succeed and those which fail. Given that the number of products, and hence the number of monopoly suppliers on product markets is given by m_t, we assign all incumbent firms who succeed in entering the market early to the interval $[n_t - \dot{n}_t, m_t]$, and all incumbent firms who fail to enter the market early to the interval $[m_t, n_t - \dot{n}_t(\varepsilon - 1)/\varepsilon]$. Evidently, only incumbent and successful emerging firms will supply consumer goods on the market.

If the number of new innovations $\dot{n}_t$, is large, the average number of successful early entries into the consumer markets, $1 - \varphi$, will equal the actual number of early market entries,

$$(1 - \varphi)\dot{n}_t = \dot{n}_t E\left(1 - \varphi_i | 1 - \tilde{\varphi}_i < \frac{\varepsilon - 1}{\varepsilon}\right) = \frac{1}{2\varepsilon}\dot{n}_t, \tag{6.19}$$

whereas the number of firms who fail to enter the market is composed of the firms who failed to pass social acceptance, and the number of firms which have chosen not to pursue early entry, as the early-entry condition (6.13) was binding,

$$\varphi\dot{n}_t = \dot{n}_t E\left(\varphi_i | \tilde{\varphi}_i \geq \frac{1}{\varepsilon}\right) + \frac{\varepsilon - 1}{\varepsilon}\dot{n}_t = \left(1 - \frac{1}{2\varepsilon}\right)\dot{n}_t, \tag{6.19'}$$

ensuring that m_t will indeed exceed the number of past innovations $n_t - \dot{n}_t$, but fall short of the number of total innovations, n_t. This allows us to establish the number of available products on the market as,

$$m_t = n_t - \varphi\dot{n}_t. \tag{6.20}$$

Apart from its immediate interpretation as an aggregate failure to early market entry, φ can be given the interpretation as an aggregate demand failure, or negative demand externality. To establish this point, define potential aggregate demand, c_t^*, as the ceteris paribus level of aggregate demand that would prevail in the absence of a positive probability to fail early entry to the market, holding everything else, in particular consumption goods sector employment, equal,

$$c_t^* = \left[\int_0^{n_t} x_{i,t}^{\frac{\varepsilon-1}{\varepsilon}}\, di\right]^{\frac{\varepsilon}{\varepsilon-1}} = n_t^{\frac{\varepsilon}{\varepsilon-1}} x_{i,t} = (n_t/m_t)^{\frac{1}{\varepsilon-1}} c_t = (1 - \varphi\hat{n}_t)^{\frac{1}{\varepsilon-1}} c_t. \tag{6.4''}$$

First, in the absence of economic growth, actual aggregate demand c_t will equal potential aggregate demand, c_t^*, for any value of the average failure rate to early entry, $1 - \varphi$, since entry will not occur in that case. Secondly, despite the fact that the demand shock is purely temporary, and only instantaneously affects demand, actual demand will always fall short of potential demand in a growing economy. Thirdly, an increase in φ widens the gap between actual and potential output, as

$$\frac{\partial c_t/c_t^*}{\partial \varphi} = -\frac{\varphi}{\varepsilon - 1}(1 - \varphi \hat{n}_t)^{\frac{1}{\varepsilon-1}-1} < 0.$$

Finally, actual output will equal potential if and only if $\varphi = 0$, hence φ describes an aggregate demand externality. Hence, social acceptance of products influences the outcome of the economy despite its purely transitory nature, because it distorts the decision of firms, which take potential failures into consideration.

6.6 Unemployment and the labor market

Ex-ante equilibrium will be ensured if every single worker is either offered a secure wage contract in an innovation firm or in an incumbent consumer goods firm at wage w_t, or an insecure contract in an emerging consumer goods firm, where the wage contract would include a risk premium. If we define the total number of labor contracts offered in the consumer goods sector as e_t^*, the labor market clears ex-ante if and only if $e_t^* + s_t = 1$, the total labor supply. Potential (or ex-ante) employment in the goods market is defined as the integral over all n_t individual monopoly suppliers of consumption goods,

$$\begin{aligned} e_t^* = \int_0^{n_t} e_{i,t} di = \int_0^{n_t - \dot{n}_t} e_{i,t} di + \int_{n_t - \dot{n}_t}^{n_t - \dot{n}_t - \varphi \dot{n}_t} e_{i,t} di \\ + \int_{n_t - \varphi \dot{n}_t}^{n_t - \dot{n}_t + \dot{n}_t/\varepsilon} e_{i,t} di + \int_{n_t - \dot{n}_t + \dot{n}_t/\varepsilon}^{n_t} e_{i,t} di, \end{aligned} \qquad (6.21)$$

where we have split the integral into four parts to capture different phases of the product life cycle. The first integral from zero to $n_t - \dot{n}_t$ captures the employment of incumbent firms. The second and the third integrals in equation (6.18) contain employment contracts offered by emerging firms which have pursued early entry, where we have used equation (6.20) to define the borders of integration. The last integral captures firms we have been refrained from pursuing early entry by condition (6.13), and corresponds to firing for profits. Given that probability to fail early market entry is equally distributed over a large number of firms, the early-entry condition implies that exactly $(\varepsilon - 1)/\varepsilon$ of all emerging firms will refrain from pursuing early entry, explaining the lower border of integration in the last integral. As these firms know ex-ante that pursuing early entry will be unprofitable, they will not offer any labor contracts, and the last term in equation (6.21) equals zero. Given symmetry on the consumption goods market, potential employment will therefore equal,

$$e_t^* = \int_0^{n_t - \dot{n}_t + \dot{n}_t/\varepsilon} e_{i,t} di = \left(1 - \hat{n}_t + \hat{n}_t/\varepsilon\right) n_t e_{i,t} = 1 - s_t = 1 - \frac{\hat{n}_t}{\phi}, \qquad (6.21)$$

Note that this implies that potential employment is constant for a constant rate of growth. But then we find that potential aggregate demand (6.4″) will equal,

$$c_t^* = n_t^{\frac{1}{\varepsilon - 1}} (n_t e_{i,t}), \qquad (6.4''')$$

where the term in parenthesis is constant for a constant growth rate, due to equation (6.19′). Taking time derivatives, we find that the growth rate of potential consumption is equal to $(\varepsilon - 1)$ times the growth rate of innovations. The same holds for the growth rate of actual aggregate consumption, from substitution of (6.4‴) and (6.20) into equation (6.4″).

Consumer good manufacturers who fail the early-entry test will evidently renege on their signed labor contracts, rendering their potential employees unemployed. As there will be no firing in the innovation sector, an ex-ante clearing labor market implies that unemployment must be the difference between potential employment and actual employment in the consumption goods sector,

$$e_t = e_t^* - u_t = \int_0^{n_t - \varphi \dot{n}_t} e_{i,t} di = (1 - \varphi \hat{n}_t) n_t e_{i,t} = 1 - u_t - s_t = 1 - u_t - \frac{\hat{n}_t}{\phi}, \qquad (6.21'')$$

The unemployment rate is therefore defined by the third integral of equation (6.21), which, given the model's symmetry of employment demand, equals

$$u_t = \int_{n_t - \varphi \dot{n}_t}^{n_t - \dot{n}_t + \dot{n}_t/\varepsilon} e_{i,t} di = \left(\varphi - \frac{\varepsilon - 1}{\varepsilon}\right) \dot{n}_t e_{i,t} = \left(\varphi - \frac{\varepsilon - 1}{\varepsilon}\right) \hat{n}_t \frac{1 - \hat{n}_t/\phi}{1 - \frac{\varepsilon - 1}{\varepsilon}\hat{n}_t}$$

$$= \left(\varphi - \frac{\varepsilon - 1}{\varphi}\right) \frac{\varepsilon - 1}{\phi}\hat{c}_t \frac{\phi - (\varepsilon - 1)\hat{c}_t}{1 - \frac{(\varepsilon - 1)^2}{\varepsilon}\hat{c}_t} \tag{6.22}$$

Equation (6.22) describes a relationship between the economic rate of growth and the unemployment rate. As it is derived both from the workers' incentive to sign up for risky but lucrative jobs in emerging firms, and by the emerging firm's incentive to renege on contracts, once the innovation has proven to be a temporary failure in the market, we shall call this locus the incentive constraint. It passes through the origin, implying that we have zero unemployment with zero growth, which is a situation when innovation is too costly to be undertaken at all. It also exhibits zero unemployment at a growth rate of $\phi/(\varepsilon - 1)$, which is when early entry is so costly that no firm will take the chance. The incentive constraint (6.22) is hump-shaped in between the nulls, with a maximum unemployment rate that would exceed unity, hence only the upward-sloping part of the incentive constraint will be of economic relevance. This allows us to linearize the incentive constraint (6.22) using a first-order MacLaurin expansion,

$$u_t = \left(\varphi - 1 + \frac{1}{\varepsilon}\right)(\varepsilon - 1)\hat{c}_t. \tag{6.22$'$}$$

Despite the fact that labor market rigidities are very limited, and concern only a fraction of the emerging firms, equation (6.22′), together with (6.19), implies that the unemployment rate equals the economic growth rate divided by twice the mark-up (6.12). Hence, for a 3 per cent growth rate and a 25 per cent mark-up, the model helps to explain 1.2 per cent percentage points of the unemployment rate.

6.7 Economic growth and venture capital markets

Innovators will have to finance their activities on bond markets. The maximal price they can achieve for an innovation equals the discounted stream of profits, which the monopoly supplier of the product can obtain in product markets. Given the symmetry of the consumption sector, the profit stream will be identical for all incumbent firms. Emerging firms, however, have to pay a risk premium out of their running profits, and still face the risk of market failure, so that their first period profits – and hence their market value – will be below the equivalent figure for an incumbent firm,

$$v_{i,t}^{*} = \int_{t}^{\infty} \pi_{i,t}^{*} e^{-r(\tau-t)} d\tau$$
$$= E_t \pi_{i,t}^{*} - \pi_{i,t} + \int_{t}^{\infty} \pi_{i,t} e^{-r(\tau-t)} d\tau = E_t \pi_{i,t}^{*} - \pi_{i,t} + v_{i,t}, \qquad (6.23)$$

where stars (*) denote values of emerging firms, and variables without stars are the corresponding values of incumbent firms. Equation (6.23) describes an intratemporal no-arbitrage condition. It states that you trade a bond of an incumbent firm, $v_{i,t}^{*}$, against a bond of an emerging firm if and only if you are compensated for the loss in expected dividends – that is, profits – in the first period. As incumbent firms will make first period profits and pay risk premia only in the case of success in marketing its product, we can reformulate the intratemporal no-arbitrage condition (6.23),

$$v_{i,t} = v_{i,t}^{*} + \tilde{\varphi}_i \pi_{i,t} + (1 - \tilde{\varphi}_i)\sigma_{i,t} = \frac{w_t}{\phi n_t} + \tilde{\varphi}_i \varepsilon \pi_{i,t}, \qquad (6.23')$$

where we have eliminated the expectation operator and the risk premium with equation (6.15), and the value of an incumbent firm with equation (6.18). Apart from incumbent and emerging firms, even firms who were refrained from early market entry by condition (6.13) have a value on the stock market, as they all benefit from a future stream of monopoly rents. Therefore, total stock market capitalization equals,

$$v_t = \int_{0}^{n_t} v_{i,t} di = \int_{0}^{n_t - \dot{n}_t} v_{i,t} di + \int_{n_t - \dot{n}_t}^{n_t - \dot{n}_t + \dot{n}_t/\varepsilon} v_{i,t} di + \int_{n_t - \dot{n}_t + \dot{n}_t/\varepsilon}^{n_t} v_{i,t} di, \qquad (6.24)$$

where we have split the integral into incumbent firms, emerging firms, and innovators who have opted not to pursue early market entry. An incumbent firm is certain that its innovation has a market, therefore its valuation on the stock market should simply equal opportunity costs of innovating a new product (6.18). By contrast, a firm which has chosen not to pursue early entry has also to forgo current profits. Finally, emerging firms face the risk of failing in the market, in which case they would not obtain running profits, but would also not have to pay risk premia.

Making use of equations (6.18), (6.10), (6.15), (6.21′) and (6.19′), we find that aggregate stock market capitalization depends on the growth rate, wages, and unemployment only,

$$v_t = \frac{w_t}{\phi} + (\varphi + \varepsilon - 1)\hat{n}_t \int_0^{n_t} \pi_{i,t} di. \tag{6.24'}$$

The first term in equation (6.24′) is familiar from the endogenous growth literature, and expresses the fact that innovations occur until revenues equal costs. The second term equals the hypothetical losses of early market failures, where a fraction φ of the emerging firms will fail early entry, thus losing their profits, and the remaining $(1 - \varphi)$ emerging firms will pay a fraction of $(\varepsilon - 1)/(1 - \varphi)$ of their profits as risk premia. It implies that as compared to the technologically determined growth models, aggregate stock market capitalization is lower in this instance. Evidently, as the growth rate of varieties increases, the gap between potential and actual aggregate stock market capitalization widens, as the chances of incurring losses increase. The second term states that as products become closer substitutes, ε increases, running profits decline, and hence the early-entry condition eliminates a larger share of potential early entrants. Finally, note that aggregate stock market capitalization, v_t, increases as the growth rate of varieties increases. Evidently, if an economy becomes more innovative, stock markets will tend to boom.

Whilst equation (6.23′) describes an intratemporal tradeoff between different types of stocks, arbitrage on stock and bond markets should also lead to an intertemporal tradeoff. In particular, investors should be indifferent between investing an amount v_t into company stocks, which yields both dividends, that is running profits, and value gains, and a safe asset, which yields interest $r_t v_t$,

$$\dot{v}_{i,t} + \pi_{i,t} = r_t v_t. \tag{6.25}$$

Dividing both sides by v_t, noting from equation (6.18) that the growth rate of a particular bond is equal to the difference between the growth rate of wages and innovations, and from integration of the intertemporal budget constraint that wages and consumption grow at the same rate, eliminating the interest rate from the intertemporal Euler condition (6.3), integrating over all n_t firms, we find upon rearrangement,

$$v_t = \frac{1}{\hat{n}_t + \rho} \int_0^{n_t} \pi_{i,t} di, \tag{6.25'}$$

which states that aggregate stock market capitalization equals potential profits, discounted at the individual rate of time preference and the innovation rate. Eliminating the aggregate stock market capitalization from the aggregate intratemporal no-arbitrage condition (6.25′), and aggregate profits from equation (6.10′) and (6.21′), we obtain a relation between the rate of innovation and the unemployment rate,

$$\Phi(\hat{n}_t) \equiv (\varepsilon - 1)(\hat{n}_t + \rho) + \varphi\varepsilon\hat{n}_t(\hat{n}_t + \rho) + \hat{n}_t = \phi(1 - u_t), \tag{6.26}$$

which, as it was derived from both limited resources on the labor and capital markets, can be referred to as a resource constraint. The function $\Phi(.)$ is decreasing in unemployment. The first term in the resource constraint (6.26) corresponds to the discount rate on an emerging firm's profits, as can be easily deduced from equations (6.25′) and (6.19). It states that as profits gets discounted faster, firms will sooner defer from pursuing early entry, and thus reducing the unemployment rate. The third term corresponds to the resource drain from the innovation sector. As the innovation sector offers more secure jobs, the labor resource base for the consumption goods sector declines, implying that reneging on labor contracts by emerging firms will affect fewer and fewer workers, thus reducing unemployment. The term in the center, finally, is an interaction term, which states that as the number of new innovations increases, a large portion of the consumption goods sector workforce will be employed in emerging firms, which evidently increases unemployment. Given that both the growth rate of innovations and the individual rate of time preference ρ are both small, the interaction term will be only of second-order importance, and we shall therefore ignore it in the following, yielding a second relation between the rate of economic growth and the unemployment rate,

$$\hat{c}_t = \frac{\phi(1 - u_t)}{\varepsilon(\varepsilon - 1)} - \frac{\rho}{\varepsilon}. \tag{6.26'}$$

6.8 Equilibrium unemployment and economic growth

The economy can be fully described by two linearized relations in the rate of economic growth and the unemployment rate, that is the incentive constraint (6.22′) and the resource constraint (6.26′). This allows us to solve for the equilibrium unemployment rate as a function of the deep parameters of the model only,

$$u_t = \frac{\left(\varphi - \frac{\varepsilon - 1}{\varepsilon}\right)[\phi - \rho(\varepsilon - 1)]}{\varepsilon + \varphi - \frac{\varepsilon - 1}{\varepsilon}}, \tag{6.27}$$

and simultaneously for the balanced rate of economic growth, which equals,

$$\hat{c}_t = \frac{\phi - \rho(\varepsilon - 1)}{\varepsilon(\varepsilon - 1) + \phi(\varepsilon - 1)\left(\varphi - \frac{\varepsilon - 1}{\varepsilon}\right)}. \tag{6.28}$$

This leads to several comparative static conclusions. First, an increase in the individual rate of time preference, unsurprisingly, reduces the rate of economic growth. In addition, however, it also contributes to lowering the equilibrium rate of unemployment. As people become more patient, they acquire a more conservative consumption profile, demanding less innovative products, and hence reducing the scope for failures in early market entry. Secondly, an increase in the innovation sector's productivity fosters economic growth, as an identical share of innovation sector workers will produce a greater number of innovations,

$$\frac{\partial \hat{c}_t}{\partial \phi} = \frac{(\varepsilon - 1)\left[\varepsilon + \rho(\varepsilon - 1)\left(\varphi - \frac{\varepsilon - 1}{\varepsilon}\right)\right]}{\left[\varepsilon(\varepsilon - 1) + \phi(\varepsilon - 1)\left(\varphi - \frac{\varepsilon - 1}{\varepsilon}\right)\right]^2} > 0.$$

However, this implies that workers are freed from innovative activities, and move particularly into emerging sector firms, where the risk of unemployment is high, thus increasing the equilibrium rate of unemployment,

$$\frac{\partial u_t}{\partial \phi} = \frac{\left(\varphi - \frac{\varepsilon - 1}{\varepsilon}\right)}{\varepsilon + \varphi - \frac{\varepsilon - 1}{\varepsilon}} > 0.$$

An increase in the price elasticity of demand ε, unambiguously reduces economic growth, since

$$\frac{\partial \hat{c}_t}{\partial \varepsilon} = \frac{-\rho\left[\varepsilon(\varepsilon - 1) + \phi(\varepsilon - 1) + \left(\varphi - \frac{\varepsilon - 1}{\varepsilon}\right)\right] - [\phi - \rho(\varepsilon - 1)]\left[2\varepsilon - 1 + \phi\left(\varphi - \frac{\varepsilon - 1}{\varepsilon}\right) - \phi\frac{\varepsilon - 1}{\varepsilon^2}\right]}{\left[\varepsilon(\varepsilon - 1) + \phi(\varepsilon - 1)\left(\varphi - \frac{\varepsilon - 1}{\varepsilon}\right)\right]^2}$$

$$< 0.$$

Evidently, as innovations yield lower rents, they will induce lower innovative effort, thus reducing the economic growth rate. In conventional endogenous growth models, this would reallocate the workforce towards an increased production of consumption goods, thus raising profits despite lower profit shares, and hence the effect is ambiguous. Here, the partial deferment of current running profits due to a demand constraint is sufficient to render the effect negative. Whilst reducing the mark-up will reduce the growth rate of the economy, it will improve the employment situation, as

$$\frac{\partial u_t}{\partial \varepsilon} = -\frac{\left(\varphi - \dfrac{\varepsilon - 1}{\varepsilon}\right)\rho + u_t}{\varepsilon + \varphi - \dfrac{\varepsilon - 1}{\varepsilon}} < 0.$$

Here, the lower number of innovations reduces the risk of getting a job offer from an emerging firm, and hence reduces unemployment.

Finally, an increase in the magnitude of the transitory demand shock will increase the aggregate demand externality φ, which in turn leads directly to an increase in the unemployment rate, as can be observed from equation (6.22′), and persists in the general equilibrium, as

$$\frac{\partial u_t}{\partial \varphi} = \frac{\varepsilon[\phi - \rho(\varepsilon - 1)]}{\varepsilon + \varphi - \dfrac{\varepsilon - 1}{\varepsilon}} > 0.$$

However, the increase in the aggregate demand externality will distort decision by firms to defer market entry, rendering less innovations lucrative at any given point in time, thus an increase in φ unambiguously reduces the economic growth rate indirectly,

$$\frac{\partial \hat{c}_t}{\partial \varphi} = \frac{-\phi(\varepsilon - 1)[\phi - \rho(\varepsilon - 1)]}{\left[\varepsilon(\varepsilon - 1) + \phi(\varepsilon - 1)\left(\varphi - \dfrac{\varepsilon - 1}{\varepsilon}\right)\right]^2} < 0.$$

This last effect sheds some new light on the discussion of unemployment benefits. As all of the distortions in firms, decisions stem from the risk premium which workers ask for in order to compensate the risk of losing a job, unemployment benefits will reduce the size of the risk premium, thus fostering economic growth, but by the same token they will also raise the average level of unemployment. In order to eliminate the entire distortionary effect, unemployment benefits are required to drive the reservation wage up to the current wage rate. The duration of unemployment benefits can, however, be short, given that labor contracts only take a short time to renegotiate.

Summarizing, we find that an increase in the individual rate of time preference, a decrease in innovation productivity and a decline in profit shares all reduce growth and unemployment, whereas a decrease in the demand externality, equivalent to an increase in aggregate failure to enter the market early, reduces growth and fosters unemployment. Therefore, whilst all growth determinants addressed by the endogenous growth literature – namely preferences, represented by the parameters ρ and ε, and technology, represented by innovation productivity ϕ – lead to a positive correlation between growth and unemployment, only shifts in aggregate demand can account for the intuitive negative correlation between growth and unemployment, as asserted in the empirical literature ever since Okun (1970). Whereas the individual rate of time preference, the elasticity of substitution, and innovation productivity may account for situations of jobless growth, only a wicked combination of these parameters, or an aggregate demand externality, can explain situations of high growth and low unemployment.

6.9 Is it Keynesian unemployment?

Three key elements form the essence of what has become known as Keynesian unemployment. First and foremost, unemployment is seen as the result of the failure of goods markets to clear. In particular, unemployment stems from a decline in effective demand. As we have already noted, an increase in the effective demand failure rate, φ, fosters unemployment in the model previously presented.

Secondly, an exogenous drop in effective demand triggers a multiplier process, leading to a further decline in effective demand and hence further aggravating the unemployment problem. Most innovation-driven endogenous growth models exhibit a multiplier process (Matsuyama, 1995; Keuschnigg, 1997). The novel feature of this model is that in this instance the multiplier process further aggravates the unemployment problem. The mechanism works as follows: An initial decline in aggregate demand leads to a fall in aggregate consumption, resulting in lower employment and higher unemployment, due to equation (6.26′). This further reduces income and hence aggregate demand, until the process fades out, leading to equations (6.27) and (6.28) in equilibrium.

Thirdly, Keynesian unemployment is not due to a failure in the price adjustment mechanism, neither because of nominal rigidities (e.g. Mankiw, 1985), nor because of real rigidities (Tobin, 1993). Keynesian unemployment is rooted in goods market failures, and regardless of changes in relative prices. The unemployment described in this chapter has been shown to be independent of price adjustment rigidities, but hinges on the failure of goods markets to accept innovative products.

The model in this chapter does not generate one of the most criticized Keynesian results, the counter-cyclicality of real wages (Ambler and Cardia, 1998). Here we find a procyclical real wage, however, a counter-cyclical real wage growth rate. Introducing the time dimension can therefore resolve the wage puzzle. Summarizing, we find that unemployment as discussed in this chapter has many of the characteristics of Keynesian unemployment. The model itself, however, is based on neoclassical foundations. Whilst there has always been an interest in integrating the Keynesian model into the Walrasian framework,[8] this model moves in the opposite direction by attempting to find a consensus model of the macroeconomy.

6.10 Conclusions

This chapter has argued that in a growing economy unemployment can be the cause of goods markets failures, even if these are purely transitory. As the economy grows, new firms wish to enter product markets. It may take some time, however, for their products to be accepted in the market, which we model as a purely transitory demand shock. This can either be due to consumers' choice to defer immediate consumption of certain products, in particular if they consider them to be dangerous to health, because of failures in the marketing of the product, or finally because of government regulation, deferring entry into the product markets.

Firms who fail early entry will renege on their job offers, thereby causing unemployment. Workers, anticipating this, will ask for a risk premium in insecure contracts, distorting the price and supply decisions of firms, and reducing incentives to invest into novel products. This process reduce, but will not eliminate, the number of precarious job offers. Thus, a transitory demand shock will lead to a persistent level of unemployment in a growing economy. Moreover, shifts in the aggregate demand externality are the only unique factor which can account for a negative correlation between the economic rate of growth and the unemployment rate, which is in line with empirical observations. Therefore, the introduction of aggregate demand externalities is important to explain the joint determinants of economic growth and unemployment.

Part II

Evidence

7
Job Creation and Destruction?

The endogenous growth literature claims that economic growth is driven by structural change. The cost associated with economic growth is structural unemployment, since structural change destroys jobs in one firm and creates jobs in another. This body of theory makes the strong prediction that the number of jobs created equals the number of jobs destroyed for any rate of economic growth, thus resulting in a constant rate of unemployment. By contrast, neoclassical growth theory suggests that exogenous productivity gains are incorporated in the factor labor, hence changes in economic growth should have no impact on the level of unemployment. This chapter presents a simple theoretical framework of intersectoral and intrasectoral change.

In the model presented here, the economy comprises two sectors. The engine of growth is labor-augmenting technical progress in the first sector, and intrasectoral structural change in the other sector. Thus, it contains both the neoclassical growth model and the endogenous growth model as special cases. The general model implies that economic growth exhibits a different impact on job creation and job destruction, depending on the relative size of the two sectors, leading to changing rates of unemployment for given rates of economic growth.

This chapter tests these two implications, using microeconomic panel data for the United Kingdom. We find that there is a significant and negative relation between unemployment and economic growth, using fixed effects panel regression methods. This implies that faster sectoral change, driven by higher rates of innovation and therefore by higher rates of economic growth, would foster structural unemployment. The test of this first hypothesis rejects the neoclassical growth model in favor of a framework which includes sectoral shifts.

If the increase in unemployment were driven entirely by intrasectoral change, we would find that the exit from employment must equal the entry to employment for every single rate of economic growth. Chi-square tests on parameter equality in logistic panel regressions for both job creation and destruction reveal that the impact of economic growth differs between exits and entries. This leads us to reject the pure intrasectoral shifts hypothesis in favor of a framework based on both inter- and intrasectoral shifts.

7.1 Motivation

The economy is permanently exposed to structural change, both within sectors and between sectors. The literature of intersectoral change finds that both employment and consumption have continuously shifted towards the service sector (Clark, 1957; Kuznets, 1957; Chenery, 1960). Echevarria (1997) attributed these facts to demand shifts due to non-homothetic preferences. By contrast, Kongsamut, Rebelo and Xie (1997) attribute the sectoral shifts to exogenous changes in productivity. Changes in productivity can account for changes in nominal and real shares of output for wide classes of preferences. In order to obtain intersectoral shifts in both employment and output, potentially leading to a transitory – but rather persistent – relation between economic growth and unemployment, they also have to deviate from homothetic preferences.

However, the employment dynamics are not mainly due to shifts between sectors, but due to shifts within sectors of the economy (Davis and Haltiwanger, 1999). The endogenous growth literature claims that economic growth drives this intrasectoral structural change – that is, a change within the sectoral composition of the economy (Romer, 1990). The introduction of new modes of production, which allow for a more efficient allocation of resources, or the innovation of a new product line itself, which augments the value of the product, form the essence of the growth process, but necessitate a simultaneous decline in existing products and production techniques. In that respect, differentiated products and markets will be more exposed to intrasectoral structural change than traditional homogenous markets and goods. The cost associated with economic growth is structural unemployment, as structural change destroys jobs in one firm and creates jobs in another (Aghion and Howitt, 1994). Firms producing a product in a declining market will lay off workers. Workers specializing in a particular mode of production will lose their jobs as new modes of production render their skills redundant. Until these workers requalify and are matched to new jobs in an expanding product segment or adapt to a new technology, they will suffer through experiencing periods of unemployment. The source of unemployment is the rate of intrasectoral structural change associated with faster economic growth. Hence the model predicts a constant unemployment rate for a given rate of economic growth. The unemployment rate would reach its lowest bound in a static economy, described by a static matching model (Mortensen and Pissarides, 1999). Higher growth induces larger structural shifts, and therefore fosters unemployment. Once we include intersectoral change, this no longer needs to be the case. Depending on the relative sizes of the traditional sector and the innovative sectors, the degree of job creation and destruction may differ, and hence the unemployment rate may change over time, even controlling for economic growth, as has been shown in chapter 4 of this book.

This view on unemployment and economic growth can, in principle, be tested. Conventional theories of economic growth (Solow, 1956) and unemployment (for a survey, cf. Layard, Nickell and Jackman, 1991) find that unemployment does not influence economic growth, and that long-run economic growth does not effect equilibrium unemployment (Blanchard, 1997). The endogenous growth and unemployment literature concludes that economic growth plays a significant role in the determination of equilibrium unemployment. This is the first hypothesis which will be tested in this chapter. In order to account for differences between individuals, sectors, and over time, a panel structure, in which we can control for both observable and unobservable components between groups, is adopted in order to estimate the impact of growth on unemployment.

The literature on endogenous growth and unemployment furthermore predicts a constant unemployment rate, and hence an equal number of job exits and entries, for a given rate of growth. The second hypothesis to be tested, therefore, is whether the coefficient for the growth rate is statistically equivalent for both exits and entries.

The chapter uses the Juvos cohort data of individual labor market exits and entries (Lawlor, 1990), and matches the cases with regionally and sectorally differentiated growth rates taken from the ONS Regional Database.

The chapter proceeds as follows. The next section will describe a simple theoretical framework of the effect of economic growth on intersectoral and intrasectoral change and unemployment. It contains both the neoclassical growth model and the Aghion and Howitt model, and is largely based on the exposition in chapter 4 of this book.[1] We will discuss the related empirical literature in section 7.3, describe the data in section 7.4, and finally present the empirical results in sections 7.5 and 7.6.

7.2 A simple theoretical framework

Consumers devote an increasing share of their nominal spending to differentiated products. Assume that agents devote a share α_t of their total spending on differentiated products, and a share $(1 - \alpha_t)$ on traditional homogenous goods. Consumer spending is then divided between the two sectors according to,

$$p_t x_t / \alpha_t = q_t y_t / (1 - \alpha_t), \tag{7.1}$$

denoting the price[2] of a typical bundle of differentiated products by p_t, aggregate demand of the innovative sector (all differentiated products) by x_t, demand for traditional goods by y_t, and their price by q_t. We can interpret a change in the differentiated product consumption share α_t as a change in consumer preferences. If relative prices reflect changes in relative productivities, the above formulation contains both the preference shifts hypothesis (Echevarria, 1997) and the technology hypothesis (Kongsamut, Rebelo and Xie, 1997) of intersectoral change. We shall argue later that it also contains the neoclassical growth model (Solow, 1956) as a special case with $\alpha_t = 0$, and the endogenous growth model (Aghion and Howitt, 1992) as a special case with $\alpha_t = 1$.

Whilst traditional goods are widely standardized, differentiated products are by definition provided in a heterogeneous variety. We argue that it is the increase in variety, indexed by n_t, which induces the shift in consumer preferences, or equivalently,

$$\alpha_t = \alpha(n_t), \tag{7.2}$$

with $\alpha(0) = 0$, $\alpha(\infty) = 1$, and $\alpha'(n_t) \geq 0$. Consumer demand for a particular differentiated product $x_{i,t}$ depends inversely on the product's relative price, with a price elasticity of demand equal to ε, and positively on aggregate demand,

$$x_{i,t} = (p_{i,t}/p_t)^{-\varepsilon} x_t. \tag{7.3}$$

This demand function contains a powerful implication for productivity-driven sectoral change. Multiplying both sides by the price for the particular product $p_{i,t}$, and aggregating over all n_t different differentiated products, we find that the aggregate innovative sector price index p_t declines for given individual product prices $p_{i,t}$. Hence variety increases productivity in the innovation sector irrespective of productivity gains by individual differentiated product suppliers. As nonstandardization implies that differentiated products produce few productivity gains, we shall ignore them altogether and assume that one unit of labor in the innovative sector, $e_{i,t}$, produces one unit of output, $x_{i,t}$. Substituting these assumptions into the demand function (7.3), taking time derivatives and rearranging terms, yields,

$$\hat{x}_t = \hat{e}_t + \frac{1}{\varepsilon - 1}\hat{n}_t, \tag{7.4}$$

where e_t is aggregate innovation sector employment to be defined below (7.8). Growth in the innovative sector is driven by an 'extensive' term, the change in employment, and an 'intensive' term, the increase in heterogeneity of differentiated products. The creation of a new differentiated product, the process of innovation, is costly, and providers of differentiated products pay for these costs by securing monopoly profits. They therefore set a price equal to a mark-up over costs, which is inversely related to the elasticity of demand,

$$p_{i,t} = \frac{\varepsilon}{\varepsilon - 1}w_t, \tag{7.5}$$

where w_t is the wage per unit of labor. The total profit $\pi_{i,t}$ of a firm in the innovative sector is equal to revenue minus costs,

$$\pi_{i,t} = \frac{1}{\varepsilon - 1}w_t e_{i,t}. \tag{7.6}$$

Given the importance of new innovations for innovation sector productivity, we shall formalize the process of innovation in a very simple manner. Suppose that s_t workers innovate a new product variety with productivity ϕn_t, then the growth rate of innovations is equal to,

$$\hat{n}_t = \phi s_t. \tag{7.7}$$

Assuming that all profits (7.6) are reinvested, then employment in the creation of new products will be a constant share of total employment in the innovative sector,

$$e_t = n_t e_{i,t} + s_t = \frac{\varepsilon}{\varepsilon - 1}n_t e_{i,t} = \varepsilon s_t. \tag{7.8}$$

As opposed to differentiated products, traditional goods are widely standardized. This standardization implies that productivity gains can be realized much more easily, and that it is easier to enter this market. For simplicity, we shall assume that manufacturers produce one unit of output with labor, l_t, as the only input, and technology a_t, under perfect competition, implying that the price q_t will equal marginal costs, w_t/a_t, and hence all revenue will go to the workers,

$$q_t y_t = w_t l_t. \tag{7.9}$$

Apart from capital, the traditional sector in this economy offers a very good representation of the competitive single-good economy as described in Solow (1956), whereas the heterogeneous monopolistically competitive innovative sector captures all essential features of the endogenous growth literature (Aghion and Howitt, 1992). Substituting traditional goods expenditure (7.9), the mark-up (7.5), and innovation employment (7.8) into consumption shares (7.1), we find that as consumers shift demand towards differentiated products, employment must follow this shift, whereas mere productivity-induced changes in relative prices, holding α constant, would not have this consequence, as

$$(1 - \alpha_t)e_t = \alpha_t l_t. \tag{7.10}$$

Defining the unemployment rate as one minus the employment rate, eliminating the traditional sector labor force from condition (7.10) above, and innovative sector employment through conditions (7.8) and (7.7), we find an inverse relation between the rate of innovation, which itself determines economic growth (7.4), and unemployment,

$$u_t = 1 - \frac{\varepsilon}{\phi \alpha_t} \hat{n}_t. \tag{H 1}$$

This structural form equation is the first testable hypothesis. Note already that this formulation contains both the Solow and the Aghion–Howitt model as special cases. In a Solow-type economy, economic growth is entirely driven by exogenous changes in factor productivity, a_t, which is equivalent to a purely traditional economy in our model, represented by a share of traditional goods in consumption $(1 - \alpha_t)$ equal to unity. In that case employment in the innovation sector will be zero due to equation (7.10), and therefore innovation growth will be zero due to equation (7.7). Therefore, as α_t converges to zero, the unemployment rate defined in (H 1) will be constant and independent of the rate of economic growth. By contrast, in an Aghion–Howitt framework economic growth is entirely driven by innovation, equivalent to a pure innovative economy, where the differentiated product share in consumption α_t equals unity. Unless the rate of substitution ε and productivity in innovation ϕ change persistently and systematically over time, unemployment rates should be identical for a given rate of economic growth. The inclusion of intersectoral shifts – where α_t evolves according to equation (7.2) – breaks the sharp prediction. The impact of new innovations on unemployment, captured by the derivative of unemployment with respect to innovation growth, becomes weaker as the level of innovation increases, as the cross derivative of unemployment with respect to innovation and innovation growth is negative, $\delta^2 u_t/\delta n_t \delta \hat{n}_t < 0$.

The model exhibits rich flow dynamics of workers in and out of employment, which are of particular interest, because they allow more efficient empirical estimates due to a higher volatility. Workers are driven out of jobs due to intersectoral shifts, leaving jobs in the traditional sector and eventually finding employment in the innovative sector. However, the larger part of employment fluctuation happens within the innovative sector as the result of intrasectoral shifts. New innovations create new jobs, but at the same time destroy existing jobs, not only in the traditional sector, but also in incumbent innovation sector firms. Job creation in this economy happens primarily in new innovation sector firms, which each employ an average of $e_{i,t}$ employees. In addition, the innovative workforce in the differentiated product sector, s_t, grows proportionally with the rest of the sector (7.8). Job creation in terms of total employment, c_t, therefore equals,

$$c_t = (\dot{n}_t e_{i,t} + \dot{s}_t)/(e_t + l_t) = \frac{\alpha_t}{\varepsilon}\hat{e}_t + \frac{(\varepsilon - 1)\alpha_t}{\varepsilon}\hat{n}_t, \qquad \text{(H 2a)}$$

where dots denote the total number of changes over time. The creation of new jobs makes existing jobs redundant at the margin, thus leading to the creative destruction of existing jobs,

$$\begin{aligned} n_t \dot{e}_{i,t}/(e_t + l_t) &= \alpha_t (n_t e_{i,t}) \hat{e}_{i,t} \\ &= \frac{(\varepsilon - 1)\alpha_t}{\varepsilon}\left[\hat{x}_t - \hat{n}_t - \frac{1}{\varepsilon - 1}\hat{n}_t\right] = \frac{(\varepsilon - 1)\alpha_t}{\varepsilon}(\hat{e}_t - \hat{n}_t). \end{aligned} \qquad (7.11)$$

Note that under the assumption $\alpha_t = 1$, equation (7.10) implies that employment is constant on a balanced growth path. The change in employment in the last expression of equation (7.11) therefore vanishes, rendering the creative destruction effect unambiguously negative. The third expression in equation (7.11) is, however, more intuitive. It captures all three effects of creative destruction, as discussed in Aghion and Howitt (1994). The second term in the square brackets is the direct effect of creative destruction. As new firms enter the market, the share of aggregate demand served by each firm declines. The third term in the square brackets is the indirect creative destruction effect. As new firms enter, aggregate prices decline faster than individual prices, thus reducing demand, and thereby indirectly destroying jobs. The first term in the square brackets represents the counteracting capitalization effect, which is due to the fact that lower aggregate prices increase aggregate demand and thus partially defer the creative destruction of jobs in incumbent firms.

As opposed to the Aghion–Howitt framework, innovation sector employment can change over time in a model, which includes intersectoral shifts for two reasons. First, the impact of growth on unemployment may differ according to the current level of innovations, hence total employment may change over time. Secondly, shifts from the traditional sector into the innovative sector can change innovation sector employment for a given rate of unemployment. In terms of employment flows, we need to incorporate the flow of workers which are driven out of the traditional sector, hence the exit rate from employment, d_t, changes to,

$$d_t = (n_t e_{i,t} + l_t)/(e_t + l_t) = \left(\frac{\alpha_t}{\varepsilon} + 1\right)\hat{e}_t - \left[\frac{(\varepsilon - 1)\alpha_t}{\varepsilon} + \frac{\partial \alpha_t}{\partial n_t}\frac{n_t}{\alpha_t}\right]\hat{n}_t, \tag{H 2b}$$

making use of equations (7.10) and (7.2). The first term merely expresses that an increase in total employment increases the number of workers who may be hit by structural change. The second term is the creative destruction effect as noted by Aghion and Howitt (1994). The third term, which is the elasticity of the innovation sector's share in total output with respect to the number of innovations, captures an indirect creative destruction effect. As the number of new innovations increases, a larger share of jobs in the traditional sector becomes redundant.

Finally, note that the direct and the indirect effect of economic growth on job creation and destruction are identical if $\alpha_t = 1$, hence the Aghion–Howitt hypothesis, $c_t = d_t$, can be considered to be a special case of a model consisting of both intersectoral and intrasectoral structural changes.[3]

7.3 Related empirical literature

Much of the empirical literature on the effect of economic growth on unemployment has focused on aggregate time series. The evidence on the choice of the correct underlying model is mixed. Topel (1999) finds time series evidence of a positive association of growth to unemployment within the Solow framework, whereas Altissimo and Violante (2001) find results favoring an association which would support an endogenous growth setting. As economic growth may influence unemployment both through the business cycle and also through its impact on the creative destruction of jobs, authors have turned their attention to panel data methods. Both Blanchard and Wolfers (2000) and Bulli (2000) use international panel data evidence, the former to test a neoclassical model, and the latter to test endogenous growth models. Both find empirical support for their respective estimates, which means that we are unable to distinguish between the two hypotheses. Time series currently available are too short to distinguish between a neoclassical growth framework with a lot of persistence, and an endogenous growth model which generates a unit root. We will therefore use microeconomic data of individual unemployment experiences, where we can control for business cycle effects, as many individuals are hit by identical shocks, in order to capture the long-run impact of economic growth on equilibrium unemployment.

The idea of using microeconomic panel data is not completely novel in an examination of growth models. Harberger (1998) has been able to assess the significance of human capital investment and innovation on the long-run growth rate of revenues of US companies, thus confirming many of the arguments within the theoretical literature on endogenous growth.

Panel data have received much greater attention in the empirical labor market literature (Bunzel et al., 1993). Bailey, Hulten and Campbell (1992) use plant-level data to estimate the effect of labor reallocation on productivity growth on the plant level, finding that more rapid changes in the labor force result in higher rates of productivity. Foster, Haltiwanger and Krizan (1998) have decomposed the impact of factor reallocation on productivity growth between exiting, entering and surviving firms, finding a similar impact of labor reallocation on productivity throughout. This has two implications for the following analysis. First, 'reallocation plays a significant role in labor productivity growth via net entry' (Davis and Haltiwanger, 1999, p. 2767), and hence for output growth. Secondly, the type of firm seems irrelevant, and hence we need not necessarily control for it, allowing us to focus solely on panel data evidence which captures employment flows.

Using UK microdata on unemployment, Layard, Nickell and Jackman (1991, p. 286ff) summarize the reasons for being unemployed. First, they find that the usual occupation and the geographical region of the unemployed exhibit a significant impact on a worker's chances of being unemployed. As some jobs and some regions are exposed to stronger structural change, it is quite evident that the process of creative destruction would lead to such a pattern. Indeed, economic growth may be the driving force behind differences in regional and occupational unemployment rates. Secondly, they find that a number of personal characteristics play an important role – in particular age, race and gender.

As the former and the latter are typically associated with additional detriments to occupational change and regional flexibility (Böheim and Taylor, 1999), we shall control for these factors explicitly. Moreover, we shall include stable relationships, such as marriages and partnerships, for the same reason, in our panel.

7.4 The data

The core of the econometric investigation in this chapter is based on the Joint Unemployment and Vacancies Online System (Juvos) database. This randomly generates a 5 per cent sample of all entries and exits into unemployment, alongside some other statistical information, for a total of 3,398,223 UK cases over a period from October 1982 to December 1999, based on daily information supplied by the Employment Service local offices (ONS, 1997). The database is longitudinal, as it assigns a code to each individual (generated to replace the National Insurance Number), and can hence be transformed into a panel structure, reporting every exit and entry to the pool of unemployed over time (Ward and Bird, 1995).

The panel contains 319,057 men and 163,555 women, with 338,082 living in a stable relationship (marriage and partnerships), and 144,530 living alone. On 1 October 1982, 4,202 individuals were over fifty, 49,987 were over forty, 79,860 were over thirty, 92,424 were over twenty, 148,707 were older than ten, and 107,432 younger than ten at the beginning of the sample.

The econometric analysis which follows uses the following dependent variables: the time series of exits, the time series of entries, and a self-generated series, labeled the individual unemployment rate. The latter captures the number of days a person spends being unemployed over the entire year, and therefore represents the closest individual correspondence to the aggregate unemployment rate.

The best individual representation of a growth rate would probably be individual wage growth. Three arguments speak against the use of this series. First, individual wage growth does not account for total value-added by the individual, unless we assume perfect competition and constant returns to scale in production. Secondly, as high wage claims by individuals will certainly lead to a higher risk of unemployment, we will face a sample selection bias. Thirdly, individual wage data cannot yet be matched with individual unemployment spells. Therefore, we have used the closest available proxy to individual value-added growth, which is the GDP growth rate of the region and the sector in which the individual is occupied.[4] The Juvos data provide the individuals' unemployment benefit office number, which can be transformed into the 11 standard statistical regions (SSR) of the United Kingdom.[5] They provide both usual (in the past) and sought (wanted) occupational codes for 1,028,396 cases or 482,612 individuals, which have been matched to the 12 industry sectors and 13 manufacturing classes as defined by the European System of Accounts (ESA 95) classification (Sweeney, 1996a).[6] GDP growth rates, taken from the ONS Regional Accounts, for these 264 observations per annum were then assigned to the individuals in the Juvos panel. The growth rates have been assigned in three different ways – by region only, by region and sought occupation, and by region and usual occupation.

Unemployment is driven by the business cycle. In order not to capture effects of the business cycle, but of economic growth, we will instrumentalize the average growth rate with the two period lagged growth rate, which exhibits the highest correlation with the current growth rate, and therefore seems an appropriate instrument.

7.5 Does economic growth determine unemployment?

This section presents estimation results and the test of the first hypothesis (H 1), which predicts a negative correlation between unemployment and economic growth, based on the empirical data presented in section 7.4. The innovation here is clearly the use of microeconomic panel data in testing this hypothesis. As discussed in section 7.2, unemployment can be viewed as the difference between flows of workers into unemployment, and flows of workers out of unemployment. Evidently, these flows are in part driven by the willingness of a particular worker to accept a job, and by the willingness of firms to hire a particular type of worker. As each worker is unique, we would like to control for these individual characteristics. Panel data allow us to control for both observable and unobservable time-invariant individual characteristics (Raj and Baltagi, 1992). As the first hypothesis (H 1) should hold in every period and for every sector, we can restate it in matrix notation,

$$U_{i,t} = N_{i,t}\gamma + X_{i,t}\beta + Y_i\theta + Z_i\delta t + v_{i,t}, \tag{7.12}$$

where $U_{i,t}$ is the dependent series, which corresponds to the individual unemployment rate, $N_{i,t}$ is the assigned growth rate, $X_{i,t}$ are other time-varying regressors and the time-varying individual characteristics, Y_i are the observable time-invariant dependent variables, Z_i are time-variant dependent variables, which may reflect underlying unobservable components which change continuously over time, γ, β, θ and δ are the associated parameters, and $v_{i,t}$ is the error term. In principle, we are faced with two types of biases in our estimation – non-stationarity and measurement errors due to unobserved components – which are correlated with the dependent variable, and we shall address these issues in turn.

Clearly, at least one regressor is non-stationary. More importantly, there may be non-stationarity in the dependent series as well, due to hysteresis in unemployment. This holds for aggregate data, where the fact that there is unemployment today is a good indicator that there will be unemployment tomorrow, but even more true in the case of individual data, where the fact that someone is unemployed today implies that she will most likely be unemployed tomorrow. This implies that lagged unemployment will be absorbed in the error term of equation (7.12), $v_{i,t} = v'_{i,t}\beta + U_{i,t-1}\rho$, where the autocorrelation coefficient ρ measures the persistence of unemployment. The unemployment rate will then exhibit persistence if $\rho < 1$, and full hysteresis, or a random walk, if $\rho = 1$. When regressing equation (7.12), this implies that the residual is correlated with the error term, and thus that all estimators are biased. We can eliminate persistence by taking first differences of equation (7.12),[7] resulting in

$$\Delta U_{i,t} = \Delta(N_{i,t}\gamma) + \Delta(X_{i,t}\beta) + \Delta(Y_i\theta) + \Delta(Z_i\delta t) + \Delta(U_{i,t-1}\rho) + \Delta v'_{i,t}, \tag{7.13}$$

which still does not eliminate the bias. However, as the time-invariant dependent variables are equivalent to their average, the third term in expression (7.13) vanishes. Moreover, as time directly influences only the time-variant dependent regressors, the fourth term simplifies to $Z_i\delta$. In order to eliminate the bias, we follow Arellano and Bond (1991), who suggest that we can account for the lagged change in the dependent variable with the twice-lagged level of the dependent variable as a valid instrument. The first stage instrumental variable (IV) estimation then equals,

$$\Delta U_{i,t-1} = U_{i,t-2}\varphi + \xi_{i,t}, \tag{7.14}$$

where $\xi_{i,t}$ is the error term. Substituting the deterministic part of the first stage IV-estimation (7.14) into equation (7.13), we obtain the second stage IV-estimator,

$$\Delta U_{i,t} = \Delta N_{i,t}\gamma + \Delta X_{i,t}\beta + Z_i\delta + U_{i,t-2}\varphi\rho + \Delta v'_{i,t}. \tag{7.15}$$

Unless φ equals unity, which we can test for in equation (7.14), this equation provides a simple unit root test for the hysteresis hypothesis of individual unemployment rates. Whilst this procedure eliminates the bias due to non-stationarity of the series, we still have to deal with the measurement error that results from unobservable components which are associated with the dependent variable.

In contrast to pure time series or cross-sectional analysis, panel data allow us to eliminate some of the measurement error. The measurement error appears because independent regressors may be correlated with unobserved individual characteristics. To give an example, it may well be the case that some workers are less mobile than others, and therefore exhibit a lower search intensity. This can be the case for individuals in stable relationships, who are much more inclined to seek work in the vicinity of their partner. Estimating equation (7.15), the unobserved individual search intensity will be absorbed in the error term, $\Delta v'_{i,t} = Z_i\varphi + \Delta v''_{i,t}$. Substituting this into equation (7.12), we find that the OLS estimator will be biased upwards by φ (Angrist and Kruger, 1999). Substituting the same information into the fixed effect panel estimator (7.13), we find that,

$$\begin{aligned}\Delta U_{i,t} - \overline{\Delta U_i} = (\Delta N_{i,t} - \overline{\Delta N_i})\gamma + (\Delta X_{i,t} - \overline{\Delta X_i})\beta + (\Delta Z_i - \overline{\Delta Z_i})(\delta + \varphi)\\ + \Delta v''_{i,t} - \overline{\Delta v''_i},\end{aligned} \tag{7.16}$$

which is unbiased due to the elimination of the fixed effects, as the third term on the right-hand side is zero by definition. Therefore, if we estimate (7.16), which is a fixed effect estimation, it does not matter whether or not we can observe the time-invariant fixed components (Baltagi, 1995, p. 10ff). Moreover, as the error terms are zero by definition, the very last term in expression (7.16) vanishes. In this respect, the error structure remains MA(1), and the double differentiation (first differences and then deviations from the mean), do not alter the error structure, and thus statistical properties of the model remain valid (Maddala, 1993). Denoting deviations from average changes by tildes, the estimated fixed effects (FE) instrumental variable panel regression ultimately equals,

$$\tilde{U}_{i,t} = \tilde{N}_{i,t}\gamma + \tilde{X}_{i,t}\beta + \Delta v''_{i,t}, \tag{7.17}$$

Table 7.1 summarizes the results of the empirical estimation of the above equation for three different methods of assigning growth rates to individual workers, equivalent to the test of hypothesis one (H 1). We could not reject hypothesis one if the coefficient on the growth rate is significant and negative.

The reported estimations can explain a remarkably large part of the variation of the dependent variable, with the relevant R^2 above 30 per cent. The F-test reveals that all regressors taken together are significant, and we find that indeed all regressors taken individually are significant at least at the one per cent significance level. This implies that we find a statistically significant impact of economic growth on unemployment at the microeconomic level. The sign is negative, as predicted by hypothesis one (H 1).

The three estimated coefficients on economic growth cannot be compared directly. Whilst the first scenario has only 11 different regional growth rates attributed in every year, the latter two scenarios attribute both regionally and sectorally differentiated growth rates to each individual. The growth rates in the first column therefore contain more averaging than the latter two, thus explaining the higher coefficient of scenario 1. If we accounted for this fact, the coefficient of the first column would be much closer to the other two.

The effect is also economically significant. Given an average individual unemployment rate of 12.5 per cent in our sample,[8] a one percentage point increase of a particular regional and sectoral growth rate would reduce unemployment by 5 per cent, or the equivalent of one working week per employee.

All time-invariant individual characteristics, such as date of birth, race and gender, have been implicitly accounted for by the fixed effect estimation. We could, however, explicitly control for all time-varying effects. We find, in particular, that both a regional migration and a change of occupation increase the individual unemployment experience. Evidently, as agents are forced to leave their region to find a job elsewhere,

Table 7.1 Change in individual unemployment experiences due to economic growth

Dependent series: individual unemployment rate in first differences (FE IV – estimation)	*Scenario 1*	*Scenario 2*	*Scenario 3*
Lagged dependent variable	−0.2398	−0.2295	−0.2299
(instrumented)	(0.0076)	(0.0076)	(0.0076)
GDP growth rate	−0.8866		
(assigned by region only)	(0.0362)		
GDP growth rate (by region		−0.0601	
and sought occupation)		(0.0050)	
GDP growth rate (by region			−0.0569
and usual occupation)			(0.0053)
Regional change	0.0425	0.0433	0.0433
	(0.0037)	(0.0037)	(0.0037)
Occupational change	0.0996	0.1007	0.1008
	(0.0019)	(0.0019)	(0.0019)
Entering a stable relationship	0.0967	0.0983	0.0987
	(0.0114)	(0.0114)	(0.0114)
Breaking up from a stable	0.0691	0.0694	0.0693
relationship	(0.0132)	(0.0132)	(0.0132)
Constant	−0.0713	−0.0708	−0.0707
	(0.0007)	(0.0007)	(0.0007)
R^2 (between) (%)	31.84	31.43	31.48
F-test	860.77	782.34	777.68
	(0.0000)	(0.0000)	(0.0000)
Unit root χ^2 test	282 511.99	281 359.80	281 285.17
	(0.0000)	(0.0000)	(0.0000)
Hausmann test for the	16 648.27	16 343.21	16 326.02
equivalent RE model	(0.0000)	(0.0000)	(0.0000)

Notes: The columns differ only in the way the regionally and sectorally different growth rates are assigned to individuals. Standard errors for coefficients and p-values for test statistics are given in parenthesis. The reported Hausmann test corresponds to the equivalent random effect model. The quasi-unit root test corresponds to a χ^2 test of the coefficient of the lagged dependent variable equaling unity. Due to endogeneity, the change in the lagged dependent variable is instrumentalized with the twice lagged level of the dependent variable, following Arellano and Bond (1991).

they will be more reluctant to move, thus prolonging the duration of their unemployment. As agents lose a job in a declining sector, employers in other sectors will be less inclined to offer them a new job, hence their probability to remain unemployed increases to the same degree.

Whilst most personal characteristics are time-invariant, we can explicitly account for changes in the marital and partnership status of individuals. We find that people entering a stable relationship will see their unemployment experience increasing on average, which may be attributable to the fact that regional flexibility in the search strategy on the labor market declines. By contrast, we find that people who leave a relationship are also more likely to become unemployed as well. This can be explained both through individual characteristics – people who are in the process of splitting up will be less focused on their job and are therefore more likely to be fired – and from employer characteristics. Employers may be less likely to hire divorced people, with only the increased regional flexibility to offset these two psychological factors. Finally, it can be noted that the instrumented lagged dependent variable has a negative impact on the current level of the variable. This implies that a bad shock to individual unemployment today will be partly offset in the next period. However, given a coefficient below unity, the negative effect of the shock is not totally reversed, implying that shocks to unemployment are indeed persistent. However, the unit root test derived from this series, which we obtain by splitting the coefficient into the autocorrelation coefficient ρ and the coefficient of the first stage IV estimation φ, rejects the hypothesis of a unit root in the individual unemployment rate. This implies that the estimation procedure adopted is valid, and not subject to spurious results.

Fixed effects estimation is based on the idea that each individual has particular time-invariant observable and unobservable characteristics, and therefore relies entirely on the information obtained from variation within each individual observation. Evidently, this leads to a loss of degrees of freedom, and therefore to inefficient estimators. In our analysis, we have suggested that we cannot observe important individual characteristics, such as search intensity, and that therefore a fixed effect model is appropriate. The most popular alternative is a random effect model, in which we treat our missing knowledge over a particular individual as individual ignorance with respect to that individual (and assume some distribution over that lack of knowledge). We can test whether it is indeed individual ignorance, by testing whether the error terms are indeed not systematically correlated, following a test procedure as described by Hausmann (1978). The Hausmann test rejects the null hypothesis that the difference in coefficients is not systematic. Therefore, we would have to reject the random effect specification in favor of something else, which gives additional support to the fixed effects modeling choice pursued here.

Summarizing, we can conclude that economic growth exhibits a significant and negative impact on unemployment. Whilst this rejects the

Solow model, it confirms both the intrasectoral shifts Aghion–Howitt framework and the intra- and intersectoral shifts framework presented in section 7.2. The estimation is rather robust with respect to the particular attribution of growth rates to individuals, hence we shall pursue by only using the last representation, by usual occupation and region. We have seen, both here and in the theoretical section 7.2, that it is important to look at flows of workers into employment and out of employment rather than at the aggregated series, which will be done in the following section.

7.6 Does economic growth exert a different impact on exits and entries?

In section 7.2, we found that the impact of economic growth on entry and exit from employment need not be identical, which leads to the formulation of hypothesis two. As our data provide information on both exits and entries into the labor market, we can in principle test the two equations (H 2a) and (H 2b) separately, and then test for parameter equality, which is our second hypothesis.

The econometric procedure is equivalent to the previous section, substituting entries $C_{i,t}$ and exits $D_{i,t}$ for the individual unemployment rates $U_{i,t}$ used in that case. There is, however, one important distinction. As agents can either be entering a new job or not, or either be leaving a job or not, both dependent variables are binary, which implies that the variance of the error term varies systematically, or that the error terms are heteroscedastic (Moffitt, 1999). We therefore estimate the model using logistic regressions, estimating the probability of an individual finding a job or losing her job, but otherwise follow the fixed effects panel data estimation procedure described in the previous section. As logit is a non-linear estimation procedure, we have to take care in interpreting the results. In particular, note that the coefficients in Table 7.2 represent the marginal effect of a unit change in independent variable from the baseline scenario, which is assumed to be $X_{i,t} = 0$.

The first two columns in Table 7.2 are the disaggregated equivalents of the last column in Table 7.1. We note from the likelihood ratio test that the model performs better than the simplest alternative, or that all coefficients taken together are highly significant.[9] Indeed, every coefficient is again significant at the one per cent significance level. The coefficient on the instrumented lagged dependent variable is positive. This implies that if you have been fired from your last job, you are more likely to be fired again from your new job. This is consistent with theories of segmented

Table 7.2 Change in exits and entries to employment due to economic growth

Dependent variables in first differences FE IV Logit estimation	*Entry to employment*	*Exit from employment*	*Entry to employment*	*Exit from employment*
Lagged entry	2.8657		2.8784	
(instrumented)	(0.0189)		(0.0191)	
Lagged exits		2.7890		2.7990
(instrumented)		(0.0192)		(0.0193)
GDP growth rate	0.4005	0.2565	0.3543	0.2234
	(0.0436)	(0.0510)	(0.0444)	(0.0520)
Change in the GDP			0.0065	0.0049
growth rate			(0.0009)	(0.0011)
Regional change	−1.2855	−1.3167	−1.2816	−1.3127
	(0.0377)	(0.0410)	(0.0378)	(0.0411)
Occupational change	−2.0232	−2.0440	−2.0259	−2.0487
	(0.0185)	(0.0207)	(0.0186)	(0.0208)
Entering stable	−1.7723	−1.6790	−1.7671	−1.6785
relationship	(0.1033)	(0.1222)	(0.1036)	(0.1224)
Breaking up from a stable	−2.5036	−2.8675	−2.5337	−2.9043
relationship	(0.1471)	(0.1686)	(0.1478)	(0.1698)
Log-likelihood	−41 801.80	−30 924.88	−41 596.73	−30 770.48
LR-χ^2 test	48 216.35	44 609.34	48 029.01	44 449.57
	(0.0000)	(0.0000)	(0.0000)	(0.0000)
Quasi-unit root χ^2 test	3 010.92	4 191.57	3 033.14	4 182.03
	(0.0000)	(0.0000)	(0.0000)	(0.0000)
Hausmann test for the	6 167.25	23 234.90	7 166.70	36 921.33
equivalent RE model	(0.0000)	(0.0000)	(0.0000)	(0.0000)
χ^2 test of parameter		25.26		47.67
equality between job		(0.00)		(0.00)
creation and destruction				

Notes: The coefficients represent the marginal effect of a unit change in independent variable from the baseline scenario, which is $X_{i,t} = 0$. Standard errors are given in parenthesis. The reported Hausmann test corresponds to the equivalent random effect model. The quasi-unit root test corresponds to a χ^2 test of the lagged dependent variable equaling unity. Due to endogeneity, the lagged dependent variable is instrumentalized with the twice lagged level of the dependent variable, following Arellano and Bond (1991).

labor markets, which find that part of the workforce will be subject to frequent job changes, and another part of the workforce will continue to enjoy long-term employment relationships (Piore, 1987; Bentolila and Dolado, 1994). Separating the coefficient into the autocorrelation coefficient ρ and the coefficient of the first stage IV estimation δ, we can again reject the hypothesis of a unit root in the individual unemployment rate.

The principal result is that we again find that economic growth exhibits a significant association with the probability to enter or leave employment. Both signs are positive, as predicted by theory – in equations (H 2a) and (H 2b). However, the coefficients are different, and a formal χ^2-test rejects the null hypothesis of parameter equality. We may therefore conclude that economic growth exhibits a different impact on job creation than job destruction, thus rejecting the pure intrasectoral change model as proposed by Aghion and Howitt (1994), in favor of a broader approach including both intra- and intersectoral change.

According to the two equations, which form hypothesis 2, exits and entries to employment depend upon both the growth rate and the change in the employment share of the innovative sector. Omitting this variable could lead to a bias in the estimation, which may be stronger in one of the two regressions, thus leading to a biased estimator of the impact on growth on job creation and job destruction.

Instead of directly including sectoral employment shift variables in the estimation, we note from equation (7.12) that a share α_t of total employment will work in the innovative sector. As the employment rate equals $1 - u_t$, we can substitute the employment share of the innovative sector, e_t, into equation (H 1), to find that employment in the innovative sector is proportional to economic growth. This is equivalent to stating that the change in the innovative sector's employment share, the second explanatory variable in both equations of hypothesis 2, is equal to the change in the rate of economic growth.

The latter variable has been included in columns 3 and 4 of Table 7.2. We find that both the rate of economic growth and the change in the rate of economic growth exhibit a positive and significant impact on both job creation and job destruction. The Hausmann test reveals again that a random effect specification for the same variables would have to be rejected. The likelihood ratio test indicates that all coefficients together are significant. The model performs slightly worse than the simpler alternative, excluding the change in the economic growth rate.

Comparing the two coefficients describing the impact of growth on job creation and destruction, they seem closer together than in the previous model – columns 1 and 2 of Table 7.2. However, in order to ensure that the impact of economic growth on the creation and the destruction of jobs offset each other, it must be the case that both coefficients together cannot be significantly different to zero. We can test this hypothesis with a standard Wald test, which is presented in the last line of Table 7.2. We find again that the null hypothesis of parameter equality has to be rejected, thus leading to a rejection of a pure model of intrasectoral change in favor of a model of both intersectoral and intrasectoral change.

Finally, note that the change in economic growth exerts a positive impact on both job creation and job destruction. As stated before, this implies that as the total employment rate increases, a larger number of workers are subject to the reallocation process of labor resources in the economy. Therefore, the number of both exits and entries to employment increases.

This result is closely related to a completely different set of evidence on the asymmetries of job creation and destruction over the course of the business cycle. Caballero and Hammour (1996) suggest that an efficient economy would concentrate its job creation and job destruction efforts during cyclical downturns. Their hypothesis was first confirmed empirically by Davis, Haltiwanger and Schuh (1998). The economic intuition is similar to the one presented in section 7.2. During a recession, just like during the process of intersectoral and intrasectoral structural change, labor reallocation is more efficient for two reasons. First, a lower number of employees have to be fired in order to compensate for changes in the demand structure. Secondly, a larger pool of unemployed facilitates hiring for firms. Therefore, the results are observationally equivalent to our findings on the positive impact of the change in economic growth on job creation and destruction, presented in Table 7.2, as the change in the economic growth rate is largest during a recession and lowest during a boom. The intuition is as follows. Both at the height of a boom and in the depths of a recession, the change in output is zero by definition. Shortly afterwards, economic growth is negative in the case of a fading boom and positive in an ending recession. The change in the economic rate of growth is therefore approaching minus infinity at the height of a boom and plus infinity in the depth of a recession. Therefore, the change in the economic growth rate presented in Table 7.2 captures the extent of the recession in the economy.

7.7 Conclusions

The aim of this chapter was to test three hypotheses about the impact of economic growth on unemployment, due to sectoral change. Section 7.2 has presented a model of both intersectoral and intrasectoral change in an endogenous growth framework with unemployment. One particular aspect of this approach was the fact that the model nested two other competing frameworks – the neoclassical Solow model and the model of intrasectoral change developed by Aghion and Howitt (1994). In this theoretical framework, we were able to derive two hypotheses about the impact of economic growth on unemployment, which allowed us to discriminate between the theories.

This chapter has presented tests of these two hypotheses, using microeconomic panel data for the United Kingdom. The results show a significant and negative relation between unemployment and economic growth, using fixed effects panel regression methods. This implies that faster sectoral change, driven by higher rates of innovation and therefore by higher rates of economic growth, would foster structural unemployment. This test rejects the neoclassical Solow model in favor of a framework, which includes sectoral shifts.

If the increase in unemployment were entirely driven by intrasectoral change, we found that the exit from employment must equal the entry to employment for every rate of economic growth. Chi-square tests on parameter equality in logistic panel regressions for both job creation and job destruction revealed that the impact of economic growth differs between exits and entries, hence rejecting the pure intrasectoral shifts hypothesis in favor of a framework based on both inter- and intrasectoral shifts.

8
On the Causality between Economic Growth and Unemployment

This chapter investigates the relation and causality of economic growth and equilibrium unemployment for the European G7 countries – France, Germany, Italy and the United Kingdom. Whilst endogenous growth models with matching frictions on the labor market predict a causal relationship from economic growth to unemployment, efficiency wage models predict the opposite direction of causality, and insider–outsider models indicate causality in both ways. Granger causality tests for the four European G7 countries indicate that France can be explained through the matching model, and Italy and Germany by the efficiency wage model. The United Kingdom follows either a union model or the efficiency wage model, depending on the number of lags included in the estimation.

8.1 Introduction

The first economist to propose a correlation between unemployment and economic growth was Arthur Okun (1970). In his seminal paper, first published in 1961, he essentially stated that a one percentage point decline in unemployment was associated with a 3 per cent increase in real output, beyond a long-run average annual growth rate of output of 2 to 3 per cent. For the research proposed here, his analysis has two major shortcomings. First, whilst he empirically describes a correlation between growth and unemployment, he fails to describe a causality in one or other direction.

Secondly, and more important, the statement that a change in unemployment leads to growth in output is equivalent to the statement that high employment is associated with a high level of output and vice versa. Hence, Okun's argument is static in nature, whilst the following research addresses a dynamic relation, whether high levels of unemployment are related to high growth rates of output or vice versa. Bean and Pissarides (1993) were the first to introduce frictional unemployment into a highly stylized endogenous growth model. They proposed a generational model with a simple Rebelo-type production function, where new members of the labor force had to be matched to a job vacancy, according to the matching approach (Pissarides, 1985). Evidently, an increase in the exogenous rate of factor productivity fosters economic growth, but also increases the rate of job creation, thus driving the unemployment rate down along the Beveridge curve (Beveridge, 1942). Bean and Pissarides therefore suggest a clear direction of causality, since innovations to economic growth (in particular through productivity shocks) lead to changes in the unemployment rate, but not vice versa. Whilst the model can explain long-run youth unemployment, they fail to give theoretical foundations for intragenerational layoffs, which account for the majority of the current level of unemployment.

Marimon and Zilibotti (1998) recently suggested that structural change is indeed the driving force behind frictional unemployment. As some industries decline, they lay off those workers who are not trained or qualified to be engaged in the emerging sectors. Aghion and Howitt (1994) realized that the second type of endogenous growth models mentioned earlier is indeed models of structural change as well. In that respect endogenous growth will affect unemployment in three distinct ways. First, there is the job creation effect, with new industries opening and hiring new workers. Second, there is the job destruction effect, as old firms leave the labor market. Third, there is an effect – which Aghion and Howitt loosely label the indirect effect – which is due to the fact that as the number of industries increases, firms can benefit less from scale effects, and production becomes more labor-intensive, a phenomenon that is widespread in the service sector. The model therefore indicates again a clear direction of causality, and it is once again economic growth which leads to a decline in unemployment, and not vice versa.

In general, we may conclude that matching models of the labor market will exhibit this unidirectional causal effect from economic growth to unemployment, as long as the matching technology is homothetic, a factor for which there is ample evidence (Mortensen and Pissarides, 1999). However, this property does not carry over for other models of endogenous growth and unemployment, in particular when different types of labor market rigidities are investigated.

The sharpest contrast to the matching models is presented in Zagler (2003), who shows that in an efficiency wage model, where efficiency considerations play an identical role both in the productive and the innovative sector, the unemployment rate will be determined purely by the non-accelerating wage rate of unemployment (Nawru). Therefore, the unemployment rate is indifferent to changes in economic growth, whereas economic growth will react to changes in the non-accelerating wage rate of unemployment. In an efficiency wage model, unemployment may therefore cause economic growth to decline, and not vice versa, thus inverting the findings of the endogenous growth and matching literature.

Combining these two strands of literature, Schaik and de Groot (1998) construct a two-sector efficiency wage model, in which the unemployed voluntarily line up to obtain a job in the efficiency wage sector. As firms in their model can exert full efficiency even in the absence of unemployment, the matching technology is once again the driving force of the correlation between unemployment and economic growth, hence it comes as little surprise that once again the causal direction is leading from economic growth to unemployment.

Both matching frictions and efficiency wages in endogenous growth models predict a unidirectional causal relation between unemployment and economic growth. By contrast, the introduction to this book has demonstrated that traditional exogenous growth models will predict no causal relationship between rates of economic growth and rates of unemployment. Shocks to productivity will alter the rate of economic growth, and shocks to the equilibrium rate of unemployment will alter the unemployment rate, leaving the other variable unaffected (Blanchard, 1997).

It has been mentioned above that the unidirectional causality from unemployment to economic growth in efficiency wage endogenous growth models relies on an identical role for efficiency considerations in all sectors of the economy. This, of course, need not necessarily be the general case. Whilst manufacturing firms will be able to control their workforce to a great degree, this is less possible in services, and definitely even worse in highly innovative firms. Therefore, the latter will rely much more heavily on efficiency wage considerations, resulting in different wage rates across the three sectors. Given that different growth rates will be associated with a different sectoral composition of the workforce, growth has a compositional impact on average wages. If average wages in the economy, and not averages within the worker's own sector, determine the outside option, growth will influence the worker's incentives, and thus alter the unemployment rate. In that respect, an efficiency wage model with a different role for efficiency considerations predicts a dual causal relation between unemployment and economic growth, as shown in chapter 2 of this book.

The channel is, however, rather hypothetical, and would probably not hold in segmented labor markets, where workers would relate to average wages in their market segment. A much more plausible theory, which can explain a causality from unemployment to economic growth and vice versa, is the insider–outsider model. The intuition is the following. First, labor is an input in production and in the innovation of new products or production techniques, which are the source of economic growth. Higher unemployment implies fewer workers in innovative activities, thus reducing economic growth. Secondly, as endogenous growth models rely on non-decreasing returns to scale with respect to reproducible factors, not all of the factors of production can be paid their marginal product, hence wages and prices will be distorted, typically resulting in less than optimal rates of growth. Forward-looking unions can work on this intertemporal tradeoff, and by moderating wages today they can induce low rates of unemployment and high rates of wage and output growth. Thus the insider–outsider model predicts a causal relation from unemployment to economic growth, and from growth to unemployment, as can be seen in Figure 5.1 of this book.

8.2 Three very stylized theoretical models

In order to outline the previous arguments more precisely, this section will present a very simple framework to develop the causal implications of the three different models of endogenous growth and unemployment – namely, a matching model, an efficiency wage model, and a union model. The matching model was first developed by Aghion and Howitt (1994), and this section presents a heavily simplified version of their framework. A more elaborate version of the efficiency wage model can be found in Zagler (2003), and a fully axiomatic representation of the union model approach with optimizing agents can be found in chapter 5.

8.2.1 Matching, growth and unemployment

In accordance with the innovation-driven endogenous growth literature, consumers in this model demand differentiated products. These products are provided by a single firm monopolistically, which enables them to pay for the costly process of innovation. Consumer demand for a particular product $x_{i,t}$ depends inversely on the products relative price, with a price elasticity of demand equal to ε, and positively on aggregate demand x_t,

$$x_{i,t} = (p_{i,t}/p_t)^{-\varepsilon} x_t. \tag{8.1}$$

We shall assume for simplicity that one unit of labor input, $l_{i,t}$, produces one unit of the product, and firms would like to hire enough workers to maximize profits, given their knowledge of demand (8.1). However, the presence of search frictions implies that finding a worker takes time, leading to a potentially suboptimal labor force. Instead of modeling the matching process explicity, we assume for simplicity that firms can outsource the search process to temporary work agencies, which charge a fixed cost $\kappa - 1$ on labor costs for their service to immediately provide employees (Mühlberger, 2000). Profit maximization implies that firms set a price equal to a mark-up over costs, which is inversely related to the elasticity of demand,

$$p_{i,t} = \frac{\varepsilon\kappa}{\varepsilon - 1} w_t, \tag{8.2}$$

where w_t is the wage per unit of labor. The total profit $\pi_{i,t}$ of a firm in the innovative sector is equal to revenue minus costs,

$$\pi_{i,t} = \frac{\kappa}{\varepsilon - 1} w_t l_{i,t}. \tag{8.3}$$

As mentioned above, the process of innovating products is costly. Suppose that s_t workers innovate a new product variety with productivity ϕn_t, then the growth rate of innovations is equal to,

$$\hat{n}_t = \phi s_t. \tag{8.4}$$

Assuming that all profits (8.3) are reinvested, then employment in the creation of new products will be proportional to total employment in the production of these products,

$$s_t = n_t \pi_{i,t}/w_t = \frac{\kappa}{\varepsilon - 1} n_t l_{i,t}. \tag{8.5}$$

Defining the unemployment rate as one minus the employment rate in the production and the creation of products, and substituting for manufacturing labor from (8.5) and innovation sector employment from (8.4), yields,

$$u_t = 1 - \frac{\varepsilon + \kappa - 1}{\phi\kappa} \hat{n}_t. \tag{8.6}$$

This equation basically states that unemployment depends inversely on economic growth. Slower economic growth will therefore cause unemployment. Equation (8.6) thus reproduces the fundamental result of the endogenous growth and matching literature, that slow economic growth causes unemployment, but not vice versa (Aghion and Howitt, 1994).

8.2.2 Efficiency wages, growth and unemployment

The introduction of efficiency wages now alters the direction of causality. Assume that instead of one unit of labor input producing one unit of output as before, now one efficiency unit of labor, $e_{i,t}l_{i,t}$, produces one unit of output. Efficiency $e_{i,t}$ is defined as

$$e_{i,t} = e^{1-\frac{\mu}{u_t} / \frac{w_{i,t}}{w_t}}, \tag{8.7}$$

where each firm can now set a different wage, $w_{i,t}$, in order to motivate their workforce. In accordance with Akerlof and Yellen (1990), both an increase in the relative wage vis-à-vis to the economy-wide average wage, $w_{i,t}/w_t$, and an increase in the unemployment rate u_t increase efficiency. Profit maximization in manufacturing implies that firms will increase their wage until the increase in effort is just offset by an alternative increase in employment, that is until the output elasticity of employment is equal to the output elasticity of the wage rate,

$$\frac{w_{i,t}}{w_t} = \frac{\mu}{u_t}, \tag{8.8}$$

implying that $e_{i,t} = 1$ from equation (8.7). Any firm will increase its wage relative to the average wage whenever unemployment exceeds μ. This will equiproportionally increase the average wage, thus inducing another round of relative wage increases, implying ultimately that wages would increase without bound, unless wage increases push the unemployment rate up to μ. The labor market will therefore only be in equilibrium if and only if $w_{i,t} - w_t$, implying $u_t = \mu$. Hence μ can be interpreted as the non-accelerating wage rate of unemployment. As opposed to the matching model, this implies that the unemployment rate is defined prior to the allocation decisions in the economy, and therefore does not depend on economic growth. The growth rate, however, will change if unemployment changes, thus indicating a causal relation from unemployment to economic growth.

After setting wages optimally to induce effort from their workforce, firms set prices in order to maximize profits,

$$p_{i,t} = \frac{\varepsilon}{\varepsilon - 1} w_t. \tag{8.2$'$}$$

The total profit $\pi_{i,t}$ of a firm in the innovative sector is now equal to,

$$\pi_{i,t} = \frac{1}{\varepsilon - 1} w_t l_{i,t}. \tag{8.3$'$}$$

Assuming once again that all profits are reinvested, we find once again that employment in the creation of new products is proportional to employment in the production process itself,

$$s_t = \frac{1}{\varepsilon - 1} n_t l_{i,t}. \tag{8.5$'$}$$

Given a constant rate of unemployment in the economy equal to μ, this implies that the number of employees working in the creation of new products is constant,

$$s_t = \frac{1 - \mu}{\varepsilon}. \tag{8.9}$$

Substituting this result into the arrival rate of new innovations (8.4), we find that the growth rate depends inversely on the equilibrium unemployment rate in the economy,

$$\hat{n}_t = \frac{\phi}{\varepsilon}(1 - \mu). \tag{8.10}$$

The efficiency wage model therefore indeed implies that shocks to the (equilibrium) unemployment rate would alter the innovation growth rate, but not vice versa. We can furthermore develop a clear relation between innovation growth and output growth.[1] First, by multiplying the demand function (8.1) with $n_t p_{i,t}$, we find that the relative price decreases with an increase in the number of innovations, $(p_{i,t}/p_t) = n_t^{1/(1-\varepsilon)}$. Substituting this back into the demand function (8.1), we find that growth in aggregate demand, x_t, equals,

$$x_t = n_t^{\frac{1}{\varepsilon - 1}} (n_t l_{i,t}). \tag{8.11}$$

Noting from equations (8.5′) and (8.9) that manufacturing employment, $n_t l_{i,t}$, is constant, we find that the growth rate of innovations is by a factor

$\varepsilon - 1$ larger than output growth, hence equation (8.10) can be modified to give a relation between unemployment and output growth,

$$\hat{x}_t = \frac{\phi(1-\mu)}{\varepsilon(\varepsilon-1)}. \tag{8.10'}$$

8.2.3 Unions, growth and unemployment

Whilst in the previous model it has been in the interest of firms to pay wages above the marginal product of labor, thus causing unemployment, unions, too, may be inclined to raise wages in order to improve the well-being of their members. Assume that there is one union operating within each manufacturing firm, then the union can choose any wage along the demand schedule for labor, which we can obtain by maximizing profits with respect to technology, $x_{i,t} = l_{i,t}$, and demand (8.1),

$$l_{i,t} = \left(\frac{\varepsilon-1}{\varepsilon}\right)^{\varepsilon} x_t (w_t/p_t)^{-\varepsilon}. \tag{8.12}$$

The demand elasticity for labor is ε, implying that a one per cent increase in wages reduces employment by ε per cent. We shall not model the union's choice, but assume that it sets wages at $w_t = w_t^*$, thus profits will equal,

$$\pi_{i,t} = \frac{1}{\varepsilon-1} w_t^* l_{i,t}. \tag{8.3''}$$

If all profits are again reinvested, employment in the innovative sector will equal

$$s_t = \frac{\overline{\omega}}{\varepsilon-1} n_t l_{i,t}, \tag{8.5''}$$

where $\overline{\omega}$ is the ratio of the manufacturing to innovation sector wage, $\overline{\omega} = w_t^*/w_t$. The manufacturing wage elasticity of innovation labor demand is negative and equal to $1-\varepsilon$, which is still negative. Hence, an increase in manufacturing wages reduces both manufacturing and innovation labor, thus unambiguously increasing unemployment. The union's choice of wages therefore has unsurprisingly a negative impact on employment. But the wage choice exhibits an impact on the economy's growth rate as well. As can be seen above, an increase in the relative union wage rate, $\overline{\omega}$, increases the number of innovative workers relative to production workers, thus altering the growth rate of the economy. In that respect, the union's choice over employment exhibits an impact on the growth rate of the economy, thus establishing a causal link from unemployment to economic growth.

For a given union wage rate, manufacturing and innovation employment are again proportional. Unemployment, defined as before, can therefore be expressed as a function of economic growth,

$$u_t = 1 - \frac{\overline{\omega} + \varepsilon - 1}{\phi \overline{\omega}} \hat{n}_t. \tag{8.6'}$$

Just as in the matching model, this relation establishes a causal relation from economic growth to unemployment, thus the union model can be characterized by dual causality between unemployment and economic growth.

8.3 The data

The aim of this chapter is to investigate the validity of the three proposed theories of economic growth and unemployment for European countries using time series methods. The number of countries was restricted due to data availability. First, time series methods require a large number of observations in order to ensure statistical inference, which reduces us to countries where quarterly data have been available for at least thirty years. The OECD provides quarterly data on growth and unemployment over that period only for G7 member countries, thus reducing the European sample to France, Germany, Italy, and the United Kingdom.

Employment data were taken from the OECD Quarterly Labor Force Survey. As the standardized unemployment rates compiled by the OECD do not date back far enough, unemployment rates were generated by dividing the seasonally adjusted stock of registered unemployed by the seasonally adjusted number of persons in Civilian Employment.

Data on Gross Domestic Product have been taken directly from the OECD Quarterly National Accounts, using the definition of GDP by Activity (with the exception of the United Kingdom, where GDP by Expenditure was used instead), seasonally adjusted, in constant prices, domestic currency, and expressed in logarithms.

For each country, the longest available time span has been used. In the case of the United Kingdom, this is from the first quarter of 1968 to the first quarter of 2000, giving a total of 129 observations. The average unemployment rate for the UK over this period was 8.3 per cent. The mean GDP growth rate over the sample period was 2.3 per cent. French data were available from the first quarter of 1970 to the second quarter of 2000 – a total of 122 observations. The mean unemployment rate over the period was 10.4 per cent. GDP was available in two separate series only, with observations from the first quarter of 1978 until the second quarter in 2000 following the OECD System of National Accounts 1993 methodology or equivalently the European System of Accounts 1995 methodology, and from the first quarter of 1970 until the fourth quarter of 1998 following older methodology. The overlap has been used to generate a linear predictor for previous periods of the SNA95 series. The mean growth rate over the sample period has been 2.4 per cent.

Italian data were available from the first quarter of 1970 to the second quarter of 2000 – a total of 122 observations. The mean unemployment rate over the period was 10.4 per cent. GDP was available in two separate series only, with observations from the first quarter of 1978 until the second quarter in 2000 following the OECD System of National Accounts 1993 methodology or equivalently the European System of Accounts 1995 methodology, and from the first quarter of 1970 until the third quarter of 1998 following older methodology. The overlap has been used to generate a linear predictor for previous periods of the SNA95 series. The mean growth rate over the sample period was 2.5 per cent.

Germany evidently poses the biggest empirical problem because of the reunification of East and West Germany. The official GDP series for Germany contains a jump in the first quarter of 1991, accounting for the inclusion of the Neue Länder in total GDP. The OECD has continued to collect a non-seasonally adjusted GDP series for the Alte Länder (West Germany) until the fourth quarter of 1997, dating back to the first quarter of 1968, giving a total of 120 observations, and we shall use this series as a proxy for German GDP. Seasonal adjustment was then performed

Table 8.1 Summary statistics

	France	*Germany*	*Italy*	*UK*
GDP (growth rate)	2.38 (1.53)	2.52 (2.38)	2.47 (2.41)	2.28 (2.27)
Unemployment rate	10.39 (4.80)	6.35 (3.57)	10.37 (2.88)	8.34 (4.33)
Number of observations	122 (1970Q1–2000Q2)	120 (1968Q1–1997Q4)	122 (1970Q1–2000Q2)	129 (1968Q1–2000Q1)

Notes: Data are expressed in per cent (%). Standard deviations are given in parenthesis.

Source: OECD (as reported in the WIFO database), own calculations.

using a ratio to moving average procedure. The average growth rate over this period was 2.5 per cent.

The unemployment rate, by contrast, did not pose as much of a problem, because both the labor force and the number of unemployed increased. The singular event of the reunification certainly triggered several effects – in particular, an increase in unemployment in the east and an increase in employment in the west – but did not visibly generate a structural break in the series. The average unemployment rate over the sample period was 6.4 per cent.

In order to further control for the reunification, appropriate dummy variables for the first quarter in 1991 have been included in all estimations.

8.4 Does slow economic growth cause unemployment, or vice versa?

Time series methods indeed allow us to test the causal relation between two variables empirically, using Granger causality tests (Granger, 1969). In order to perform Granger causality tests, we first need to ensure that all series are stationary after subsequent differencing.

8.4.1 Stationarity

Note that equation (8.10′) implies that at least the time series for output is difference stationary, or stationary after differencing the series once. This hypothesis of the model can in principle be tested. Given that the growth rate of a variable is equal to the first difference of the logarithm of the series, we can rewrite equation (8.10′) to read,

$$\ln x_t = \beta + \rho \ln x_{t-1} + v_t, \tag{8.10''}$$

where $\beta = \phi(1-\mu)/[\varepsilon(\varepsilon-1)]$, ρ would be one, and we can interpret v_t as measurement error. If ρ would indeed be unity, then equation (8.10″) would no longer be stationary, and any test on the properties of ρ would be biased. We can avoid the problem of non-stationarity simply by subtracting the lagged dependent variable (Gujarati, 1995), resulting in,

$$\ln x_t - \ln x_{t-1} = \beta + (\rho - 1)\ln x_{t-1} + v_t. \tag{8.13}$$

Equation (8.13) presents the bases for a formal test of stationarity, the so-called Dickey–Fuller test (Dickey and Fuller, 1979), which tests the null hypothesis whether $\rho - 1 = 0$. Table 8.2 presents Dickey–Fuller tests for

Table 8.2 Dickey–Fuller tests

In levels	*France*	*Germany*	*Italy*	*UK*
GDP	−1.94	−1.81	−1.67	−0.18
	(−2.89)	(−2.89)	(−2.89)	(−2.88)
Unemployment rate	−1.79	−1.46	−1.58	−2.13
	(−2.89)	(−2.89)	(−2.89)	(−2.88)
In first differences				
GDP	−5.22	−12.99	−5.70	−7.81
	(−2.89)	(−2.89)	(−2.89)	(−2.88)
Unemployment rate	−3.41	−4.31	−8.08	−2.67
	(−2.89)	(−2.89)	(−2.89)	(−2.88)*

Notes: Numbers are the *t*-values of the Dickey–Fuller test with one lag. Numbers in parenthesis are the critical values for stationarity at the 5 per cent significance level, taken from MacKinnon (1990).
* The critical value at the 10 per cent level is 2.58.

GDP and unemployment rates in all four countries, both in levels and first differences. According to the table, we can clearly reject stationarity in levels for both (the logarithm of) real GDP and the unemployment rate for all four countries. Both GDP and unemployment rates have been rejected as stationary in recent empirical work (Altissimo and Violante, 2001).

The unit root property has been widely acknowledged for the GDP series. The fact that variance of a difference stationary series converges to infinity as time goes to infinity implies that the unemployment rate may surpass its theoretical boundaries of zero and unity in finite time. However, a time series may very well be stationary over very long horizons, but only difference stationary over shorter period of times – even in the absence of structural breaks (Johansen, 1995).

With the exception of the British unemployment rate, all series are stationary in first differences at the 5 per cent significance level. We cannot reject difference stationarity for the UK unemployment rate at the 10 per cent significance level. Furthermore, the inclusion of further lags (as discussed below) implies we should not reject difference stationarity for any series in any country investigated at the 5 per cent significance level.

For Germany, non-stationarity has the implication that a conventional dummy included in the estimation of a differenced series would continue to show thereafter in the integrated series. This may be desirable in the case of Germany, where one may argue that we have experienced a systems shift, but would not be appreciated if we consider reunification to be primarily a statistical problem. All reported estimations have therefore used a dummy which takes the value unity in the first quarter of 1991 and the value minus unity in the second quarter of 1991, with zero otherwise. Including a stepdummy, which takes the value unity in the first quarter of 1991 and zero otherwise, does not alter the results substantially, however.

Agiakoglu and Newbold (1992) have noted that the size and power properties of the Dickey–Fuller tests change as different lags of the dependent variable or the error term enter the estimation of equation (8.13). Without any prior knowledge from theory on the distribution of residuals, autocorrelation of the error term may be present in our estimation in the form of moving average terms. If some of the deep parameters of the model are related to past values of the dependent series, we may even observe autoregressive components in equation (8.13). The literature therefore suggests including further lagged values of the dependent series in the estimation, a development known as the Augmented Dickey–Fuller test (Said and Dickey, 1984).

This implies that we face a choice of the optimal number of lags to be included in the Augmented Dickey–Fuller test. As the inclusion of an additional lag increases the power of the test, but reduces the parsimonious use of additional regressors, we face a tradeoff which enables us to select an optimal number of lags. Schwert (1989) proposes a rule based on the total number of observations, and suggests using $(12T/100)^{1/4}$ lags, where T is the number of observations. Maddala and Kim (1998, p. 77f) suggest to weigh parsimony against power directly and suggest to minimize the following objective function,

$$\log \sigma^2(k) + k\frac{C}{T}, \tag{8.14}$$

where σ^2 is the sum of square residuals in the estimation of equation (8.13) upon inclusion of k lags, and C is based on an information criterion, where the Akaike Information Criterion chooses $C = 2$, and the Schwarz Baysian Criterion would select $C = \sqrt{T}$. Appendix 1 presents Augmented Dickey–Fuller tests in levels, first and second differences, up to a lag length of nine for both GDP and unemployment in all four countries, together with the three criteria for the optimal lag length. We find that for any choice of the selection criterion, all processes in all countries are shown to be integrated of order one, or difference stationarity.

8.4.2 Optimal lag length

Unit root tests investigate an important univariate property of time series. We have seen in the preceding theoretical section that unemployment and economic growth are indeed related, and should therefore be treated as a system. However, we are interested here in whether slow economic growth causes unemployment or vice versa, or even both, which implies that we have to analyse at least bivariate systems.

In a bivariate system, a variable is said to Granger cause another variable if the information contained in past realizations of the variable helps to improve the forecast of the other variable. For our purposes, consider the following stationary bivariate vector autoregressive system,

$$\begin{pmatrix} \hat{x}_t \\ \Delta u_t \end{pmatrix} = \begin{pmatrix} \beta_1 \\ \beta_2 \end{pmatrix} + \begin{pmatrix} A(L) & B(L) \\ C(L) & D(L) \end{pmatrix} \begin{pmatrix} \hat{x}_{t-1} \\ \Delta u_{t-1} \end{pmatrix} + \begin{pmatrix} v_{1,t} \\ v_{2,t} \end{pmatrix}, \tag{8.15}$$

where $A(L)$, $B(L)$, $C(L)$ and $D(L)$, are potentially infinite lag polynomials. Then GDP growth does not Granger cause unemployment if and only if all elements in the lag polynomial $C(L)$ are zero. Equivalently, unemployment does not Granger cause GDP growth if and only if all elements in the lag polynomial $B(L)$ are zero. Granger causality tests the hypotheses whether all elements in $C(L)$ and all elements in $B(L)$ are zero. In that respect, Granger causality tests whether shocks that first only realize in the GDP growth rate, subsequently influence the unemployment rate, and whether shocks which first realize in the unemployment rate subsequently affect the GDP growth rate. For this reason, Granger causality tests indeed test precedence of shocks rather than true causality.

For our purpose, however, this is sufficient. As shocks to the unemployment rate should never exhibit an impact on the GDP growth rate in the endogenous growth matching model, and as shocks to the GDP growth rate should not change the unemployment rate in an efficiency wage endogenous growth model, whereas shocks to either the unemployment or the growth rate should subsequently effect the other variable in an insider–outsider endogenous growth model, we can use Granger causality tests to discriminate between the rival theories.

As we do not have enough observations to include an infinite number of lags, we have to select the number of lags prior to performing the Granger causality tests. Maddala and Kim (1998, p. 164f) suggest to select the model with the lowest information criterion. The two most common information criteria are the Akaike Information Criterion and the

Schwarz Baysian Criterion, which are both based on the log-likelihood and penalize the inclusion of additional regressors.

Alternatively, the literature suggests the use of a likelihood ratio test. The test statistic is generated by dividing the likelihood of the restricted model by the likelihood of the more general model, where the latter contains a larger number of lags, then taking logs and multiplying by -2. The resulting test statistic is χ^2 distributed, with the degrees of freedom equal to the number of zero restrictions. For two variables, unemployment and GDP, two equations, and one additional lag, the total number of zero restrictions on coefficients in the estimation of the system (8.15) to reduce the general model to the restricted model is four. We would reject the restricted model for the more general model if the test statistic exceeds the critical value at the 5 per cent significance level, or if the *p*-value is above the 5 per cent critical value. Starting from a lag length of 8, or two full years, we choose the number of lags at the level when we first reject the restricted model for the more general model.

Appendix 2 at the end of this book presents the results for all three procedures in full detail. Table 8.3 summarizes these results by presenting the optimal lag length in a bivariate unrestricted VAR of GDP growth and change in the unemployment rate for all four countries.

In all four countries, the Schwarz Baysian and the Likelihood Ratio Test Criterion agree on the optimal number of lags to be included in a VAR, and hence also in the Granger causality test. In all countries, with the exception of Germany, the optimal number of lags is one. The optimal number of four lags in Germany points to the fact that seasonal adjustment using the ratio to moving average method, which has been adopted for German GDP only, may have been insufficient.

Table 8.3 Optimal number of lags in a bivariate unrestricted VAR for growth and unemployment

	France	*Germany*	*Italy*	*UK*
Akaike Information Criterion	1	6	3	4(2)
Schwarz Baysian Criterion	1	4	1	1
Likelihood Ratio Test Criterion	1	4	1	1

Note: Numbers in parenthesis correspond to local minima.

The optimal number of lags is typically longer for the Akaike Information Criterion, as it penalizes additional regressors less than the Schwarz Baysian Criterion. Whilst in the United Kingdom the global minimum (up to lag 8) for the Akaike Information Criterion is four, we do find a local minimum at two lags. Once again, the long number of lags for Germany can be attributed to insufficient seasonal adjustment.

8.4.3 Granger causality

This chapter has set out to answer the question whether there is evidence that slow economic growth indeed causes unemployment, or vice versa, as suggested by economic theory. This allows us to address this question

Table 8.4 Granger causality tests

	France	*Germany*	*Italy*	*UK*
Does economic growth cause unemployment?				
1 lag	21.75*		0.96	9.36*
	($8.3E^{-6}$)		(0.328)	(0.003)
2 lags				1.58
				(0.209)
3 lags			0.53	
			(0.661)	
4 lags		1.93		3.73*
		(0.111)		(0.007)
6 lags		2.04		
		(0.067)		
Does unemployment cause economic growth?				
1 lag	0.17		7.45*	4.41*
	(0.683)		(0.007)	(0.037)
2 lags				7.82*
				(0.001)
3 lags			1.73	
			(0.164)	
4 lags		10.09*		3.12*
		($5.8E^{-7}$)		(0.018)
6 lags		3.45*		
		(0.004)		

Notes: Numbers are the F-Statistic for the pairwise Granger causality test. Numbers in parenthesis are the corresponding *p*-value. Granger causality cannot be rejected at the 5 per cent significance level if the *p*-value is below 0.05, marked by an asterisk (*). *E* is equal to 10.

with the help of Granger causality tests. Table 8.4 presents the results for Granger causality tests for all the selected choices of lag length indicated in Table 8.3.

We find a remarkably heterogeneous picture of the causal relationship between unemployment and economic growth in Europe. Among the selected countries, France is the only instance in which we find a clear direction of causality from economic growth to unemployment, but no causal relation from unemployment to economic growth. In that respect, France seems to be the only major European country which adheres to the endogenous growth matching model of unemployment and growth, suggested by Aghion and Howitt (1994).

In Italy, by contrast, we find evidence that unemployment causes economic growth, but not vice versa, if we include only one lag in the estimation, as suggested by both the Schwarz Baysian and the Likelihood ratio criterion. This gives the surprising indication that Italy can best be explained by the efficiency wage model. Upon the inclusion of two additional lags, we find neither a causal relation from growth to unemployment nor the other way around. Hence Italy may be the only country which lacks a relationship, which can theoretically only be explained by an exogenous growth model with labor market frictions (Blanchard, 1997).

In Germany, we find that unemployment Granger causes GDP for both four and six lags, whilst the inverse does not hold. This implies that Germany adheres to the efficiency wage model of growth and unemployment, as well.

In the United Kingdom, finally, we do observe causality in both directions, with the exception of two lags, where we cannot discern a causal relation from economic growth to unemployment. Once again, this allow us to conclude that the preferred endogenous growth and equilibrium unemployment model for the United Kingdom is either an insider model or an efficiency wage model. The reason for this ambivalence may be attributed to the point that under certain conditions, as discussed in the introduction, an efficiency wage model may generate a dual causality between economic growth and unemployment. An additional reason for this ambivalence can be found in the switch from a union-dominated economy to an efficiency wage relation during the Thatcher years.

8.5 Conclusions

This chapter has tried to investigate whether slow economic growth may have been the reason for high unemployment in Europe, or whether the causality has been in the opposite direction. The most important result that we can find is that there is no unifying pattern for the relationship across Europe. Whilst it seems that slow economic growth may have indeed been the reason for high unemployment in France, the exact opposite holds for Italy and Germany, whereas in the United Kingdom we cannot fully reject the idea that unemployment and growth mutually influence each other.

This has allowed us to shed some light on the underlying economic explanation of unemployment in the selected European countries. Whilst the evidence suggests that the main argument for unemployment in France should be attributed to problems in the matching process of workers to vacant jobs, we should seek the reason for German and Italian unemployment in the fact that firms wish to pay some of their workforce wages above the marginal product in order to ensure effort. One intuitive explanation can, of course, be found in the regional division of Italy, where firms in the north overpay workers instead of moving their plants to the *mezzogiorno*, where labor would be cheaper, but where the extraction of effort is much more difficult. Depending on the number of lags considered in the Granger causality tests, the United Kingdom can either be explained by an efficiency wage or a union endogenous growth model.

Summarizing, we find that unemployment in Europe cannot be fully explained by a single factor, having different causes in different countries, and potentially even within a single country. This has clear implications for policy. First, because there is no single explanation that explains the phenomena of slow growth and high unemployment over recent decades in Europe, there is no single solution to the problem. Secondly, the direction of causality has major implications for economic policy. Whilst for some countries – the example in our analysis would be France – the solution to the unemployment problem may be found in fostering economic growth, in other countries, in particular Italy and Germany, and in some respect also the United Kingdom, the unemployment problem can only be solved in the labor market.

9
The Dynamics of Economic Growth and Unemployment

This chapter analyses a vector error correction model of economic growth and unemployment in four major European economies – France, Germany, Italy and the United Kingdom. We find that unemployment and economic growth are cointegrated, and driven by the same autoregressive unit root present in most endogenous growth models. In the long run, economic growth and unemployment are positively correlated, as suggested by recent economic theories on endogenous growth and unemployment. In the short run, an increase in the equilibrium unemployment rate leads to a decline in economic growth rates. The short-run dynamics of economic growth and unemployment therefore remain consistent with Okun's law. Okun's coefficient is in line with previous estimates for all countries except in the case of the United Kingdom, whose labor market appears to be much more flexible in accommodating adverse transitory shocks than continental labor markets.

9.1 Motivation

Over the past few decades, Europe has experienced both an increase in its unemployment figures and a decline in economic rates of growth. This apparent long-run correlation, known as Eurosclerosis, did not hold in the short run. Indeed, the empirical evidence in recent years has typically tended to contradict Okun's law, the once-fundamental insight that a one per cent per annum increase in GDP (in excess of 2 to 3 per cent GDP growth) would reduce the unemployment rate by a third to one fifth of a per cent (Okun, 1970). This chapter addresses the question of why we have observed an apparent breakdown in the short-run relation between output and unemployment. The ambition is to empirically test a theoretically convincing explanation, which can explain a breakdown of a short-run relationship between unemployment and economic growth, without necessarily rejecting a long-run relation.

The long-run relationship between unemployment and economic growth has received renewed attention in the literature due to the emergence of endogenous growth literature. Whilst neoclassical exogenous growth literature postulates that there is no long-run relationship between economic growth and unemployment, the endogenous growth literature finds a clear relationship between economic growth and unemployment in the long run, with potential implications even for shorter horizons.

The presence of a long-run relationship between unemployment and economic growth, as suggested by the endogenous growth literature and the soft evidence presented above, is known as cointegration in the empirical literature, and can in principle be tested. Moreover, once we have detected a long-run relationship between economic growth and unemployment, we can continue to analyse their short-run behavior without the need to invoke much theory. If adjustment to the long-run equilibrium is slow, we may observe a very different behavior over the short run than over the longer horizon, thus potentially explaining the breakdown of Okun's law.

9.2 Related literature

For a long time, economists – and in particular macroeconomists – have tended to separate their explanations of the cyclical and the trend behavior of the economy. This view was challenged in a seminal paper by Campbell and Mankiw (1987), who find that shocks to US output are persistent, and that by separating trends and cycles, some important information on the behavior of the economy may be lost. Campbell and Mankiw (1989) repeat the univariate time series analysis for a range of countries, and find once again that shocks to output are persistent or – equivalently – that output is characterized by a unit root process.

Blanchard and Quah (1989) and Evans (1989) both challenge the analysis of Campbell and Mankiw, claiming that output is hit by both transitory and persistent shocks. By assuming a single type of shock, the persistence of output shocks in Campbell and Mankiw may be explained by a combination of these shocks. Both Blanchard and Quah (1989) and Evans (1989) separate transitory from permanent shocks by introducing a second time series, the unemployment rate. However, they still find that output is characterized by a unit root process, thus the principal conclusion in Campbell and Mankiw (1987), that we cannot separate the analysis of trends from the analysis of cycles, remains valid.

These two papers have stimulated empirical research on growth and unemployment. Given that few theoretical models have given a sound foundation for the joint cyclical and trend behavior of an economy, an atheoretical vector autoregression approach has been widely adopted. Dolado and Jimeno (1997) analyse the reasons for Spanish unemployment in a structural VAR model resulting from aggregate demand, productivity, price and labor supply shocks. They find no evidence that productivity shocks, which are the growth propagation mechanism in their model, play a major role in the explanation of unemployment. Gali (1999) presents US and international evidence on the impact of technology on employment, and finds that technology shocks, which are the growth propagation mechanism in his approach, tend to reduce working hours. Finally, in a recent contribution Blanchard and Wolfers (2000) present evidence from structural VAR on the relationship between unemployment and output, but impose the long-run restriction of no correlation between productivity and unemployment.

The unit root property of output in all of the papers cited above is introduced exogenously through the stochastic elements, and is therefore not explained from within the economic model. It is therefore rather surprising that we find similar evidence across the world. However, as shown in Lau (1999), a unit root is an intrinsic property of every endogenous growth model. Moreover, Lau demonstrates that in every bivariate endogenous growth model where both variables exhibit a unit root, there will be exactly one cointegrating vector, or one long-run relationship between the two time series (Lau, 1999, p. 10).

Whilst the unit root properties of output are well known, recent evidence on the United States (Altissimo and Violante, 2001) and Europe (see chapter 8) show that the unemployment rate also exhibits a unit root pattern. If we do not reject a unit root in either series, we are bound to find a cointegrating relationship between unemployment and output, thus invalidating VAR models in first differences (Banerjee and Hendry, 1992). One possible solution is to estimate a VAR in levels, as suggested by Bulli (2000). The problem in this approach is that nonstationarity invalidates conventional statistical inference, and one has to resort to little-known test procedures. The other approach, which we shall follow here, is to estimate a vector error correction model, where we explicitly account for the cointegration vector in the VAR estimation. In the next section, we will theoretically motivated two dynamic equations, and then develop the corresponding error correction representation.

9.3 A simple theoretical framework

9.3.1 The resource constraint

Economic growth in this model is driven by the intentional decision to invest in the innovation of new products. To motivate this incentive, we need to assume that consumers demand differentiated products. There is a total of n_t products available at time t, and each product is provided by a single firm monopolistically. Firms produce one unit of the product with one unit of labor input, $l_{i,t}$, which they hire at the current market wage w_t. The monopoly supplier of a particular product obtains rents, which enables it to pay for the costly process of innovation. Consumer demand for a particular product $x_{i,t}$ depends inversely on the product's relative price, with a price elasticity of demand equal to ε, and positively on aggregate demand x_t,

$$x_{i,t} = (p_{i,t}/p_t)^{-\varepsilon} x_t. \tag{9.1}$$

We can furthermore develop a clear relationship between innovation growth and output growth. First, by multiplying the demand function (9.1) with $n_t p_{i,t}$, we find that the relative price decreases with an increase in the number of innovations, $(p_{i,t}/p_t) = n_t^{1/(1-\varepsilon)}$. Substituting this back into the demand function (9.1), we find that the growth rate of aggregate demand equals,

$$\hat{x}_t = \frac{1}{\varepsilon - 1}\hat{n}_t, \tag{9.2}$$

where we have assumed that the labor market is in equilibrium, that is the change in total employment in production, $n_t l_{i,t}$, is zero.

Maximizing profits with respect to demand yields a mark-up pricing rule for firms,

$$p_{i,t} = \frac{\varepsilon}{\varepsilon - 1} w_t. \tag{9.3}$$

The total profit $\pi_{i,t}$ of a firm in the innovative sector is equal to revenue minus costs,

$$\pi_{i,t} = \frac{1}{\varepsilon - 1} w_t l_{i,t}. \tag{9.4}$$

Innovation takes time and effort. We shall assume that new innovations are created by s_t workers with productivity ϕn_t, where productivity depends positively on the existing number of products, n_t. The arrival rate of new innovations therefore equals,

$$\hat{n}_t = \phi s_t. \tag{9.5}$$

Assuming that all profits (9.4) are reinvested, then employment in the creation of new products will be proportional to total employment in the production of these products,

$$s_t = n_t \pi_{i,t}/w_t = \frac{1}{\varepsilon - 1} n_t l_{i,t}. \tag{9.6}$$

Defining the unemployment rate as one minus the employment rate in the production and the creation of products, and substituting the allocation of labor relation (9.6) into the arrival rate of new products (9.5) and the growth rate of the economy (9.2), gives

$$\hat{x}_t = \frac{\phi}{\varepsilon(\varepsilon - 1)}(1 - u_t). \tag{9.7}$$

This equation relates the growth rate of an economy to its employed resources. As unemployment declines, or employment increases, more labor resources will be available for both productive and innovative activities, thus promoting the growth of product variety and output, and thereby describing the resource constraint of the economy.

9.3.2 The incentive condition

The resource constraint describes one, downward-sloping, relationship between unemployment and economic growth. However, the resource constraint does not explain the presence of unemployment in the first place. A number of labor market theories can be invoked to derive a second relationship between unemployment and economic growth. Most prominently, Aghion and Howitt (1994) show that a search model would generate the second condition required to solve the model. The difference to conventional matching models (Mortenson, 1986; Pissarides, 1990) is that the equilibrium unemployment rate is now sensitive to changes in economic growth. As the sensitivity of the equilibrium unemployment rate depends on the incentives for individuals to seek employment and the incentives for firms to offer vacancies, we may refer to this relationship between unemployment and economic growth as an incentive condition. A similar incentive condition emerges upon inclusion of efficiency wages (Zagler, 2003), or union insider power, as shown in chapter 5, into an innovation-driven endogenous growth model.

Here, we shall sketch a fourth version of the incentive condition, motivated by aggregate demand externalities.[1] We shall assume that consumers, for reasons of fatigue or some other cause, cease to demand a fraction φ of all available products irrespective of their time of innovation, including, for the sake of simplicity, all newly innovated products. This changes the growth rate of the number of firms to,

$$\hat{n}_t = \phi s_t - \varphi, \tag{9.5'}$$

and hence the growth rate of the economy, or the resource constraint, to,

$$\hat{x}_t = \frac{\phi}{\varepsilon(\varepsilon - 1)}(1 - u_t) - \frac{\phi\varphi}{\varepsilon - 1}. \tag{9.7'}$$

If the labor market is able to adjust instantaneously, this aggregate demand externality need not necessarily generate unemployment. We shall assume, however, that workers and firms have to sign employment contracts one period in advance. With the lack of knowledge which particular firm will be hit by the aggregate demand externality, some workers will always be unemployed. In equilibrium, the number of unemployed workers will equal $\varphi n_t l_{i,t}$. The adjustment dynamics of employment can be described by the difference between the flow of workers out of employment, d_t, and the flow of unemployed into employment, c_t, or

$$\Delta u_t = d_t - c_t. \tag{9.8}$$

Job creation happens in the newly emerging firms, which will employ an average of $l_{i,t}$ workers each, hence

$$c_t = \dot{n}_t l_{i,t} = \frac{1}{\phi}(\varepsilon - 1)\hat{n}_t(\hat{n}_t + \varphi). \tag{9.9}$$

Job destruction, by constrast, has two components. First, workers in firms whose product vanishes from the market will face unemployment, totaling $\varphi n_t l_{i,t}$ workers. Secondly, surviving firms in the product market will have to lay off a proportional share of their workforce, as demand is diverted to new products. Job destruction will therefore equal,

$$d_t = -\varphi n_t l_{i,t} + n_t \dot{l}_{i,t} = -\frac{\varphi}{\phi}(\varepsilon - 1)\hat{n}_t(\hat{n}_t + \varphi) - \frac{1}{\phi}(1 - \varphi)(\varepsilon - 1)\hat{n}_t(\hat{n}_t + \varphi). \tag{9.10}$$

Substituting this result back into the dynamics of unemployment (9.8), we find that the change in unemployment depends on the rate of growth,

$$\Delta u_t = \frac{1}{\phi}(\varepsilon - 1)\left[\hat{x}_t^2/(\varepsilon - 1)^2 - \varphi^2\right]. \tag{9.8'}$$

This incentive condition expresses a nonlinear relationship between the change in unemployment and the growth rate of output. As opposed to Okun's law, but in accordance with the literature on economic growth and unemployment (Aghion and Howitt, 1994), it indicates a positive tradeoff between economic growth and the change in unemployment.

9.4 The data

This chapter investigates time series properties of economic growth and unemployment for selected European countries. The number of countries was restricted due to data availability. First, time series methods require a large number of observations in order to ensure statistical inference, which means that we are limited to countries where quarterly data have been available for at least 30 years. The OECD provides quarterly data on growth and unemployment over that period only for G7 member countries, thus reducing the European sample to France, Germany, Italy and the United Kingdom. The data are identical to chapter 8, and we therefore refer to section 8.3 for a description of the data and the summary statistics.

Stationarity will again be an important issue in the following econometric analysis, and here we will therefore explore the order of integration – that is, the minimal number of times a series has to be differenced until it is stationary. Assume that a time series y_t can be described by a simple autoregressive process,

$$y_t = C + \rho y_{t-1} + e_t, \tag{9.11}$$

where C is a constant, ρ is the autocorrelation coefficient and e_t is an error term. If ρ were set to unity, then equation (9.11) would no longer be stationary, and any test on the properties of ρ would be biased. We can avoid the problem of non-stationarity simply by subtracting the lagged dependent variable from equation (9.11), resulting in,

$$y_t - y_{t-1} = C + (\rho - 1)y_{t-1} + e_t. \tag{9.11'}$$

Equation (9.11′) presents the bases for a formal test of stationarity, the so-called Dickey–Fuller test (Dickey and Fuller, 1979), which tests the null hypothesis whether $\rho - 1 = 0$. The test have been carried out in chapter 8 of this book, and were presented in Table 8.2. According to that table, we can clearly reject stationarity in levels for both (the logarithm of) real GDP and the unemployment rate for all four countries, but cannot reject stationarity in first differences for any series.

9.5 The dynamic system in a vector error correction representation

Equations (9.7′) and (9.8′) present a dynamic system in two variables – GDP and unemployment. Summarizing parameters and adding an error term, equation (9.7′) can be written as

$$\Delta y_t = A - \alpha u_t + e_t, \tag{9.7''}$$

where y_t is the logarithm of x_t, and hence Δy_t the growth rate of output, the parameters A and α would be defined as $A = (\phi - \varphi\varepsilon)/[\varepsilon(\varepsilon - 1)]$, and $\alpha = \phi/[\varepsilon(\varepsilon - 1)]$, and e_t is an error term. Note that (9.7″) is equal to (9.11), with $\rho = 1$, and $C = A - \alpha u_t$. In a similar fashion, we can rewrite the incentive condition (9.8′), linearized and in levels, to equal,

$$y_t = \beta u_t - B + v_t, \tag{9.8''}$$

where v_t is once again a stochastic disturbance. In order to potentially account for hysteresis in unemployment, that is, the fact that past shocks to unemployment exhibit a long-run effect, we shall assume that v_t is serially correlated,

$$v_t = \rho v_{t-1} + \xi_t. \tag{9.12}$$

By consecutive substitution of equation (9.12) into (9.8″), lagged once more after each substitution, we obtain the distributed lag representation of the unemployment rate, as

$$u_t = (B + y_t)/\beta - 1/\beta \sum_{n=0}^{\infty} (\rho^n \xi_{t-n}). \tag{9.13}$$

Evidently, the second component is the impact of past disturbances on the unemployment rate, and captures hysteresis in unemployment. In that respect, the first element in equation (9.14) is the permanent component in the explanation of unemployment, and we may therefore interpret it as the equilibrium unemployment rate,

$$u_t^* = (B + y_t)/\beta, \tag{9.14}$$

where the equilibrium is relative, because it depends on the state of the economy.

Expressing both equations in terms of y_t, the dynamic system described by equations (9.7″) and (9.8″) is complete and can in principle be estimated. Two important issues need to be addressed prior to this activity – namely the dynamic nature of the system, where output appears both in levels and growth rates, and the exact formulation of the error terms.

It is important to note that (9.7″) contains an autoregressive unit root, and hence the system may not be stationary, thus implying that we should estimate the system with dynamic methods. The first possibility would be to difference the variables until they are stationary, and then to apply vector autoregression methods in order to estimate the system. The problem with this approach is that we may eliminate cointegrating relations, which are stationary relationships between nonstationary series such as output and unemployment in all the countries investigated here. Should we detect cointegration in the data, the more promising approach would evidently be to estimate a vector error correction model, and we shall pursue this methodology, and present the dynamic system (9.7″) and (9.8″) in a vector error correction representation below. With respect to the stochastic elements, theory gives us little indication. However, we can relax one important assumption that is present in all estimations of exogenous growth models, which had to assume a unit root in one of the error terms in order to explain the trending behavior of output, empirically verified for our data in the previous section. As the system already contains an autoregressive unit root in equation (9.7″), we can drop the assumption of a moving average unit root. In that respect, we may assume i.i.d. errors in both equation (9.7″) and equation (9.8″). Therefore, the serial correlation introduced in equation (9.12) is not completely necessary, and certainly need not be fixed at $\rho = 1$, and we can always eliminate it by setting the coefficient of correlation, ρ, to zero. Taking first differences of equation (9.8″), we arrive at the linearized version of the incentive condition (9.8′),

$$\Delta y_t = \beta \Delta u_t + \Delta v_t. \tag{9.15}$$

Eliminating output growth with the help of the resource constraint (9.7″), and eliminating the first difference of the error term with the help of its definition (9.13), yields upon rearrangement,

$$\Delta u_t = \phi A - \alpha\phi u_{t-1} + \phi(1-\rho)v_{t-1} + \phi(e_t - \xi_t), \tag{9.16}$$

where $\phi = 1/(\alpha+\beta)$. In order to eliminate the serially correlated terms, we substitute the lagged incentive condition (9.8″) for the unemployment rate, and the lagged resource constraint for the error term v_{t-1}, to obtain the vector autoregressive representation of the unemployment rate,

$$\Delta u_t = \theta(y_{t-1} + B - \beta u_{t-1}) + \phi \Delta y_{t-1} + \phi(\Delta e_t - \xi_t), \tag{9.16'}$$

where $\theta = \phi(1 - \rho)$. Substituting (9.16′) into (9.15), and eliminating the serially correlated error term again by first substituting the definition of the moving average error (9.12), and then the lagged incentive condition (9.8″) yields,

$$\Delta y_t = -\alpha\theta(y_{t-1} + B - \beta u_{t-1}) + \phi\beta \Delta y_{t-1} + \phi(\beta \Delta e_t + \alpha \xi_t). \tag{9.17}$$

Equations (9.16′) and (9.17) are the vector autoregression representations of the system, as they express the changes in the endogenous variables resulting from past changes in both variables and serially uncorrelated – but across equations correlated – error terms. In a pure VAR in first differences, the expression in parenthesis, which appears in both equations, would be omitted. The expression in parenthesis is the cointegration relationship – that is, the only relationship between output and the unemployment rate, which is stationary, as can be inferred from the equilibrium unemployment rate (9.14). By substituting the equilibrium unemployment rate, we can express the change in the unemployment rate in vector error correction form,

$$\Delta u_t = \Delta u_t^* + \beta\theta(u_t^* - u_{t-1}) - \phi(\alpha/\beta)\Delta y_{t-1} + \phi(\Delta e_t - \xi_t). \tag{9.16''}$$

The change in the unemployment rate is due to changes in the equilibrium unemployment rate, adjustment due to past disequilibria in unemployment at speed $\theta\beta$, and past changes in the endogenous variables due to moving average components in the error term. As we only have one moving average element, one lagged endogenous variable is sufficient. A further inclusion of moving average processes into the original system (9.7″) and (9.8″) would merely lead to a further inclusion of lagged endogenous variables. In a similar fashion, we could express the change in output in VECM form, from equation (9.17),

$$\Delta y_t = -\alpha\beta\theta(u_t^* - u_{t-1}) + \phi\beta\Delta y_{t-1} + \phi(\beta\Delta e_t + \alpha\xi_t), \tag{9.17'}$$

where the change in output is due to adjustments from past disequilibria and past changes in the endogenous variables due to the moving average component in one of the error terms. To complete the analysis of the system, in addition to the equilibrium relation between unemployment and economic growth (9.14), we can also describe the dynamic adjustment path. Multiplying (9.16′) with α, summing equations (9.16′) and (9.17), and taking expectations yields after some rearrangement,

$$\mathrm{E}\Delta y_t + \alpha \mathrm{E}\Delta u_t = (\alpha + \beta)\phi \mathrm{E}\Delta y_{t-1}, \tag{9.18}$$

Given that $(\alpha + \beta)\phi = 1$, we find that $\mathrm{E}\Delta^2 y_t / \mathrm{E}\Delta u_t = -\alpha$, or that the expected change in the growth rate of output per unit of change in the unemployment rate is equal to $-\alpha$. The slope of the dynamic adjustment path in a growth–unemployment plane would therefore be $-\alpha$. One possible adjustment path is described by the resource constraint (9.7″). Whilst the incentive condition therefore describes the equilibrium locus of the economy, the resource constraint would describe its dynamic adjustment path.

9.6 Testing for cointegration

The model presented in the previous section clearly indicates the existence of a cointegrating relationship. In principle, we can test for the presence of cointegration, using the conventional Johansen Maximum Likelihood Test (Johansen, 1995). Before performing this test, we need to make an assumption about the number of lags to be included. In the previous section we saw that the number of lags to be included depends upon the number of lags in the moving average processes of the error terms in our dynamic system, equations (9.7″) and (9.8″). As theory gives no clear indication about the order of the MA process, we must investigate the optimal number of lags empirically.

9.6.1 Optimal lag length

Maddala and Kim (1998, p. 164f) suggest selecting the model with the lowest information criterion. The two most common information criteria are the Akaike Information Criterion and the Schwarz Baysian Criterion, both of which are based upon the log-likelihood and penalize the inclusion of additional regressors.

Alternatively, the literature suggests the use of a likelihood ratio test. The test statistic is generated by dividing the likelihood of the restricted model by the likelihood of the more general model, where the latter contains a larger number of lags. We then take logs and multiply by -2. The resulting test statistic is χ^2 distributed, with the degrees of freedom equal

Table 9.1 Optimal number of lags in a bivariate unrestricted VAR for growth and unemployment

	France	*Germany*	*Italy*	*UK*
Akaike Information Criterion	1	6	3	4 (2)
Schwarz Baysian Criterion	1	4	1	1
Likelihood Ratio Test Criterion	1	4	1	1

Note: Numbers in parenthesis correspond to local minima.

to the number of zero restrictions. For two variables – unemployment and GDP – two equations, and one additional lag, the total number of zero restrictions on coefficients in the estimation of the VAR system to reduce the general model to the restricted model is four. We would reject the restricted model for the more general model if the test statistic exceeds the critical value at the 5 per cent significance level, or if the p-value is above the 5 per cent critical value. Starting from a lag length of 8, or two full years, we choose the number of lags at the level when we first reject the restricted model for the more general model. Appendix 2 at the end of this book presents the results for all three procedures in full detail. Table 9.1 summarizes these results by presenting the optimal lag length in a bivariate unrestricted VAR of GDP growth and change in the unemployment rate for all four countries.

In all four countries, the Schwarz Baysian and the Likelihood Ratio Test Criterion agree on the optimal number of lags to be included in a VAR, and hence also in the Granger causality test. In all countries, with the exception of Germany, the optimal number of lags is one. The optimal number of four lags in Germany points to the fact that seasonal adjustment using the ratio to moving average method, which has been adopted for German GDP only, may have been insufficient.

The optimal number of lags is typically longer for the Akaike Information Criterion, as it penalizes additional regressors less than the Schwarz Baysian Criterion. Whilst in the United Kingdom the global minimum (up to lag 8) for the Akaike Information Criterion is four, we do find a local minimum at two lags. Once again, the long number of lags for Germany can be attributed to insufficient seasonal adjustment.

9.6.2 Cointegration tests

Consider the system in vector autoregressive representation, as given by equations (9.16′) and (9.17), repeated here for convenience in vector notation,

$$\begin{pmatrix}\Delta y_t \\ \Delta u_t\end{pmatrix} = \theta\begin{pmatrix}1 \\ -\alpha\end{pmatrix}(1-\beta)\begin{pmatrix}y_{t-1} \\ u_{t-1}\end{pmatrix} + \theta\begin{pmatrix}1 \\ -\alpha\end{pmatrix}B$$

$$+\begin{pmatrix}\phi & \beta\phi \\ 0 & 0\end{pmatrix}\begin{pmatrix}\Delta y_{t-1} \\ \Delta u_{t-1}\end{pmatrix} + \begin{pmatrix}\phi & -\phi \\ \beta\phi & \alpha\phi\end{pmatrix}\begin{pmatrix}\Delta e_{1,t} \\ \xi_{2,t}\end{pmatrix}. \qquad (9.19)$$

As noted in section 9.4.2, all elements in the VAR are stationary, with the exception of the first element on the right-hand side, the vector of the lagged dependent variable in levels, which is integrated of order one. One possibility for equation (9.19) to remain consistent would be that $\theta = 0$, which can only be the case if $\rho = 1$. Note that this implies that equation (9.7″) still contains an autoregressive unit root, and in addition equation (9.8″) now contains a moving average unit root. Both series would therefore be integrated of order one, as shown empirically in section 9.4.2, without any cointegrating relationship between them. The other possibility for equation (9.19) to remain consistent would be if the matrix $(1, -\alpha)'(1, -\beta)$ is not of full rank. If θ is different from zero, equation (9.8″) is stationary, and hence so is $(1, -\beta)(y_{t-1}, u_{t-1})'$. The latter, of course, is the cointegrating relationship, and $(1, -\beta)$ is the cointegrating vector, and $-\alpha$ is the adjustment parameter, as shown in section 9.5.

There are three possible scenarios for the explanation of the economic system, depending on the rank of the matrix $M = \theta(1, -\alpha)'(1, -\beta)$. First, if all dependent variables are stationary in levels, the matrix M would be of full rank, and we could consistently estimate the system using VAR methods. This would be consistent with an exogenous growth model in the absence of a moving average unit root. Secondly, if the system exhibits endogenous balanced growth,[2] Lau (1999, p. 10) has demonstrated that in the absence of unit root cancellation, the rank of the matrix is M equal to unity, and hence the number of cointegrating relationships for a bivariate system must be equal to one. Finally, if the rank of the matrix M is zero, the variables would not be cointegrated, but individual components would be integrated (Lau, 1999, p. 11).

In order to determine the rank of the matrix M, Johansen (1991) suggests a likelihood ratio test, which tests the restrictions implied by the reduced rank matrix against an unrestricted model, where the matrix M is assumed to be of full rank. The trace test for the number of cointegrating relations suggests to estimated the following likelihood ratio statistic for the hypothesis of rank zero, or equivalently no cointegrating relation,

$$LR_0 = -T[ln(1 - \lambda_1) + ln(1 - \lambda_2)], \tag{9.20}$$

where λ_1 is the smaller and λ_2 is the larger eigenvalue of the matrix M, and T is the number of observations. Similarly, the likelihood ratio statistic for the hypothesis of rank one or equivalently a single cointegrating relation is equal to,

$$LR_1 = -T[ln(1 - \lambda_1)]. \tag{9.20'}$$

To determine the number of cointegrating relations, we can proceed by sequentially comparing the likelihood ratio test statistic to the critical values as tabulated in Osterwald-Lenum (1992), until we fail to reject. We would assume the matrix to be of full rank if we reject all of the hypothesis.

Table 9.2 summarizes the cointegration tests for all four countries and all the different lag lengths suggested by the VAR method (Table 9.1). For completeness, Appendix 3 presents all eigenvalues and likelihood ratio test statistics up to 8 lags, or for 2 full years.

We find that we can reject rank zero, or that all variables are integrated but that there is no cointegration, in all four countries for all possible lag lengths. However, we find that we cannot reject rank one, or one cointegrating relation for all countries and all lags at the one per cent significance level, and with the exception of Germany at 4 lags, also at the 5 per cent significance level.

Note that a rejection of rank one for four lags in Germany would imply that both GDP and the unemployment rate would be stationary. This would be in clear contradiction to the unit root properties of both series, as discussed in section 9.4.2.

This is a further indication not to reject the hypothesis of rank one even in this case. Summarizing, this implies that we indeed find cointegration in the system described by equations (9.7″) and (9.8″), and that we therefore have to estimate the system using vector error correction methods (Banerjee et al., 1993).

9.7 Cointegration and dynamic adjustment

Given that we found in the previous section that the system is to be estimated by a vector error correction model (VECM), we once again

Table 9.2 Johansen cointegration test

Hypothesis: rank = 0 *(No cointegrating relation)*	*France*	*Germany*	*Italy*	*UK*
1 lag	55.94		26.92	52.93
2 lags				59.51
3 lags			29.09	
4 lags		40.86		41.10
6 lags		25.80		
Hypothesis: rank = 1 *(1 cointegrating relation)*	*France*	*Germany*	*Italy*	*UK*
1 lag	2.43**		3.58**	4.55**
2 lags				7.22**
3 lags			4.05**	
4 lags		9.81*		4.63**
6 lags		8.40**		

Notes: Numbers are the likelihood ratio test statistic as presented in equation (9.20) and (9.20′) for the Johansen cointegration trace test. The benchmark (unrestricted) model is of full rank, rank = 2. Critical values under the assumption of a constant in the cointegrating relation and no intercept in the VAR for rank zero are 19.96 at the 5 per cent significance level and 24.60 at the one per cent significance level. Critical values for rank one are 9.24 (12.97) at the 5 per cent (1 per cent) significance level (Osterwald-Lenum, 1992). ** implies that we cannot reject the hypothesis at the 5 per cent significance level, and * implies that we cannot reject the hypothesis at the one per cent significance level.

Table 9.3 Optimal number of lags in a bivariate unrestricted VECM for growth and unemployment

	France	*Germany*	*Italy*	*UK*
Akaike Information Criterion	1	4	5	4 (2)
Schwarz Baysian Criterion	1	4	1	1
Likelihood Ratio Test Criterion	1	3	3	1

Note: Numbers in parenthesis correspond to local minima.

have to ask how many lags should be included in the VECM. Since theory fails to give a clear indication, we once again adopt the same procedure as in section 9.6.1, but estimate the system as a VECM instead of VAR. Table 9.3 summarizes the results according to the different criteria used. A more detailed table of the results for all lags up to 8, or two full years, is given in Appendix 4.

Once again, the Akaike Information Criterion suggests the largest number of lags to be included. With the exception of Germany and Italy, the other two criteria suggest estimating the VECM with a single lag. Whilst the Likelihood Ratio Test Criterion suggests the inclusion of three lags in the case of Italy, the Schwarz Baysian Criterion would still suggest the inclusion of one lag. This is, of course, exactly identical to the VECM system presented in equations (9.16′) and (9.17′). In order to select a specific number of lags for the estimation of the VECM, we use the dominant number of lags for each country, and hence use one lag for France and the United Kingdom, and four lags for Germany. Given that the Schwarz Baysian Criterion is the only asymptotically efficient criterion, we select one lag also for Italy. Table 9.4 summarizes the results, omitting higher order lags and the reunification dummy for Germany. The complete results for Germany can be found in Appendix 5.

Table 9.4 Vector error correction models for growth and unemployment in Europe

	France	*Germany*	*Italy*	*UK*
Cointegration equation				
(Dependent: unemployment)	1	1	1	1
GDP	−0.754	−0.057	−0.179	−0.243
	(0.517)	(0.054)	(0.039)	(0.093)
Constant (B)	10.897	0.602	2.220	2.933
	(7.612)	(0.741)	(0.505)	(2.576)
VECM: unemployment (Δ)				
Cointegration equation	0.003	−0.013	0.026	0.002
	(0.001)	(0.004)	(0.015)	(0.002)
Lagged change in unemployment	0.712	0.581	−0.136	0.793
	(0.074)	(0.074)	(0.094)	(0.05)
Lagged change in GDP	−0.068	−0.034	−0.046	−0.043
	(0.033)	(0.014)	(0.047)	(0.0324)
VECM: GDP growth rate				
Cointegration equation	0.021	−0.082	0.122	0.050
	(0.003)	(0.029)	(0.026)	(0.007)
Lagged change in unemployment	−0.593	−2.570	−0.015	−0.731
	(0.215)	(0.667)	(0.164)	(0.214)
Lagged change in GDP	0.198	−0.305	0.381	−0.102
	(0.097)	(0.099)	(0.082)	(0.092)

Notes: Numbers are the coefficients of the standardized ($u_t = 1$) cointegrating relation or the VECM. Numbers in parenthesis are standard errors.

From the first part of the cointegrating relation, we find that the equilibrium unemployment rate would increase with higher output. This is equivalent to stating that equilibrium unemployment has increased over time, given that output has increased over the period of analysis.

From the two error correction equations, we can derive the slope of the adjustment path α by dividing the two coefficients in the cointegrating relation. In all cases, we find that the adjustment parameter is positive, which is the sign predicted by theory, equation (9.7′).

The adjustment parameter α is equal to 7.81 in France, 6.14 in Germany, 4.73 in Italy, but a remarkable 32.83 in the United Kingdom. Whilst the coefficient for France, Germany and Italy is in line with older estimates of the Okun coefficient, which is known to lie between 3 and 5, the estimate for the United Kingdom falls out of line. This high value implies a remarkable speed of adjustment from labor market disequilibria in the UK economy. One reason why the United Kingdom has been able to recover fastest from Eurosclerosis may therefore be found in the speed at which the UK economy recovers from temporary shocks to unemployment.

9.8 Conclusions

This chapter has analysed the dynamics of economic growth and unemployment in four major European economies – France, Germany, Italy and the United Kingdom. We find that unemployment and economic growth can only be explained jointly and in a dynamic model. In particular, we find that unemployment and output are cointegrated, and driven by the same autoregressive unit root present in most endogenous growth models, such as the innovation-driven endogenous growth model discussed in section 9.3.1.

We find that in the long run, economic growth and unemployment are positively correlated, as suggested by recent economic theories on endogenous growth and unemployment, notably the matching model due to Aghion and Howitt (1994) and the aggregate demand model presented in section 9.3.2.

In the short run, an increase in the equilibrium unemployment rate leads to a decline in economic growth rates. The short-run dynamics of economic growth and unemployment therefore remain consistent with Okun's law. The recent empirical failure may therefore be due to the fact that the impact of changes in the long-run equilibrium unemployment rate has not been properly accounted for. Moreover, it has to be pointed out that the coefficients of adjustment, the closest correspondence to

Okun's coefficient, are in line with previous estimates, except in the case of the United Kingdom, where a remarkably high coefficient points to the fact that the labor market in the United Kingdom can recover much faster from adverse transitory shocks to unemployment, or that the UK labor market is much more flexible in accommodating adverse transitory shocks than continental labor markets.

10
Conclusions and Policy Recommendations

The ambition of this book was to investigate the interaction between changes in the level of unemployment and changes in the rate of economic growth. There is good reason to analyse the causes of unemployment themselves. As stated in the introduction, unemployment is, first and foremost, a social problem, but it also deprives the economy of part of its resource base, and thus has a clearly detrimental effect on well-being.

It may be equally rewarding to determine the engine of growth for an economy. 'If one could foster growth only by a 0.1 percentage point per year [starting at 3% p.a.], this would increase the ten year compound growth rate by 1.3 percentage points. [...] Having fostered economic growth initially, a "normal" recession[1] would still exhibit a GDP which is higher than at three per cent constant growth without fluctuations' (Zagler, 1999a). Higher long-run growth can therefore ameliorate bad times in the short run.

Whilst there is good reason to analyse economic growth and unemployment separately, there are several important reasons – theoretical, empirical and political – to investigate their interaction. On theoretical grounds, we have seen that economic growth is driven by structural change. Structural change, however, implies a higher rate of job creation and job destruction, and in that respect, higher rates of growth may lead to higher levels of unemployment (Hagemann, 1993). On a larger scale, economic growth means an increase in the level of available economic resources. The prospect of higher future income may induce agents to rethink their behavior in the labor market, and it may well alter the level of unemployment in the economy.

Because unemployment deprives the economy of part of its resource base, it will potentially reduce productivity-enhancing activities, thus reducing the resource base for economic growth. Moreover, the presence of unemployment will alter the motivation and incentives of economic agents in many ways. It may induce agents to work harder in order not to lose one's job, but it may just as easily lead to a shift away from innovative towards routine tasks. Accordingly, higher unemployment can either increase or reduce the rate of economic growth. It may induce agents to revise their wage claims, potentially influencing the sectoral composition of the economy, which may or may not foster economic growth.

On empirical grounds, unemployment and economic growth have been systematically negatively correlated over time and across countries. However, in recent decades, this stable relationship seems to have broken down, and phenomena such as jobless growth, which cannot be explained by conventional theories of unemployment and economic growth, require new theoretical explanations.

Finally, on political grounds, economic growth and unemployment have been key issues in the policy debate in recent years – particularly in Europe. Policy makers have realized that many policy strategies exhibit an impact on both unemployment and economic growth. Indeed, it is hard to imagine strategies which would not. In that respect, policy makers tend to address both issues simultaneously. It should therefore be of significant interest to have an understanding of the relationship between economic growth and unemployment.

The following four sections of this chapter attempt to summarize the theoretical and empirical insights offered by this book. Given the vast amount of novel material presented, this summary cannot be considered to be comprehensive. Instead, the following four sections will focus on presenting a simple and unifying framework, which should give an insight into the theoretical and empirical part of the book. After representing the orthodox view from the introduction for completeness, and in order to give an understanding of the current state of the art, section 10.2 presents the resource constraint, which summarizes the effects of unemployment on economic growth.

Whilst the resource constraint has appeared in all models of growth and unemployment in a fairly similar fashion, the incentive condition, discussed in section 10.3, will take a different form, depending on the particular labor market failure imposed for its derivation. It turns out that the diversity of this incentive condition is not detrimental for any dynamic interpretation of the relationship between economic growth and unemployment and its empirical application, both presented in section 10.4. In the dynamic interpretation, we find that the resource constraint describes the dynamic adjustment path, and the incentive condition merely determines the dynamic equilibrium along the resource constraint, where the unemployment rate and the rate of economic growth do not change any more.

This book predominantly deals with issues of positive economics, trying to determine the governing economic laws of the relationship between economic growth and unemployment. It would be ignorant, however, to assume that this work has no implications for economic policy. Consequently, political issues are addressed in the second part of this concluding chapter. Section 10.5 will first establish the types of externalities which are intrinsically present in the models developed in this book. We will discuss the knowledge externality present in endogenous growth models, which results in suboptimally low rates of economic growth, and the labor market externality, which results in suboptimally high rates of unemployment. The section then analyses first-best policy options to foster economic growth and unemployment, and its respective limits. Section 10.6 will consider the shape of the market in which policy should be best constituted. We argue that this is primarily an empirical question, depending on whether slow economic growth can be considered to cause unemployment, or vice versa. Whereas labor market policies should be promoted in the latter instance, policies on the product markets, in particular to encourage entrepreneurs to enter the market, should characterize the first situation. In the absence of explicit policy parameters in most theoretical models, section 10.7 discusses the workings of traditional policy instruments, such as supply-side, demand and incomes policy. Section 10.8 offers some concluding comments.

10.1 The orthodox view of unemployment and economic growth

Section 1.1 of this book presented the orthodox view of unemployment and economic growth. In the conventional view, long-run unemployment and economic growth are determined quite separately. Economic growth is driven by the exogenous rate of technical change. Technical progress is required to be labor augmenting in order not to contradict the stylized facts on economic growth (Kaldor, 1961). But if technical progress is incorporated in the factor labor, changes in technical progress should not alter the rates of job turnover or employment. That is, in the long run, GDP per capita would grow at the exogenously determined rate of technical progress, irrespective of the level of unemployment or the dynamics of the labor market along the adjustment path.

Similarly, we can trace back unemployment to factors relating to the destruction of jobs the creation of jobs and to the imperfect process of matching unemployed workers to job vacancies. As technical change is incorporated in the factor labor, economic growth in the orthodox view is not considered to alter job creation, job destruction or the matching process. In that respect, most theories of unemployment will predict a constant rate of unemployment in the long run, irrespective of the rate of economic growth.

In transition to the long-run equilibrium, the orthodox view of growth and unemployment predicts a negatively sloped adjustment path. This is due to the fact that a change in unemployment changes the amount of employed labor resources, and therefore exhibits an impact on growth accounting (Blanchard, 2000), as seen from equation (1.5) in the introduction. Figure 10.1 presents the orthodox view graphically, once again.

This model exhibits several empirical shortcomings. First, whilst it can predict both periods of high growth and periods of low unemployment, as well as periods of low growth and low unemployment, it fails to explain periods of high growth and high unemployment, or phases of jobless growth, which have characterized the European situation. Secondly, the transition path can be interpreted as Okun's law, a stable relationship between economic growth and unemployment. The strong empirical evidence against Okun's law therefore translates into the empirical failure of the orthodox model (Bishop and Havemann, 1979; Courtney, 1991; Erber, 2001).

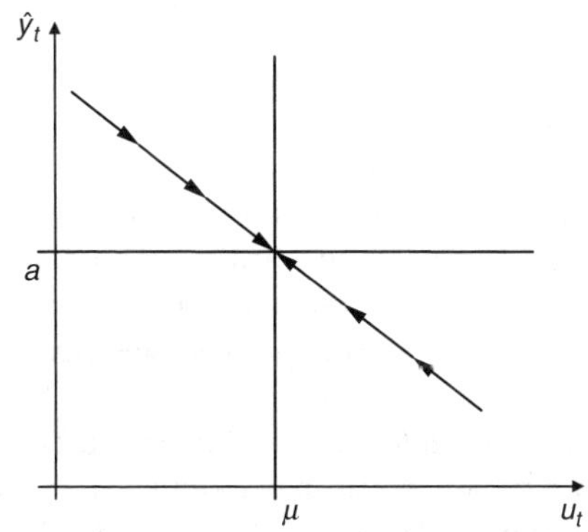

Figure 10.1 The orthodox model of equilibrium unemployment and economic growth: short-run dynamics and long-run neutrality

10.2 Innovation-driven endogenous growth models and the resource constraint

In the previous chapter, economic growth was due to a stroke of fortune, as technical progress happened to the economy out of mere chance. Technical progress was considered to be non-appropriable, hence once technology improved, and everybody could benefit without incurring any costs at all.

By contrast, it has now become the consensus view that economic growth does not happen by chance, but that it takes time and effort to generate productivity increases, which would enable the economy to produce a larger quantity of output with a given number of inputs. In accordance with the literature, we shall call all productivity-enhancing activities, which are actively pursued and costly, an innovation. In order to finance the cost of the innovation, it must at least in part be privately appropriable. At least two types of innovations qualify for this – product innovations (Romer, 1990) and production process innovations (Grossman and Helpman, 1991b). In the first case, the innovator benefits from an at least temporary monopoly over the product, which she can exploit to finance the cost of the innovation. In the latter case, the innovator benefits from a cost advantage over her competitors, which she can exploit to finance the cost of innovation as well.

Throughout this book, and in this summary, we focus on product innovations for the following reason. Whereas process innovations typically occur within existing firms, product innovations are the key to the entry of new firms and the decline of incumbent firms. As some firms emerge whilst others decline, some workers will lose their jobs whereas others will find employment. This process of structural change due to product innovations can therefore contribute to our understanding of the flow approach to unemployment.

Both product and process innovations require scarce resources for their creation. In that respect, innovations compete with production for labor resources, and restore the conventional assumption that economic growth is consumption forgone. The presence of unemployment, however, reduces the resource base for both consumption and innovation activities, and can therefore be detrimental to economic growth. To formalize this point, which has been elaborated extensively in the theoretical part of this book, consider an economy with n_t different products available at time t, where consumption demand for a particular product, $x_{i,t}$, depends inversely on the relative price of that particular product $p_{i,t}$, with a price elasticity of demand equal to ε, and aggregate demand y_t,

$$x_{i,t} = (p_{i,t}/p_t)^{-\varepsilon} y_t. \tag{10.1}$$

Suppose further, that each unit of the product can be produced with one unit of labor input, $l_{i,t}$, at cost w_t, and that the innovator of a particular product i has a permanent monopoly over the provision of the product. Then profit maximization with respect to demand (10.1) implies,

$$p_{i,t} = \frac{\varepsilon}{\varepsilon - 1} w_t, \tag{10.2}$$

or that the monopolist innovator sets the price with a mark-up over marginal costs, w_t. The monopolist then receives a stream of profits $\pi_{i,t}$, defined as total revenues $p_{i,t}x_{i,t}$, minus total costs $w_t l_{i,t}$, equal to,

$$\pi_{i,t} = \frac{1}{\varepsilon - 1} w_t l_{i,t}, \tag{10.3}$$

which is used to pay back the cost of the innovation. As mentioned before, innovations take time and effort. New products Δn_t, are innovated by employing e_t workers at wage w_t over a period Δt at productivity ϕn_t. The arrival rate of new innovations is then equal to

$$\hat{n}_t = \phi e_t. \tag{10.4}$$

Whilst innovations yield a constant flow of income in the future (10.3), they bear an initial cost of investment equal to $w_t e_t$. The initial cost is financed on the capital market, which is in equilibrium when all savings are invested. Assuming, as in the introduction, that households save a constant proportion, s, of their income, y_t, then

$$w_t e_t = s y_t = s\left(w_t e_t + w_t n_t l_{i,t} + \frac{1}{\varepsilon - 1} w_t n_t l_{i,t}\right), \tag{10.5}$$

where income is defined as labor income for e_t workers in the innovative activities, labor income for $n_t l_{i,t}$ workers in productive activities, and total profit income, $n_t \pi_{i,t}$. The investment equals savings locus (10.5) implies that employment in innovative and productive activities is proportional. Normalizing the labor force to unity, we can define employment $1 - u_t$, as employment in innovative and productive activities,

$$1 - u_t = e_t + n_t l_{i,t}, \tag{10.6}$$

where u_t is the unemployment rate. The labor market clearing condition (10.6) and the investment equals savings locus (10.5) imply that employment in innovative activities is proportional to the total labor force, hence the arrival rate of innovations (10.4) can be expressed as a function of unemployment and deep parameters of the model only,

$$\hat{n}_t = \frac{\phi \varepsilon s}{s + \varepsilon - 1}(1 - u_t). \tag{10.4$'$}$$

A decline in unemployment evidently increases the resources available for innovative activities, and therefore boosts the innovation rate. But it exhibits a positive impact on output growth as well. The intuition is the following. An increase in the number of products, n_t, reduces the monopoly power of each monopolist, hence reducing every individual price $p_{i,t}$. The impact on aggregate prices is even greater due to market entry, thus increasing the relative price charged by each firm. This can most easily be demonstrated by multiplying the demand function (10.1) by $n_t p_{i,t}$, and then eliminating aggregate spending, $p_t y_t = n_t p_{i,t} x_{i,t}$, on both sides. This implies that the relative price increases with an increase in the number of innovations, since $(p_{i,t}/p_t) = n_t^{1/(\varepsilon-1)}$.

Substituting this back into the demand function (10.1), we find that the growth rate of aggregate demand equals,

$$\hat{y}_t = \frac{1}{\varepsilon - 1}\hat{n}_t = \frac{\varepsilon}{\varepsilon - 1}\frac{\phi s}{s + \varepsilon - 1}(1 - u_t), \tag{10.7}$$

where we have assumed that the labor market is in equilibrium – that is, the change in total employment $1 - u_t$, and hence of employment in production, $n_t l_{i,t}$, is zero. An increase in unemployment leads to a decline in economic growth, because less aggregate employment implies less employment in innovative resources. In that respect, we may refer to equation (10.7) as the resource constraint.

10.3 Labor market imperfections and the incentive condition

Throughout this book, the dynamics of the labor market have been characterized by flows of workers out of employment and flows of the unemployed into employment. If workers who leave employment are not instantaneously matched to a new vacant job, unemployment arises. The unemployment rate will be constant, or in equilibrium, if the number of workers who leave employment is identical to the numbers of the unemployed who find employment. In this framework, equilibrium unemployment may increase for three reasons. First, the number of vacancies posted may be voluntarily held low. Secondly, the number of unemployed may be held high on purpose. Finally, the matching process itself may deteriorate.

All of the theories of labor market imperfections introduced in this book can be seen as falling into one of these three categories, and can therefore be thought of as special cases of the flow approach to the labor market. The pure search model, introduced in chapter 4 of this book, assumes that the matching process is imperfect, and that at every point in time neither can all vacancies be filled nor can all of the unemployed be assigned to a job, whichever is the smaller number. Instead, the search model assumes that the probability of matching an unemployed person to a vacant job increases both in vacancies and unemployment, and the only possibility for full employment – the permanent posting of an infinite number of vacancies – is prevented by the cost of posting vacancies and hiring workers on behalf of firms (Mortenson, 1986; Pissarides, 1990).

The efficiency wage model, as presented in chapter 2, claims that firms withhold part of their job offers, hence the number of vacancies will be held low, fostering unemployment. Firms deliberately reduce the number of vacancies, and prefer to pay a wage above the marginal product, as this induces effort on behalf of the workers (Akerlof and Yellen, 1990; Shapiro and Stiglitz, 1984).

Unions, by contrast, may withhold part of the workforce from applying for vacant jobs, thus increasing their bargaining power, but at the same time reducing the number of available unemployed to the matching process, and thereby fostering unemployment (McDonald and Solow, 1985). Similarly, as argued in chapter 6 of this book, the number of job seekers may be held low deliberately because of advance contracts between workers and firms. Given that all labor market rigidities in this book can be reduced to the matching model, we shall discuss it more explicitly.

As mentioned above, the number of unemployed, which can be matched to a vacant job, m_t, depends positively on the number of unemployed, u_t, and the number of vacancies, v_t. As both the number of vacancies and the number unemployed double, we would expect twice as many matchings to occur. The matching function should therefore exhibit constant returns to scale, which allows us to pull out one argument, hence $m_t = v_t m(u_t/v_t)$, where $m(.)$ describes the probability for a firm to find an unemployed person to fill its vacancy. Introducing a measure of labor market tightness, $\theta_t = u_t/v_t$, we find quite realistically that the probability of finding a worker increases with an increase in the tightness of the labor market. We have argued in the introduction, equation (1.1), that in the absence of an impact of economic growth on the matching technology, and for a given cost of posting a job, the proportion of unemployed who find a job is constant, or $m_t = \eta u_t$. This implies that labor market tightness is constant, and solves for $\eta = \theta_t^{-1} m(\theta_t)$.

In the orthodox view of economic growth and unemployment, not only job creation, but also job destruction was considered to be constant and exogenous. The previous chapter, however, has shown that job destruction happens endogenously. As some firms reduce their market share, they reduce their employment level proportionally, given constant returns to scale, while other firms enter the product market. The rate of job destruction can therefore be derived from the growth rate of an individual firm's output (10.1). Given that the relative price depends positively on the number of innovations, $(p_{i,t}/p_t) = n_t^{1/(\varepsilon-1)}$, the growth rate of individual output, or the rate of job destruction, is the negative of the innovation rate,

$$\hat{x}_{i,t} = \hat{l}_{i,t} = \frac{-\varepsilon}{\varepsilon - 1}\hat{n}_t + \hat{y}_t = -(\varepsilon - 1)\hat{y}_t, \tag{10.8}$$

where we have made use of the relation between the growth rate of innovation and the growth rate of output (10.7). Evidently, only workers in productive activities are affected by this process of the creative destruction of jobs (Aghion and Howitt, 1994).

In order to compare this result to the orthodox model, we can continue to express job destruction in terms of total employment, by using the relation between innovative and productive workers (10.5), yielding,

$$d_t = \hat{l}_{i,t}(n_t l_{i,t}) = (\varepsilon - 1)\hat{y}_t(n_t l_{i,t}) = \frac{(1-s)(\varepsilon-1)^2}{s+\varepsilon-1}\hat{y}_t(1-u_t) = \delta'\hat{y}_t(1-u_t), \tag{10.9}$$

where the δ' has been chosen to distinguish it from the constant δ in the orthodox model of growth and unemployment in the introduction. In equation (10.9), job destruction would be zero in the absence of economic growth, but positive for any positive rate of economic growth. In that respect, unemployment is due to creative destruction, because the pursuit of new business opportunities causes unemployment. The labor market is in equilibrium when the number of unemployed who have been matched to a new job, m_t, is equal to the number of workers who have been laid off, d_t, resulting in a equilibrium unemployment rate, which we obtain by solving equations (10.8) and (10.9) for unemployment,

$$u_t = \delta' \hat{y}_t / (\eta + \delta' \hat{y}_t). \tag{10.10}$$

What has been hidden in the derivation of equation (10.10) is the fact that a match requires both a job-seeking worker and a vacancy-posting firm to agree on a wage, after finding each other. Evidently, a higher wage offer will encourage the worker to accept the offer, whereas a higher wage demand may induce the firm to withdraw the offer. In that respect, equation (10.10) summarizes the incentives for the worker to accept a job and the incentives for the firm to fill a vacancy, and can thus be labeled the incentive condition.

The incentive condition (10.10) describes an upward-sloping line in an unemployment–economic growth plane and, together with the resource constraint (10.7), should give a unique solution for the equilibrium unemployment rate and the steady-state growth rate of the economy. Whilst the resource constraint summarizes the effects of unemployment on economic growth, the incentive condition (10.10) describes the impact of economic growth on the equilibrium unemployment rate, due to rigidities on the labor market. Figure 10.2 presents the long-run equilibrium of economic growth and unemployment, as presented throughout this book.

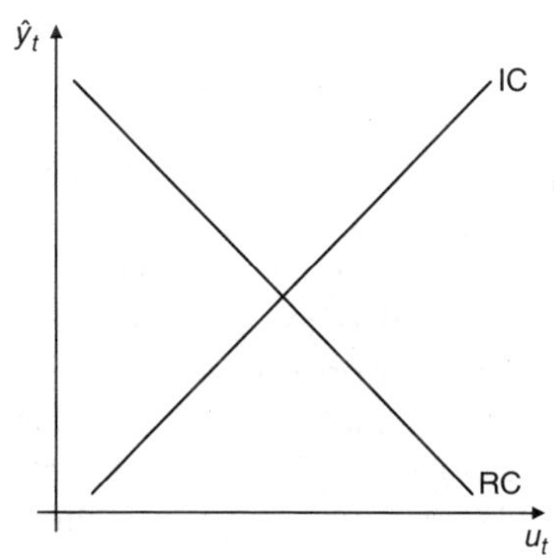

Figure 10.2 Resource constraint (RC) and incentive condition (IC) in the determination of the equilibrium unemployment rate and steady-state rate of economic growth

Whilst the resource constraint has been established in a similar fashion throughout the theoretical models presented in this book, the incentive condition may take very different shapes. In order to highlight this, consider an efficiency wage model, in which the productivity of a worker in the productive sector is not unity as assumed in section 10.2, but instead is given by,

$$a_{i,t} = e^{1-\frac{\mu}{u_t} \Big/ \frac{w_{i,t}}{w_t}}. \tag{10.11}$$

Each firm can now set a different wage, $w_{i,t}$, in order to motivate its workforce. In accordance with Akerlof and Yellen (1990), both an increase in the relative wage with relation to the economy-wide average wage, $w_{i,t}/w_t$, and an increase in the unemployment rate u_t increase efficiency. Profit maximization in manufacturing implies that firms will increase their wage rate until the increase in effort is just offset by an alternative increase in employment – that is, until the output elasticity of employment is equal to the output elasticity of the wage rate, or

$$w_{i,t}/w_t = \mu/u_t, \tag{10.12}$$

implying that in equilibrium productivity $a_{i,t}$ is again unity (10.11), and the analysis of section 10.2 can be carried through without alterations. However, equation (10.12) implies that the wage incentives set by firms to motivate their workers already determines the unemployment rate. The intuition is the following. Any firm will increase its wage relative to the average wage whenever unemployment exceeds μ. This will equiproportionally increase the average wage, thus inducing another round of relative wage increases, implying that wages would ultimately increase without bound, unless wage increases push the unemployment rate up to μ. The labor market will therefore only be in equilibrium if and only if $w_{i,t} = w_t$. In contrast to the matching model, this implies that the unemployment rate is defined prior to the allocation decisions in the economy, and therefore does not depend upon economic growth. Indeed, just as in the case of job destruction (10.9), job creation now also depends on economic growth, because every worker set free allows firms to reduce wages or hire a new worker without altering the potential to induce optimal effort from its existing workforce. Formally, the rate of job creation has to be equal to $\eta = \delta'\hat{y}_t(1-\mu)/\mu$, reducing the equilibrium unemployment rate to,

$$u_t = \delta'\hat{y}_t/(\eta + \delta'\hat{y}_t) = \mu. \tag{10.10'}$$

The incentive condition would then be a vertical line, not much different from the equilibrium unemployment rate in the orthodox model. In these circumstances, the difference between the two models can then only be determined by the position of the resource constraint. Given the importance of the resource constraint in the selection of the appropriate model of economic growth and unemployment, an entire chapter of this book has been devoted to the empirical examination of this relationship. Using microeconomic panel data on regional and sectoral growth rates and individual unemployment experiences, chapter 7 tests the hypothesis as to whether the resource constraint is indeed downward sloping, a hypothesis which we could not reject.

Apart from the vertical incentive condition in the efficiency wage model, an upward-sloping incentive condition has been found in the insider–outsider models presented in chapter 5, as well as for the aggregate demand model in chapter 6.

It turns out that the incentive condition is hump-shaped in the case of the search model presented in chapter 4, which is based on a growth model of intra- and intersectoral change, discussed in chapter 3. Moreover, we find that the resource constraint would shift outwards initially, with both growth and unemployment increasing. The resource constraint would shift back after economic growth has reached its peak, thereby reducing unemployment again. The intuition for the peak in the unemployment rate is the following. Consider a sector with a high intersectoral labor turnover, like that described in section 10.2, and a sector with a relatively low labor turnover, which is diminishing in size. As the labor force shifts from the low turnover sector to the high turnover sector, unemployment increases for two reasons. On the one hand, workers leave jobs in the low turnover sector and seek employment in the high turnover sector, and on the other workers leave jobs in the high turnover sector in order to seek new jobs in the same sector. Evidently, because the structural shift is complete, the unemployment rate will decline again, as the intersectoral reallocation of labor ceases.

This model has some empirical relevance, for three reasons. First, it can explain why unemployment may have risen over long periods, and then started to decline. Secondly, it can explain a stylized fact uncovered by Jones (1998, p. 85), namely that the number of employees in innovative activities has risen steadily over the years without fostering economic growth, contradicting the implications of equation (10.4) in the absence of intersectoral change. Thirdly, it predicts that the resource constraint shifts systematically through time, and generates the vector field which we have estimated in the vector error correction model, chapter 9.

Despite the diversity of the incentive conditions, all of the models of economic growth and unemployment could be estimated within the same dynamic macroeconometric framework. This is due to the fact that the incentive condition only holds in labor market equilibrium, where the change in the unemployment rate is zero. The resource constraint, by contrast, should hold at every point in time, and can therefore describe the dynamic adjustment path of the economy. The only information required on the position of the incentive condition is its intercept with the resource constraint, and whether unemployment would increase or decline off the incentive condition. Given that all models predict a unique intercept, we have been able to estimate a vector error correction model (VECM) that would correspond to all theoretical models of unemployment and economic growth, with the exception of the heterodox model. Instead of the incentive condition, the cointegrating relation would determine the equilibrium unemployment rate, and the resource constraint would be a particular adjustment path within the vector field of the vector autoregression estimator.

10.4 The dynamics of economic growth and unemployment

In chapter 9 of this book, we presented a VECM of economic growth and unemployment for the four major European countries – France, Germany, Italy and the United Kingdom. In this section, our emphasis is on relating the results obtained from the empirical estimation of these four countries to the unifying model presented so far. The idea behind a vector error regression model is that there is a stationary relationship between trending variables, and that the economy gradually adjusts to the equilibrium relation – called the cointegrating relationship – along specified predetermined paths, called the vector field.

It turns out that cointegration between output and unemployment is supported by evidence. From the cointegrating relationship, which takes the general form,

$$u_t - \alpha y_t + \beta = 0, \tag{10.13}$$

we can derive equilibrium unemployment rates by substituting average output levels, and find an equilibrium unemployment rate for France of 9.5 per cent, 13.4 per cent for Germany, 7.2 per cent for Italy and 5 per cent for the United Kingdom. The high value for Germany may be due to estimation problems in the face of reunification.

Given these equilibrium values, we could then estimate the dynamic adjustment path, along which the economy would converge to the equilibrium unemployment rate and the steady-state growth rate. The estimation procedure is to estimate a vector autoregressive system for the change in the unemployment rate and the growth rate of output, which includes adjustment from past disequilibria, or which contains the estimator of the cointegrating relation (10.13), named the error correction component, as one argument. We can derive the slope of the adjustment path as the ratio of the coefficients on the error correction component from the two equations in the autoregressive system. It turns out that the slope of the adjustment path is equal to 7.81 in France, 6.14 in Germany, 4.73 in Italy, but a remarkable 32.83 in the United Kingdom. The resource constraint is negatively sloped in all four countries, and thus consistent with theory. For France, Germany and Italy, the coefficient is in line with estimates of Okun's law that do not use a dynamic approach (Holloway, 1989). As opposed to recent conventional estimators of Okun's law, the coefficients are statistically highly significant, implying that it may have been shocks to the long-run equilibrium relationship between unemployment and economic growth which lead to some of the rejections of Okun's law. The high coefficient for the United Kingdom implies that the UK unemployment rate reacts strongly to changes in economic growth, which seems entirely consistent with the habit of hiring and firing in Anglo-Saxon economies.

Figure 10.3 summarizes the dynamics of output and unemployment by including the cointegrating relation and the dynamic adjustment

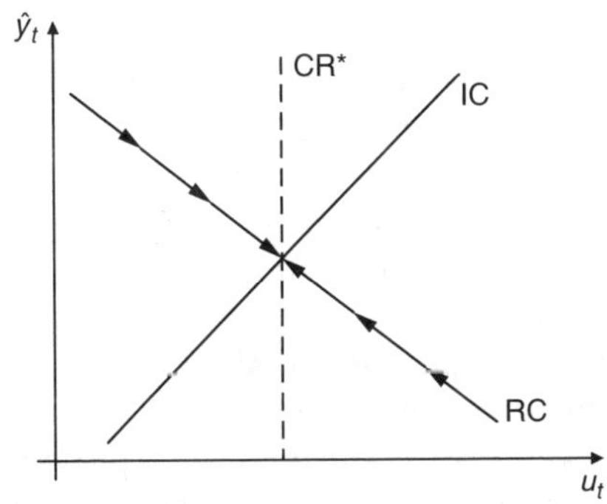

Figure 10.3 The dynamics of unemployment and economic growth: resource constraint (RC), incentive condition (IC), and the solution to the cointegrating relation (CR*)

into Figure 10.2. The empirical analysis has revealed that the model presented in sections 10.2 and 10.3 is consistent with the facts. We do find a long-run relationship between unemployment and economic growth, or evidence for cointegration. In the short run, unemployment and economic growth are negatively related, which is consistent with the resource constraint. Together with the microeconometric evidence presented in chapter 7, this provides ample evidence in favor of an endogenous growth model with labor market frictions.

10.5 The scope for economic policy

The previous sections have sketched a unifying framework for the discussion of economic growth and unemployment, and presented some favorable evidence. We find that the relation between economic growth and unemployment can best be described as an innovation-driven endogenous growth model with imperfect matching in the labor market. Both innovation-driven endogenous growth models and search models of unemployment contain an intrinsic externality, which implies that the economy will exhibit a suboptimally low rate of growth and a suboptimally high rate of unemployment, thus presenting great opportunities for welfare-improving economic policy interventions.

The externality in the growth process is a knowledge externality. Knowledge – or at least its economically relevant parts – is very limited in the model economy described in the previous sections. Indeed, agents only know, and only need to know, the different types of consumption goods in the economy. In that respect, we may consider n_t to be an index of knowledge in the economy. This knowledge is not totally worthless, as innovators can build on existing knowledge to create novel products.[2] The good news for innovators is that knowledge is non-appropriable, so they have access to this information for free.

The bad news for innovators, however, is that they cannot sell the knowledge gathered from an innovation to future potential innovators. Whilst innovators pay for the labor resources required to create a novel product, they do not reward the previous innovators for their contribution, nor will they receive any monetary rewards from future innovators for their contribution to common knowledge.

The knowledge externality in the innovation process therefore implies that innovators account for neither the knowledge inputs nor the knowledge output in their optimization process. These two effects of the knowledge externality do not exactly offset each other. If they did, the economy would not be distorted after all, because the future stream of profits (10.6) required would be identical whether there was an externality or not. However, as we have shown in section 6.9 of this book, this is not the case. The proof involves the hypothetical introduction of a clearing house for knowledge, which would buy and sell the available knowledge to innovating firms and monopoly producers of particular products at market clearing, or optimal, prices. We find that the price for an innovation that should be charged from a monopoly producer is too high, or that current innovators should receive more from future innovators than they should pay for the existing stock of knowledge. The suboptimal pricing behavior is equivalent to a barrier to market entry. If current products would not require all profits to finance their innovation, additional innovations would be possible. Hence, the knowledge externality implies that the rate of innovation and, given equation (10.7), the rate of economic growth, are too low.

The second externality intrinsic in an endogenous growth model with unemployment is labor market rigidity. In the stylized model of section 10.3, we introduced a search externality with the peculiar feature that the number of market participants – both those seeking employment and the vacancy-offering firms – matters for the market outcome (Diamond, 1982). Pissarides (1990, p. 6) points out that this trading externality cannot be eliminated by flexible price adjustments, given that there will be a positive probability that a firm does not find an unemployed person seeking work and an unemployed person does not find a hiring firm at the same point in time and for every positive wage rate. We can consider this trading externality to be a form of congestion, where despite the existence of both unsatisfied supply and demand, some traders do not get through to each other to be in the position to reach a deal.

In the absence of a search externality, we would expect the market to yield a maximal amount of matches for a given number of vacancies and unemployment, or $m_t = min(u_t, v_t)$. If the number of unemployed is lower than the number of vacancies, all unemployed people would be instantaneously matched to a job, hence we would have $u_t = 0$. Despite the fact that the probability for a firm of finding a matching unemployed person converges to zero in this situation, $m(0) = 0$, it can be demonstrated that the job creation rate, $\eta = \theta_t^{-1} m(\theta_t)$, would converge to infinity, thus equation (10.10) implies zero unemployment, indeed. In the model outlined in chapter 10.3, there would always be a wage so that the number of vacancies exceeds the number of unemployed. Unless wages are prevented from falling due to the actions of unions, efficiency considerations, or government legislation, we would therefore never observe positive rates of unemployment in the absence of a trading externality.

Both the knowledge externality and the matching externality give ample scope for welfare-improving policy interventions. The first-best solutions are evidently to directly create incentives for private agents to replicate the socially optimal outcome within the market. Given that innovators have to advance financial funds for future profits, innovations resemble investments, and we may therefore in analogy consider an investment subsidy to resolve the suboptimal rate of growth (Keuschnigg, 1997). In the case of the innovation externality, the optimal policy would evidently be a subsidy to innovators of new products in order to compensate them for their contribution to the stock of knowledge. There are two problems associated with an innovation subsidy that do not arise in the context of an investment externality. First, it is hard to judge what constitutes a new product innovation, and secondly, it is hard to quantify its contribution to further innovations. Moreover, firms will be eager to declare costs that are typically not associated with innovating to the innovation process in order to receive a larger share of the subsidy, and we would evidently observe an unintentional mushrooming of product innovations. Even if the problem of correctly establishing the subsidy base could be solved, we would face a permanently increasing subsidy rate, as the impact of current innovations on future innovations exceeds the impact of past innovations on current innovations, thus deserving a higher subsidy, even relative to GDP.

Whilst we could at least theoretically devise an optimal knowledge subsidy, this is completely unrealistic in the case of the labor market externality. The only possible way of eliminating the congestion of the trading externality in the matching model would be an unlimited supply of vacancies. This would ensure, in a manner equivalent to the perfect matching in a congestion-free market economy, that the job creation rate, $\eta = \theta_t^{-1} m(\theta_t)$, converges to infinity as the number of vacancies goes to infinity, given that $\theta_t^{-1} = v_t/u_t$ would converge to infinity. However, the only subsidy which would encourage firms to post an infinite amount of vacancies would be a zero wage and no costs for posting the vacancies – hence government would end up subsidizing the entire wage bill and all hiring costs. Given that the search externality arises only in the productive sector, a full wage subsidy would interfere in the optimal allocation decision of labor, and hence even this extreme subsidy would not be optimal.

Given that first-best policies are both impractical and unfeasible, it makes sense to consider the alternatives. The following section discusses whether the focus of attention for policy intervention should be on the labor market or on the product markets. Thereafter, we shall discuss traditional macroeconomic policy instruments – such as fiscal or incomes policy – which may yield welfare-improving results in the framework discussed here.

10.6 The focus of economic policy

In the previous section, we demonstrated that the knowledge externality leads to too little growth, and the search externality to too much unemployment. However, the knowledge externality also has an impact on unemployment, and the search externality influences economic growth. As argued, the knowledge externality implies that there is too little investment in innovation. But this must also imply that there is too little employment in innovatory activities and, given that there is a higher labor turnover of employment in productive activities, the knowledge externality therefore induces a higher level of unemployment. Similarly, the search externality exhibits a negative impact on economic growth. Once a monopoly producer has purchased a product innovation, she has to staff a production firm. Thus she is posting vacancies, which is costly, implying that innovators receive a lower share of profits, and cannot invest enough in the creation of product innovations, thereby reducing economic growth. This implies that the knowledge externality and the growth externality reinforce each other, or that unemployment would be even higher and economic growth would be even lower than optimal. The positive aspect of this mutual reinforcement is that any policy that would reduce the influence of either would also benefit the other. Thus economic policy aimed at reducing unemployment may also boost economic growth, and policy aimed at fostering economic growth will also reduce equilibrium unemployment.

The question therefore arises as to whether it is preferable to pursue growth policies or employment policies, where employment policy instruments would also affect incentives in the labor market, and growth policy instruments would also interfere in the product markets. In the European context, this is equivalent to asking whether policy should preferably pursue the common market project or the Essen program and intensify its focus on National Action Plans for Employment.

This question can only be answered empirically. We will have to consider whether the cross-effect of growth policies on unemployment and the employment policy effects on economic growth are existent and economically significant.

Chapter 8 of this book has presented Granger causality tests between economic growth and unemployment. If we assume that growth policies would first be visible in growth rates and only subsequently in unemployment rates, whilst employment policies would first be visible on the labor market and only afterwards on the product market, we can apply Granger causality tests to test the cross-impact. The results for the four major European countries were mixed. We have found Granger causality from unemployment to economic growth in Germany, Italy and the United Kingdom, and from economic growth to unemployment in France and the United Kingdom. This implies that employment policies should foster growth in Germany and Italy, but not in France, whereas growth policies should exhibit an impact on unemployment in France and the United Kingdom.

In that respect, the public spending experiment in France at the beginning of the 1980s, which aimed to foster economic growth, though ill performed, certainly had its merits (Zagler, 1992). By contrast, Germany, which has always been reluctant to engage in extensive public spending programs, or – God forbid – loose monetary policy, to stimulate economic growth, may not have been missing too much of an opportunity. The United Kingdom is the only country in which Granger causality leads both ways, hence the United Kingdom could do little wrong, with the exception of doing nothing at all. Italy, finally, has always run a flexible fiscal policy, stimulating the product market, but with little effect on employment. By contrast, the austerity program in the light of Maastricht did not harm the labor market either, as growth policies exhibit no influence on unemployment in Italy. They would probably be better advised to focus on labor market policies – such as promoting regional mobility – in order to ameliorate unemployment and economic growth. Summarizing, we find a very heterogeneous picture across Europe, where some countries should focus on economic growth, whilst others should predominately tackle the problem of unemployment.

10.7 Traditional policy instruments

Section 10.5 made it clear that there are no straightforward policy instruments available to solve the problem of low growth and high unemployment in Europe or elsewhere. Despite the concentration on the explanatory – or positive – aspects of the interaction between economic growth and unemployment throughout this book, the models in the theoretical part suggest several policy measures which could ameliorate the problem. Moreover, the models give fruitful indications about the workings of traditional policy instruments, on both the supply and the demand side of the economy, which will be discussed in this section.

On the supply side, as has already been mentioned, innovation subsidies play a central role. It is socially preferable to subsidize novel innovations in this economy, and many countries in Europe follow this path. On the European level, the European structural funds provide assistance – usually financial – to less favorable target regions. In the model presented, product innovations go hand in hand with the market entry of new firms. This evidently need not be the case, but is very likely to happen. Therefore, overly strict product market regulations, which work in a similar manner to a lump-sum tax on profits (Messina-Granovsky, 2000), may be detrimental to innovation and growth. On the other hand, overly loose product market regulations may precipitately introduce competition for a particular innovator, and thus prematurely destroy monopoly rents, thereby discouraging potential innovators, and again reducing economic growth. The task for the policy maker is therefore to strike a balance between the negative consequences of both too loose and too tight product market regulations.

In the labor market, one ambition can certainly be to implement policies which reduce congestion in the matching process, or to render search activities more successful. This particular form of active labor market policy can be undertaken either by making both employers and employees more eager to accept a job contract, or by facilitating searches, so that searching unemployed and vacancy-posting firms find one another more easily. The search process can also be improved by the standardization of professions, e.g. through specific government-endorsed training programs and apprenticeships, and the reform of employment offices. Employers can be motivated to accept job applicants more eagerly by offering employment subsidies, a policy which has been implemented in several countries, in particular for the long-term unemployed and special risk groups, such as young workers. One reason why firms may be reluctant to hire additional workers may be efficiency wage considerations. In section 10.3, we saw that firms cease to hire additional workers when the output of the additional employee no longer outweighs the output loss due to losses in efficiency from the incumbent workforce. Evidently, if firms promote activities which will foster internal efficiency, as outlined in chapter 2, they need to rely less on outside threats to ensure efficiency, thereby reducing unemployment. Of course, workers can be motivated to accept a job offer by increasing the opportunity cost of rejecting an offer, in particular by reducing the length of unemployment benefits, which is supported by the facts, as opposed to reducing the amount of the benefit (Ball, 1997).

Whilst supply-side policies have always been considered to potentially exhibit a positive impact on the long-run performance of the economy, this is much less the case for demand-side policies. However, within the framework discussed throughout this book, demand stimuli may exhibit permanent effects. In chapter 6, we have argued that unemployment may be the cause of the unexpected obsolescence of certain products, and the rigidity of the labor market to accommodate these shocks. One possibility would, of course, be to remove the labor market rigidity, with all the difficulties discussed above.

The other alternative is to adopt a range of demand-side policies, depending on the nature of the shock, in order to counteract the effects of the demand externality. If demand shocks are idiosyncratic and purely transitory, or if demand for a particular product would only decline for a limited period, it may be in the interests of the public to support demand for this particular product. Examples of actual policies which target transitory shocks to demand of particular products, can be subsidies to affected industries, or export promotion programs to substitute foreign demand for domestic demand (Ambler, Cardia and Farazli, 1999). If consistent, such a policy strategy would retain existing jobs, and thus reduce unemployment, as well as guaranteeing a stream of future profits, thereby encouraging investment into innovation and economic growth.

Of course, perfect markets could enable private agents to insure against a decline in product demand or a risk of unemployment, if demand shocks are indeed idiosyncratic. This does not hold if demand shocks are not idiosyncratic, but indeed occur more frequently at some times than others. Under such circumstances, government intervention can then improve welfare by counter-cyclical fiscal policy, once again concentrating on those industries that are suffering the most. If demand shocks would be persistent, and certain industries become permanently obsolescent, government intervention in order to ensure the employment of those workers affected would have to be permanent, and would probably burst the financial limits of financing. This does not imply that government should not intervene at all, but it may well be the case that a deferred retreat, which would allow workers to anticipate obsolescence and seek employment elsewhere in due time, may be preferable.

Finally, an often-neglected policy instrument holds some interesting insights in the context of the economic growth and unemployment framework. Throughout this book, labor, at least in efficiency terms, was considered to be a homogeneous factor. Therefore, we have assumed an equal wage rate per efficiency unit of labor, and the only reason for an unequal distribution of income, apart from unemployment, would have been an unequal distribution of efficiency units, or labor resources, across workers. The assumption of homogeneous labor may be extreme, in particular considering potential differences between productive and innovative activities. However, even if we assume that innovators have a preference for the most productive workers, the wage per efficiency unit would be identical across sectors, as the worker with the highest efficiency endowment in productive activities would otherwise challenge the worker with the lowest efficiency endowment in the innovative activities. The only difference would therefore be that the number of workers per head would be lower in innovative activities, and the income per capita in innovative activities would be higher.

Active income policy would therefore aim at redistributing income from workers with a high endowment of efficiency units of labor towards workers with a lower endowment of efficiency units of labor. Whilst in a perfect economy this policy would certainly exhibit distortionary effects and therefore reduce welfare, this need not be the case in the presence of externalities (Acemoglu, Aghion and Violante, 2000), such as the knowledge externality or the search externality discussed in section 10.5.

There is some theoretical indication that active income policy may indeed be welfare improving within the framework discussed throughout this book. In chapter 5, we analysed the impact of production sector trade unions on the interaction between changes in the level of unemployment and changes in the economic rate of growth. In essence, a trade union which organizes the productive workforce in order to increase their wage rate is carrying out an active income policy. If workers in productive activities indeed possess fewer labor resources, the initial redistribution effect is positive. The impact of the redistributional policy on growth and unemployment crucially depends upon the level of the bargaining process. Decentralized bargaining leads to the leapfrogging of wage claims, and thus fosters unemployment and reduces economic growth. In centralized bargaining, the union is in a position to take the macroeconomic knowledge externality into account, apart from internalizing the leapfrogging externality. By setting wages in the unionized production sector above wages in the non-unionized innovative sector, they increase profits for monopoly producers, but reduce costs for innovators. In that respect, a union wage mark-up works similarly to an innovation subsidy as discussed in section 10.5, with the additional benefit that the wage mark-up can remain constant through time, as opposed to an ever-increasing innovation subsidy. In that respect, incomes policy can lead to an increase in economic growth and a decline in unemployment, and thus foster economic well-being.

10.8 Concluding remarks

This book has investigated the interaction between changes in the level of unemployment and changes in the rate of economic growth. In this chapter, instead of presenting a comprehensive summary of the results throughout the theoretical and empirical parts, we have focused on presenting a stylized version of a unified framework of the dynamics and the long-run equilibrium of economic growth and unemployment. In contrast to the conventional view, economic growth and unemployment are related in the long run. We found that we can determine the long-run equilibrium and the transitional dynamics from a resource constraint, which is downward sloping in an unemployment–economic growth space, and an incentive condition, which is upward sloping in this unemployment–economic growth space, a framework which is supported by the facts.

This novel view on growth and unemployment has important implications for policy. First, the model intrinsically contains at least two externalities. A knowledge externality in innovative activities implies that the growth rate will be too low in equilibrium, and a search externality in the labor market implies that the unemployment rate is too high in equilibrium, compared to the social optimum. Moreover, the two externalities enforce each other, leading to an additional increase in unemployment and decline in economic growth.

This provides ample scope for policy interventions, which have been discussed in the second part of this chapter. We have noted that first-best policy measures will not work for reasons of practicality and feasibility. Therefore, this chapter has analysed the preferable focus of policy – that is, whether to conduct policies aimed at fostering economic growth or policies targeted at reducing unemployment. The answer was given empirically, and we found a surprisingly heterogeneous picture across Europe. Unemployment and economic growth should be a major concern for policy makers, but the strategies needed to address these issues are not straightforward and differ considerably across nations.

Appendixes

Appendix 1: Augmented Dickey–Fuller test statistics

Dependent series: GDP, France, in constant prices, domestic currency (mill. FF), and logarithms, taken from OECD National Accounts

	DF(1)	*ADF(2)*	*ADF(3)*	*ADF(4)*	*ADF(5)*	*ADF(6)*	*ADF(7)*	*ADF(8)*	*ADF(9)*
in Levels	−1.9409	−1.4794	−1.1613	−1.7525	−1.1865	−1.2125	−1.0401	−1.2166	−0.9195
(Critical Value)	(−2.8855)	(−2.8857)	(−2.8859)	(−2.8861)	(−2.8863)	(−2.8865)	(−2.8868)	(−2.8870)	(−2.8872)
Opt. Lag Length (T)	1.956	**1.956**	1.956	1.956	1.956	1.956	1.956	1.956	1.956
Opt. Lag Length (AIC)	−10.513	−10.511	−10.491	−10.524	**−10.536**	−10.531	−10.504	−10.486	−10.481
Opt. Lag Length (SBC)	**−10.490**	−10.465	−10.422	−10.432	−10.421	−10.393	−10.343	−10.302	−10.275
in First Differences	−5.2210	−4.4143	−4.4840	−3.9075	−4.2484	−3.5258	−3.6932	−2.8589	−2.4989
(Critical Value)	(−2.8857)	(−2.8859)	(−2.8861)	(−2.8863)	(−2.8865)	(−2.8868)	(−2.8870)	(−2.8872)	(−2.8874)
Opt. Lag T	1.952	**1.952**	1.952	1.952	1.952	1.952	1.952	1.952	1.952
Opt. Lag AIC	−10.517	−10.504	−10.521	**−10.548**	−10.542	−10.519	−10.497	−10.498	−10.479
Opt. Lag SBC	**−10.494**	−10.458	−10.452	−10.456	−10.426	−10.380	−10.335	−10.313	−10.271
in Second Differences	−12.0113	−7.9284	−8.1282	−6.5137	−6.8198	−5.5718	−6.4205	−6.4615	−6.0137
(Critical Value)	(−2.8859)	(−2.8861)	(−2.8863)	(−2.8865)	(−2.8868)	(−2.8870)	(−2.8872)	(−2.8874)	(−2.8877)
Opt. Lag T	1.948	**1.948**	1.948	1.948	1.948	1.948	1.948	1.948	1.948
Opt. Lag AIC	−10.372	−10.381	−10.443	−10.413	−10.433	−10.399	**−10.447**	−10.444	−10.445
Opt. Lag SBC	−10.348	−10.335	**−10.374**	−10.320	−10.317	−10.259	−10.284	−10.258	−10.236

Notes: The first line in each block gives the Augmented Dickey–Fuller test statistics. Numbers in parenthesis are the critical values at the 5 per cent level, taken from MacKinnon (1990). The three criteria for the optimal lag length are given below, with the optimum marked in bold. The T criterion is computed as $(12T/100)^{1/4}$, the *AIC* criterion is computed as $log\ \sigma^2(k) + 2/T$, and the *SBC* criterion as $\sigma^2(k) + 1/\sqrt{T}$.

Dependent series: Unemployment rate (number of persons in unemployment/number of persons in employment), France, from QLFS

	DF(1)	*ADF(2)*	*ADF(3)*	*ADF(4)*	*ADF(5)*	*ADF(6)*	*ADF(7)*	*ADF(8)*	*ADF(9)*
in Levels	−1.7891	−1.8582	−1.8575	−1.9033	−1.8935	−1.7866	−1.8208	−1.7910	−1.7721
(Critical Value)	(−2.8855)	(−2.8857)	(−2.8859)	(−2.8861)	(−2.8863)	(−2.8865)	(−2.8868)	(−2.8870)	(−2.8872)
Opt. Lag Length (T)	1.956	**1.956**	1.956	1.956	1.956	1.956	1.956	1.956	1.956
Opt. Lag Length (AIC)	**−12.685**	−12.672	−12.639	−12.610	−12.590	−12.588	−12.562	−12.584	−12.558
Opt. Lag Length (SBC)	**−12.661**	−12.626	−12.570	−12.518	−12.476	−12.450	−12.401	−12.400	−12.351
in First Differences	−3.413992	−3.167657	−3.148224	−2.357850	−1.512833	−1.727250	−0.844628	−0.464081	−0.587754
(Critical Value)	(−2.8857)	(−2.8859)	(−2.8861)	(−2.8863)	(−2.8865)	(−2.8868)	(−2.8870)	(−2.8872)	(−2.8874)
Opt. Lag T	1.952	**1.952**	1.952	1.952	1.952	1.952	1.952	1.952	1.952
Opt. Lag AIC	**−12.667**	−12.634	−12.604	−12.584	−12.583	−12.556	−12.578	−12.553	−12.519
Opt. Lag SBC	**−12.644**	−12.586	−12.534	−12.491	−12.467	−12.418	−12.417	−12.368	−12.311
in Second Differences	−8.3825	−6.9446	−7.1855	−7.5297	−5.7475	−6.5925	−6.1737	−5.0138	−4.8938
(Critical Value)	(−2.8859)	(−2.8861)	(−2.8863)	(−2.8865)	(−2.8868)	(−2.8870)	(−2.8872)	(−2.8874)	(−2.8877)
Opt. Lag T	1.948	**1.948**	1.948	1.948	1.948	1.948	1.948	1.948	1.948
Opt. Lag AIC	−12.574	−12.544	−12.559	**−12.587**	−12.553	−12.596	−12.575	−12.541	−12.518
Opt. Lag SBC	**−12.551**	−12.498	−12.489	−12.494	−12.437	−12.457	−12.412	−12.356	−12.309

Notes: The first line in each block gives the Augmented Dickey–Fuller test statistics. Numbers in parenthesis are the critical values at the 5 per cent level, taken from MacKinnon (1990). The three criteria for the optimal lag length are given below, with the optimum marked in bold. The *T* criterion is computed as $(12T/100)^{1/4}$, the *AIC* criterion is computed as $\log \sigma^2(k) + 2/T$, and the *SBC* criterion as $\sigma^2(k) + 1/\sqrt{T}$.

Dependent series: GDP, Germany (West), in constant prices, domestic currency (mill. DM), and logs, taken from OECD National Accounts

	DF(1)	*ADF(2)*	*ADF(3)*	*ADF(4)*	*ADF(5)*	*ADF(6)*	*ADF(7)*	*ADF(8)*	*ADF(9)*
in Levels	−1.8093	−1.9426	−2.2585	−1.2440	−0.9425	−0.8183	−0.9506	−1.3069	−0.8378
(Critical Value)	(−2.8859)	(−2.8861)	(−2.8863)	(−2.8865)	(−2.8868)	(−2.8870)	(−2.8872)	(−2.8874)	(−2.8877)
Opt. Lag Length (T)	1.948	**1.948**	1.948	1.948	1.948	1.948	1.948	1.948	1.948
Opt. Lag Length (AIC)	−7.926	−8.157	−8.196	−8.540	−8.525	−8.511	−8.538	−8.548	**−8.579**
Opt. Lag Length (SBC)	−7.903	−8.111	−8.127	**−8.447**	−8.409	−8.372	−8.375	−8.362	−8.370
in First Differences	−12.9957	−10.4445	−3.9050	−3.6672	−3.9170	−4.5901	−3.9259	−3.8540	−3.6339
(Critical Value)	(−2.8861)	(−2.8863)	(−2.8865)	(−2.8868)	(−2.8870)	(−2.8872)	(−2.8874)	(−2.8877)	(−2.8879)
Opt. Lag T	1.944	**1.944**	1.944	1.944	1.944	1.944	1.944	1.944	1.944
Opt. Lag AIC	−8.150	−8.177	−8.551	−8.542	−8.530	−8.554	−8.557	−8.598	**−8.561**
Opt. Lag SBC	−8.126	−8.130	**−8.481**	−8.449	−8.413	−8.414	−8.393	−8.411	−8.351
in Second Differences	−14.86785	−24.35074	−11.44077	−7.956978	−5.627532	−5.443853	−5.766453	−5.425657	−5.436845
(Critical Value)	−2.8863	−2.8865	−2.8868	−2.8870	−2.8872	−2.8874	−2.8877	−2.8879	−2.8882
Opt. Lag T	1.940	**1.940**	1.940	1.940	1.940	1.940	1.940	1.940	1.940
Opt. Lag AIC	−7.522	−8.447	−8.451	−8.421	−8.395	−8.442	**−8.485**	−8.461	−8.445
Opt. Lag SBC	−7.499	**−8.400**	−8.380	−8.327	−8.278	−8.301	−8.321	−8.273	−8.233

Notes: The first line in each block gives the Augmented Dickey–Fuller test statistics. Numbers in parenthesis are the critical values at the 5 per cent level, taken from MacKinnon (1990). The three criteria for the optimal lag length are given below, with the optimum marked in bold. The T criterion is computed as $(12T/100)^{1/4}$, the AIC criterion is computed as $\log \sigma^2(k) + 2/T$, and the SBC criterion as $\sigma^2(k) + 1/\sqrt{T}$.

Dependent series: Unemployment rate (number of persons in unemployment/number of persons in employment), Germany, from QLFS

	DF(1)	*ADF(2)*	*ADF(3)*	*ADF(4)*	*ADF(5)*	*ADF(6)*	*ADF(7)*	*ADF(8)*	*ADF(9)*
in Levels	−1.4589	−1.6369	−1.7368	−1.7086	−1.6487	−1.6948	−1.7093	−1.5393	−1.603
(Critical Value)	(−2.884)	(−2.8842)	(−2.8844)	(−2.8845)	(−2.8847)	(−2.8849)	(−2.8851)	(−2.8853)	(−2.8855)
Opt. Lag Length (T)	1.987	**1.987**	1.987	1.987	1.987	1.987	1.987	1.987	1.987
Opt. Lag Length (AIC)	**−12.369**	−12.352	−12.325	−12.293	−12.282	−12.254	−12.222	−12.199	−12.173
Opt. Lag Length(SBC)	**−12.347**	−12.308	−12.259	−12.205	−12.171	−12.121	−12.068	−12.023	−11.975
in First Differences	−4.3076	−3.9018	−3.6897	−4.029	−3.5175	−3.3545	−3.5453	−3.5055	−3.89
(Critical Value)	(−2.8842)	(−2.8844)	(−2.8845)	(−2.8847)	(−2.8849)	(−2.8851)	(−2.8853)	(−2.8855)	(−2.8857)
Opt. Lag T	1.984	**1.984**	1.984	1.984	1.984	1.984	1.984	1.984	1.984
Opt. Lag AIC	**−12.354**	−12.324	−12.292	−12.282	−12.253	−12.221	−12.201	−12.174	−12.167
Opt. Lag SBC	**−12.331**	−12.279	−12.225	−12.193	−12.142	−12.088	−12.046	−11.996	−11.968
in Second Differences	−9.9569	−8.0643	−6.2927	−6.4045	−5.9517	−5.1045	−4.8775	−4.215	−4.6516
(Critical Value)	(−2.8844)	(−2.8845)	(−2.8847)	(−2.8849)	(−2.8851)	(−2.8853)	(−2.8855)	(−2.8857)	(−2.8859)
Opt. Lag T	1.980	**1.980**	1.980	1.980	1.980	1.980	1.980	1.980	1.980
Opt. Lag AIC	**−12.229**	−12.208	−12.177	−12.175	−12.15	−12.119	−12.091	−12.06	−12.059
Opt. Lag SBC	**−12.207**	−12.164	−12.11	−12.086	−12.038	−11.985	−11.935	−11.882	−11.859

Notes: The first line in each block gives the Augmented Dickey–Fuller test statistics. Numbers in parenthesis are the critical values at the 5 per cent level, taken from MacKinnon (1990). The three criteria for the optimal lag length are given below, with the optimum marked in bold. The T criterion is computed as $(12T/100)^{1/4}$, the *AIC* criterion is computed as $\log \sigma^2(k) + 2/T$, and the *SBC* criterion as $\sigma^2(k) + 1/\sqrt{T}$.

Dependent series: GDP, Italy, in constant prices, domestic currency (bill. Lit), and logarithms, taken from the OECD National Accounts

	DF(1)	*ADF(2)*	*ADF(3)*	*ADF(4)*	*ADF(5)*	*ADF(6)*	*ADF(7)*	*ADF(8)*	*ADF(9)*
in Levels	−1.6722	−1.5544	−2.1574	−2.2796	−2.9078	−2.719	−2.6314	−2.7676	−3.0855
(Critical Value)	(−2.8855)	(−2.8857)	(−2.8859)	(−2.8861)	(−2.8863)	(−2.8865)	(−2.8868)	(−2.887)	(−2.8872)
Opt. Lag Length (T)	1.956	**1.956**	1.956	1.956	1.956	1.956	1.956	1.956	1.956
Opt. Lag Length (AIC)	−9.66	−9.628	**−9.675**	−9.652	−9.7	−9.668	−9.633	−9.61	−9.628
Opt. Lag Length (SBC)	**−9.637**	−9.582	−9.606	−9.56	−9.585	−9.53	−9.472	−9.426	−9.421
in First Differences	−5.7047	−5.9235	−5.5256	−6.1226	−5.0998	−4.3687	−4.2196	−3.4971	−3.1083
(Critical Value)	(−2.8857)	(−2.8859)	(−2.8861)	(−2.8863)	(−2.8865)	(−2.8868)	(−2.887)	(−2.8872)	(−2.8874)
Opt. Lag T	1.952	**1.952**	1.952	1.952	1.952	1.952	1.952	1.952	1.952
Opt. Lag AIC	−9.632	**−9.659**	−9.631	−9.651	−9.626	−9.594	−9.563	−9.563	−9.532
Opt. Lag SBC	−9.609	**−9.613**	−9.562	−9.558	−9.511	−9.456	−9.402	−9.378	−9.324
in Second Differences	−9.3301	−8.336	−6.75	−7.4442	−7.5658	−6.7419	−7.0207	−6.6199	−6.3134
(Critical Value)	(−2.8859)	(−2.8861)	(−2.8863)	(−2.8865)	(−2.8868)	(−2.887)	(−2.8872)	(−2.8874)	(−2.8877)
Opt. Lag T	1.948	**1.948**	1.948	1.948	1.948	1.948	1.948	1.948	1.948
Opt. Lag AIC	−9.416	−9.415	−9.382	−9.436	−9.454	−9.43	−9.475	**−9.465**	−9.453
Opt. Lag SBC	**−9.393**	−9.369	−9.313	−9.343	−9.338	−9.291	−9.312	−9.279	−9.244

Notes: The first line in each block gives the Augmented Dickey–Fuller test statistics. Numbers in parenthesis are the critical values at the 5 per cent level, taken from MacKinnon (1990). The three criteria for the optimal lag length are given below, with the optimum marked in bold. The T criterion is computed as $(12T/100)^{1/4}$, the *AIC* criterion is computed as $\log \sigma^2(k) + 2/T$, and the *SBC* criterion as $\sigma^2(k) + 1/\sqrt{T}$.

Dependent series: Unemployment rate (number of persons in unemployment/number of persons in employment), Italy, taken from QLFS

	DF(1)	*ADF(2)*	*ADF(3)*	*ADF(4)*	*ADF(5)*	*ADF(6)*	*ADF(7)*	*ADF(8)*	*ADF(9)*
in Levels	−1.5771	−1.4758	−1.5983	−1.6066	−1.6657	−1.7177	−1.5937	−1.3792	−1.3444
(Critical Value)	(−2.8855)	(−2.8857)	(−2.8859)	(−2.8861)	(−2.8863)	(−2.8865)	(−2.8868)	(−2.887)	(−2.8872)
Opt. Lag Length (T)	1.956	**1.956**	1.956	1.956	1.956	1.956	1.956	1.956	1.956
Opt. Lag Length (AIC)	**−10.829**	−10.797	−10.788	−10.805	−10.779	−10.761	−10.732	−10.72	−10.695
Opt. Lag Length (SBC)	**−10.806**	−10.751	−10.719	−10.713	−10.665	−10.623	−10.571	−10.536	−10.488
in First Differences	−8.0761	−5.5254	−6.0814	−4.7355	−3.6977	−3.2131	−3.5095	−3.648	−3.129
(Critical Value)	(−2.8857)	(−2.8859)	(−2.8861)	(−2.8863)	(−2.8865)	(−2.8868)	(−2.887)	(−2.8872)	(−2.8874)
Opt. Lag T	1.952	**1.952**	1.952	1.952	1.952	1.952	1.952	1.952	1.952
Opt. Lag AIC	−10.804	−10.79	**−10.806**	−10.779	−10.758	−10.733	−10.727	−10.702	−10.676
Opt. Lag SBC	**−10.781**	−10.744	−10.737	−10.687	−10.643	−10.595	−10.565	−10.518	−10.468
in Second Differences	−15.3391	−9.1199	−9.5406	−9.3163	−8.1352	−6.2692	−5.3739	−5.7208	−5.6027
(Critical Value)	(−2.8859)	(−2.8861)	(−2.8863)	(−2.8865)	(−2.8868)	(−2.887)	(−2.8872)	(−2.8874)	(−2.8877)
Opt. Lag T	1.948	**1.948**	1.948	1.948	1.948	1.948	1.948	1.948	1.948
Opt. Lag AIC	−10.578	−10.546	−10.619	−10.664	**−10.666**	−10.64	−10.605	−10.608	−10.592
Opt. Lag SBC	−10.555	−10.5	−10.549	**−10.571**	−10.55	−10.501	−10.442	−10.422	−10.383

Notes: The first line in each block gives the Augmented Dickey–Fuller test statistics. Numbers in parenthesis are the critical values at the 5 per cent level, taken from MacKinnon (1990). The three criteria for the optimal lag length are given below, with the optimum marked in bold. The *T* criterion is computed as $(12T/100)^{1/4}$, the *AIC* criterion is computed as $log\ \sigma^2(k) + 2/T$, and the *SBC* criterion as $\sigma^2(k) + 1/\sqrt{T}$.

Dependent series: GDP, UK, in constant prices, domestic currency (mill. UKP), and logarithms, taken from the OECD National Accounts

	DF(1)	*ADF(2)*	*ADF(3)*	*ADF(4)*	*ADF(5)*	*ADF(6)*	*ADF(7)*	*ADF(8)*	*ADF(9)*
in Levels	−0.1846	−0.153	−0.1668	−0.1971	−0.2221	−0.3059	−0.3787	−0.2119	−0.1217
(Critical Value)	(−2.8822)	(−2.8824)	(−2.8825)	(−2.8827)	(−2.8828)	(−2.883)	(−2.8832)	(−2.8833)	(−2.8835)
Opt. Lag Length (T)	2.028	**2.028**	2.028	2.028	2.028	2.028	2.028	2.028	2.028
Opt. Lag Length (AIC)	**−9.145**	−9.119	−9.137	−9.112	−9.082	−9.065	−9.039	−9.053	−9.025
Opt. Lag Length (SBC)	**−9.124**	−9.078	−9.074	−9.028	−8.978	−8.939	−8.892	−8.885	−8.837
in First Differences	−7.8098	−5.1939	−4.9721	−4.527	−3.7455	−3.6492	−4.234	−4.0661	−3.8396
(Critical Value)	(−2.8824)	(−2.8825)	(−2.8827)	(−2.8828)	(−2.883)	(−2.8832)	(−2.8833)	(−2.8835)	(−2.8837)
Opt. Lag T	2.025	**2.025**	2.025	2.025	2.025	2.025	2.025	2.025	2.025
Opt. Lag AIC	−9.141	**−9.159**	−9.133	−9.104	−9.086	−9.059	−9.074	−9.047	−9.017
Opt. Lag SBC	**−9.12**	−9.116	−9.07	−9.02	−8.981	−8.933	−8.927	−8.879	−8.828
in Second Differences	−16.5717	−10.6306	−9.0859	−8.9125	−7.4686	−5.6193	−5.4802	−5.4173	−5.3559
(Critical Value)	(−2.8825)	(−2.8827)	(−2.8828)	(−2.883)	(−2.8832)	(−2.8833)	(−2.8835)	(−2.8837)	(−2.8838)
Opt. Lag T	2.021	**2.021**	2.021	2.021	2.021	2.021	2.021	2.021	2.021
Opt. Lag AIC	−8.995	−8.982	−8.978	**−9.003**	−8.979	−8.96	−8.94	−8.922	−8.903
Opt. Lag SBC	**−8.974**	−8.94	−8.914	−8.918	−8.874	−8.833	−8.793	−8.753	−8.713

Notes: The first line in each block gives the Augmented Dickey–Fuller test statistics. Numbers in parenthesis are the critical values at the 5 per cent level, taken from MacKinnon (1990). The three criteria for the optimal lag length are given below, with the optimum marked in bold. The T criterion is computed as $(12T/100)^{1/4}$, the *AIC* criterion is computed as $\log \sigma^2(k) + 2/T$, and the *SBC* criterion as $\sigma^2(k) + 1/\sqrt{T}$.

Dependent series: Unemployment rate (number of persons in unemployment/number of persons in employment), UK, taken from QLFS

	DF(1)	*ADF(2)*	*ADF(3)*	*ADF(4)*	*ADF(5)*	*ADF(6)*	*ADF(7)*	*ADF(8)*	*ADF(9)*
in Levels	−2.1288	−2.5618	−2.5677	−2.0079	−1.8867	−1.8466	−1.8388	−1.7014	−1.7995
(Critical Value)	(−2.8842)	(−2.8844)	(−2.8845)	(−2.8847)	(−2.8849)	(−2.8851)	(−2.8853)	(−2.8855)	(−2.8857)
Opt. Lag Length (T)	1.984	**1.984**	1.984	1.984	1.984	1.984	1.984	1.984	1.984
Opt. Lag Length (AIC)	−11.974	**−11.99**	−11.961	−12.003	−11.979	−11.946	−11.912	−11.902	−11.882
Opt. Lag Length (SBC)	**−11.952**	−11.946	−11.894	−11.915	−11.868	−11.813	−11.757	−11.724	−11.683
in First Differences	−2.6752	−2.6635	−3.5143	−3.6764	−3.5218	−3.3508	−3.7235	−3.1122	−3.2932
(Critical Value)	(−2.8844)	(−2.8845)	(−2.8847)	(−2.8849)	(−2.8851)	(−2.8853)	(−2.8855)	(−2.8857)	(−2.8859)
Opt. Lag T	1.980	**1.980**	1.980	1.980	1.980	1.980	1.980	1.980	1.980
Opt. Lag AIC	−11.962	−11.93	−11.994	**−11.971**	−11.94	−11.907	−11.899	−11.876	−11.854
Opt. Lag SBC	**−11.939**	−11.886	−11.927	−11.882	−11.828	−11.773	−11.743	−11.698	−11.653
in Second Differences	−8.9157	−5.4595	−4.8595	−4.7881	−4.7381	−4.0637	−4.6349	−4.1427	−4.2318
(Critical Value)	(−2.8845)	(−2.8847)	(−2.8849)	(−2.8851)	(−2.8853)	(−2.8855)	(−2.8857)	(−2.8859)	(−2.8861)
Opt. Lag T	1.976	**1.976**	1.976	1.976	1.976	1.976	1.976	1.976	1.976
Opt. Lag AIC	−11.897	**−11.919**	−11.886	−11.861	−11.836	−11.805	−11.815	−11.782	−11.758
Opt. Lag SBC	**−11.875**	−11.874	−11.819	−11.771	−11.724	−11.671	−11.658	−11.602	−11.557

Notes: The first line in each block gives the Augmented Dickey–Fuller test statistics. Numbers in parenthesis are the critical values at the 5 per cent level, taken from MacKinnon (1990). The three criteria for the optimal lag length are given below, with the optimum marked in bold. The *T* criterion is computed as $(12T/100)^{1/4}$, the *AIC* criterion is computed as $\log \sigma^2(k) + 2/T$, and the *SBC* criterion as $\sigma^2(k) + 1/\sqrt{T}$.

Appendix 2: Optimal lag length in a bivariate unrestricted VAR

Dependent series: GDP and unemployment rate, France

Number of lags	*AIC*	*SBC*	*Loglikelihood*	*χ^2 statistic*	*p-value*
1	**−17.550**	**−17.411**	1059.026	*	*
2	−17.529	−17.295	1052.967	−12.118	1.00
3	−17.487	−17.159	1045.758	−14.419	1.00
4	−17.461	−17.036	1039.484	−12.548	1.00
5	−17.480	−16.958	1035.838	−7.2923	1.00
6	−17.478	−16.857	1030.963	−9.7510	1.00
7	−17.425	−16.705	1023.201	−15.524	1.00
8	−17.406	−16.585	1017.436	−11.530	1.00

Notes: The three selection criteria for the optimal number of lags to be included in a VAR are (a) at the minimum value for the Akaike Information Criterion, (b) at the minimum value of the Schwarz Baysian Criterion, or (c) at the highest number of lags where we would reject the restricted model in favor of the more general model (where the more general model includes one additional lag). Rejection is based on a likelihood ratio test, where the test statistic is generated by dividing the likelihood of the restricted model by the likelihood of the more general model, then taking logs and multiplying by −2. The resulting test statistic is χ^2 distributed, with the degrees of freedom equal to the number of zero restrictions. * implies that there is no more restricted model available, and we would never reject the most specific model, with only one lag.

Dependent series: GDP and unemployment rate, Germany

Number of lags	*AIC*	*SBC*	*Loglikelihood*	*χ^2 statistic*	*p-value*
1	−14.677	−14.537	871.966	*	*
2	−14.765	−14.528	873.726	3.521	0.474
3	−14.692	−14.360	866.130	−15.192	1.00
4	−15.368	**−14.939**	901.668	**71.076**	**$1.34E^{-14}$**
5	−15.425	−14.897	901.201	−0.935	1.00
6	**−15.429**	−14.801	897.735	−6.931	1.00
7	−15.371	−14.643	890.801	−13.869	1.00
8	−15.428	−14.598	890.251	−1.100	1.00

Notes: The three selection criteria for the optimal number of lags to be included in a VAR are (a) at the minimum value for the Akaike Information Criterion, (b) at the minimum value of the Schwarz Baysian Criterion, or (c) at the highest number of lags where we would reject the restricted model in favor of the more general model (where the more general model includes one additional lag). Rejection is based on a likelihood ratio test, where the test statistic is generated by dividing the likelihood of the restricted model by the likelihood of the more general model, then taking logs and multiplying by −2. The resulting test statistic is χ^2 distributed, with the degrees of freedom equal to the number of zero restrictions. * implies that there is no more restricted model available, and we would never reject the most specific model, with only one lag.

Dependent series: GDP and unemployment rate, Italy

Number of lags	*AIC*	*SBC*	*Loglikelihood*	χ^2 *statistic*	*p-value*
1	−14.764	**−14.625**	891.842	*	*
2	−14.701	−14.467	884.708	−14.269	1.00
3	**−14.767**	−14.438	885.233	1.050	0.902
4	−14.737	−14.312	880.111	−10.244	1.00
5	−14.748	−14.225	877.360	−5.502	1.00
6	−14.715	−14.095	872.139	−10.441	1.00
7	−14.662	−13.942	865.747	−12.784	1.00
8	−14.592	−13.771	858.425	−14.644	1.00

Notes: The three selection criteria for the optimal number of lags to be included in a VAR are (a) at the minimum value for the Akaike Information Criterion, (b) at the minimum value of the Schwarz Baysian Criterion, or (c) at the highest number of lags where we would reject the restricted model in favor of the more general model (where the more general model includes one additional lag). Rejection is based on a likelihood ratio test, where the test statistic is generated by dividing the likelihood of the restricted model by the likelihood of the more general model, then taking logs and multiplying by −2. The resulting test statistic is χ^2 distributed, with the degrees of freedom equal to the number of zero restrictions. * implies that there is no more restricted model available, and we would never reject the most specific model, with only one lag.

Dependent series: GDP and unemployment rate, United Kingdom

Number of lags	*AIC*	*SBC*	*Loglikelihood*	χ^2 *statistic*	*p-value*
1	−15.627	**−15.492**	998.288	*	*
2	−15.709	−15.484	999.687	2.796	0.592
3	−15.709	−15.392	995.782	−7.809	1.00
4	**−15.734**	−15.325	993.512	−4.540	1.00
5	−15.663	−15.160	985.282	−16.460	1.00
6	−15.631	−15.033	979.469	−11.626	1.00
7	−15.558	−14.865	971.277	−16.384	1.00
8	−15.548	−14.758	966.865	−8.824	1.00

Notes: The three selection criteria for the optimal number of lags to be included in a VAR are (a) at the minimum value for the Akaike Information Criterion, (b) at the minimum value of the Schwarz Baysian Criterion, or (c) at the highest number of lags where we would reject the restricted model in favor of the more general model (where the more general model includes one additional lag). Rejection is based on a likelihood ratio test, where the test statistic is generated by dividing the likelihood of the restricted model by the likelihood of the more general model, then taking logs and multiplying by −2. The resulting test statistic is χ^2 distributed, with the degrees of freedom equal to the number of zero restrictions. * implies that there is no more restricted model available, and we would never reject the most specific model, with only one lag.

Appendix 3: Johansen cointegration tests

Dependent series: GDP and unemployment rate, France

Number of lags	*1. Eigenvalue*	*2. Eigenvalue*	*LR: No CE*	*LR: 1 CE*
1	0.360	0.020	55.938	2.432**
2	0.298	0.021	44.592	2.466**
3	0.270	0.022	39.810	2.626**
4	0.303	0.019	44.539	2.281**
5	0.245	0.024	35.438	2.773**
6	0.243	0.028	35.283	3.282**
7	0.231	0.028	33.147	3.196**
8	0.308	0.029	44.846	3.274**

Notes: The second and third columns present the two eigenvalues of the matrix *M*. Columns 4 and 5 are the likelihood ratio test statistic as presented in equation (20) and (20′) for the Johansen cointegration trace test. The benchmark (unrestricted) model is of full rank, rank = 2. Critical values under the assumption of a constant in the cointegrating relation and no intercept in the VAR for rank zero are 19.96 at the 5 per cent significance level and 24.60 at the one per cent significance level. Critical values for rank 1 are 9.24 (12.97) at the 5 per cent (1 per cent) significance level (Osterwald-Lenum, 1992). ** implies that we cannot reject the hypothesis at the 5 per cent significance level, and * implies that we cannot reject the hypothesis at the one per cent significance level.

Dependent series: GDP and unemployment rate, Germany

Number of lags	*1. Eigenvalue*	*2. Eigenvalue*	*LR: No CE*	*LR: 1 CE*
1	0.200	0.072	35.052	8.754**
2	0.385	0.060	64.066	7.269**
3	0.562	0.071	104.494	8.603**
4	0.237	0.082	40.861	9.812*
5	0.172	0.059	28.367	6.874**
6	0.143	0.072	25.802	8.403**
7	0.172	0.074	29.735	8.621**
8	0.159	0.060	26.096	6.810**

Notes: The second and third columns present the two eigenvalues of the matrix *M*. Columns four and five are the likelihood ratio test statistic as presented in equation (20) and (20′) for the Johansen cointegration trace test. The benchmark (unrestricted) model is of full rank, rank = 2. Critical values under the assumption of a constant in the cointegrating relation and no intercept in the VAR for rank zero are 19.96 at the 5 per cent significance level and 24.60 at the one per cent significance level. Critical values for rank one are 9.24 (12.97) at the 5 per cent (one per cent) significance level (Osterwald-Lenum, 1992). ** implies that we cannot reject the hypothesis at the 5 per cent significance level, and * implies that we cannot reject the hypothesis at the 1 per cent significance level.

Dependent series: GDP and unemployment rate, Italy

Number of lags	*1. Eigenvalue*	*2. Eigenvalue*	*LR: No CE*	*LR: 1 CE*
1	0.177	0.029	26.923	3.578**
2	0.141	0.027	21.271	3.207**
3	0.191	0.034	29.093	4.054**
4	0.205	0.022	29.406	2.576**
5	0.273	0.022	39.558	2.546**
6	0.236	0.030	34.458	3.520**
7	0.216	0.031	31.343	3.565**
8	0.188	0.031	27.107	3.547**

Notes: The second and third column present the two eigenvalues of the matrix M. Columns four and five are the likelihood ratio test statistic as presented in equation (20) and (20′) for the Johansen cointegration trace test. The benchmark (unrestricted) model is of full rank, rank = 2. Critical values under the assumption of a constant in the cointegrating relation and no intercept in the VAR for rank zero are 19.96 at the 5 per cent significance level and 24.60 at the one per cent significance level. Critical values for rank 1 are 9.24 (12.97) at the 5 per cent (one per cent) significance level (Osterwald-Lenum, 1992). ** implies that we cannot reject the hypothesis at the 5 per cent significance level, and * implies that we cannot reject the hypothesis at the one per cent significance level.

Dependent series: GDP and unemployment rate, United Kingdom

Number of lags	*1. Eigenvalue*	*2. Eigenvalue*	*LR: No CE*	*LR: 1 CE*
1	0.317	0.035	52.927	4.552**
2	0.340	0.056	59.506	7.219**
3	0.287	0.051	48.867	6.547**
4	0.255	0.037	41.099	4.633**
5	0.220	0.031	34.336	3.826**
6	0.172	0.027	26.411	3.312**
7	0.158	0.026	23.891	3.133**
8	0.191	0.022	28.043	2.660**

Notes: The second and third column present the two eigenvalues of the matrix M. Columns four and five are the likelihood ratio test statistic as presented in equation (20) and (20′) for the Johansen cointegration trace test. The benchmark (unrestricted) model is of full rank, rank = 2. Critical values under the assumption of a constant in the cointegrating relation and no intercept in the VAR for rank 0 are 19.96 at the 5 per cent significance level and 24.60 at the one per cent significance level. Critical values for rank one are 9.24 (12.97) at the 5 per cent (one per cent) significance level (Osterwald-Lenum, 1992). ** implies that we cannot reject the hypothesis at the 5 per cent significance level, and * implies that we cannot reject the hypothesis at the one per cent significance level.

Appendix 4: Optimal lag length in a bivariate unrestricted VECM

Dependent series: GDP and unemployment rate, France

Number of lags	*AIC*	*SBC*	*Loglikelihood*	χ^2 *statistic*	*p-value*
1	**−17.675**	**−17.466**	1069.511	*	*
2	−17.670	−17.367	1064.376	−10.271	1.00
3	−17.633	−17.234	1057.359	−14.032	1.00
4	−17.667	−17.171	1054.493	−5.734	1.00
5	−17.638	−17.044	1047.986	−13.012	1.00
6	−17.621	−16.928	1042.187	−11.599	1.00
7	−17.579	−16.787	1035.011	−14.351	1.00
8	−17.650	−16.757	1034.240	1.543	1.00

Notes: The three selection criteria for the optimal number of lags to be included in a VECM are (a) at the minimum value for the Akaike Information Criterion, (b) at the minimum value of the Schwarz Baysian Criterion, or (c) at the highest number of lags where we would reject the restricted model in favor of the more general model (where the more general model includes one additional lag). Rejection is based on a likelihood ratio test, where the test statistic is generated by dividing the likelihood of the restricted model by the likelihood of the more general model, then taking logs and multiplying by −2. The resulting test statistic is χ^2 distributed, with the degrees of freedom equal to the number of zero restrictions. * implies that there is no more restricted model available, and we would never reject the most specific model, with only one lag.

Dependent series: GDP and unemployment rate, Germany

Number of lags	*AIC*	*SBC*	*Loglikelihood*	χ^2 *statistic*	*p-value*
1	−14.816	−14.557	885.115	*	*
2	−15.165	−14.810	902.125	34.019	$7.39E^{-7}$
3	−15.432	−14.981	914.075	**23.902**	**0.00**
4	**−15.551**	**−15.002**	917.193	6.234	0.18
5	−15.525	−14.877	911.947	−10.490	1.00
6	−15.494	−14.746	906.435	−11.024	1.00
7	−15.471	−14.621	901.358	−10.154	1.00
8	−15.512	−14.560	899.894	−2.929	1.00

Notes: The three selection criteria for the optimal number of lags to be included in a VECM are (a) at the minimum value for the Akaike Information Criterion, (b) at the minimum value of the Schwarz Baysian Criterion, or (c) at the highest number of lags where we would reject the restricted model in favor of the more general model (where the more general model includes one additional lag). Rejection is based on a likelihood ratio test, where the test statistic is generated by dividing the likelihood of the restricted model by the likelihood of the more general model, then taking logs and multiplying by −2. The resulting test statistic is χ^2 distributed, with the degrees of freedom equal to the number of zero restrictions. * implies that there is no more restricted model available, and we would never reject the most specific model, with only one lag.

Dependent series: GDP and unemployment rate, Italy

Number of lags	*AIC*	*SBC*	*Loglikelihood*	χ^2 *statistic*	*p-value*
1	−14.775	**−14.566**	895.521	*	*
2	−14.699	−14.395	887.592	−15.857766	1.00
3	−14.781	−14.382	889.093	3.002	0.56
4	−14.768	−14.272	884.939	−8.310	1.00
5	**−14.819**	−14.225	884.498	−0.881	1.00
6	−14.780	−14.088	878.857	−11.283	1.00
7	−14.725	−13.933	872.326	−13.062	1.00
8	−14.643	−13.750	864.351	−15.950	1.00

Notes: The three selection criteria for the optimal number of lags to be included in a VECM are (a) at the minimum value for the Akaike Information Criterion, (b) at the minimum value of the Schwarz Baysian Criterion, or (c) at the highest number of lags where we would reject the restricted model in favor of the more general model (where the more general model includes one additional lag). Rejection is based on a likelihood ratio test, where the test statistic is generated by dividing the likelihood of the restricted model by the likelihood of the more general model, then taking logs and multiplying by −2. The resulting test statistic is χ^2 distributed, with the degrees of freedom equal to the number of zero restrictions. * implies that there is no more restricted model available, and we would never reject the most specific model, with only one lag.

Dependent series: GDP and unemployment rate, United Kingdom

Number of lags	*AIC*	*SBC*	*Loglikelihood*	χ^2 *statistic*	*p-value*
1	−15.633	**−15.432**	1001.706	*	*
2	−15.705	−15.413	1002.435	1.458	0.83
3	−15.686	−15.302	997.399	−10.071	1.00
4	**−15.719**	−15.241	995.581	−3.636	1.00
5	−15.652	−15.081	987.628	−15.906	1.00
6	−15.605	−14.939	980.934	−13.388	1.00
7	−15.530	−14.767	972.542	−16.784	1.00
8	−15.551	−14.692	970.090	−4.905	1.00

Notes: The three selection criteria for the optimal number of lags to be included in a VECM are (a) at the minimum value for the Akaike Information Criterion, (b) at the minimum value of the Schwarz Baysian Criterion, or (c) at the highest number of lags where we would reject the restricted model in favor of the more general model (where the more general model includes one additional lag). Rejection is based on a likelihood ratio test, where the test statistic is generated by dividing the likelihood of the restricted model by the likelihood of the more general model, then taking logs and multiplying by −2. The resulting test statistic is χ^2 distributed, with the degrees of freedom equal to the number of zero restrictions. * implies that there is no more restricted model available, and we would never reject the most specific model, with only one lag.

Appendix 5: VECM: Germany, 4 lags and a reunification dummy

Dependent series	Δu_t	Δy_t
Cointegrating Equation	−0.013	−0.082
	(0.004)	(0.029)
Δu_{t-1}	0.582	−2.570
	(0.096)	(0.667)
Δu_{t-2}	−0.117	1.432
	(0.106)	(0.740)
Δu_{t-3}	0.045	0.227
	(0.103)	(0.720)
Δu_{t-4}	0.002	−0.202
	(0.087)	(0.612)
Δy_{t-1}	−0.034	−0.305
	(0.014)	(0.099)
Δy_{t-2}	−0.034	−0.240
	(0.015)	(0.104)
Δy_{t-3}	−0.035	−0.124
	(0.014)	(0.097)
Δy_{t-4}	−0.027	0.457
	(0.013)	(0.092)
Dummy 1991Q1	−0.007	0.006
	(0.001)	(0.010)

Comments: Numbers are the coefficients of the VECM. Numbers in parenthesis are standard errors.

Notes

1 Introduction and Overview

1. In the course of this book, we will present results in terms of unemployment levels and growth rates. However, these are not robust, and the introduction of certain parameters, such as exogenous productivity rates, will induce a level shift in the results. What remains robust, despite the inclusion of these parameters, will be the interdependency between changes in unemployment and changes in growth rates, the focus of our analysis.
2. To be discussed below.
3. We may think of search costs in terms of output forgone, which would imply that savings must exceed investment by exactly that amount. Assuming that search costs grow proportionally with output – otherwise search costs would become negligible in a growing economy – this implies that savings must exceed investment by a constant proportion. We may therefore think of the savings rate s above as taking already account of this fact.

3 A Model of Economic Growth and Structural Change

1. To be defined below.
2. As the number of manufacturers is undetermined, we normalize it to unity, assuming perfect competition nonetheless.
3. This may explain the US hype over international property rights.

4 Structural Change and Search Frictions

1. To be defined below.
2. As the number of manufacturers is undetermined, we normalize it to unity, assuming perfect competition nonetheless.

6 Aggregate Demand and Keynesian Unemployment

1. That is, a particular product is available if and only if one would devote infinite resources for its procuration, or pay an infinite price.
2. We will give a more precise interpretation for m_t below.
3. A more precise formulation in the spirit of the endogenous growth literature is presented in chapter 4.
4. Note that as τ converges to zero, $\dot{n}_t$ also represents the change from time t to $t + \tau$.
5. Note that we are deriving this result under the assumption that households suspend savings for a single period, which is not crucial along the equilibrium path (Blanchard and Fischer, p. 42).

6. This is equivalent to stating that ϵ in equation (6.8) is unknown at the time wage contracts are signed.
7. Indeed, a negative impact can be justified as well. In particular, if one assumes that the number of potential innovations is limited, and the easiest innovations have been tackled first, then a large number of already innovated products imply that it takes more and more effort to achieve an additional innovation.
8. These models data back to the neoclassical synthesis approach of most modern macroeconomic textbooks. For a recent survey and a unifying framework, see Klausinger (2000).

7 Job Creation and Destruction?

1. The emphasis here is on simplicity rather than rigor. For a more precise and rigorous exposition, see chapter 4 of this book.
2. To be discussed below.
3. Indeed, an even less stringent condition, $\alpha' = 0$ is required to obtain equality of job creation and destruction. Hence a mixed economy with homothetic preferences (as in Kongsamut, Rebelo and Xie, 1997) is in that respect analytically equivalent to Aghion and Howitt (1994).
4. In contrast to the prediction of the convergence hypothesis, even highly integrated regions may well exhibit very different growth rates, provided persistent stochastic supply shocks would be large enough to give one region an unrecoverable competitive advantage (Maier, 1999).
5. These are the North, North West, Yorkshire and Humberside, East Midlands, West Midlands, East Anglia, South East, South West, Wales, Scotland and Northern Ireland.
6. Note that we have eliminated all individual cases which are still seeking employment (53,464 cases), as well as all individuals which have not returned to work for some reason or another. This leaves us with a sample of 238,036 cases, or about 40 per cent of the unemployed, who return to jobs (Sweeney, 1996b), whereas the remaining 60 per cent cannot be termed structurally unemployed in the spirit of Mortensen (1986) or Pissarides (1990). The industries are agriculture, hunting, forestry and fishing; mining and quarrying, including oil and gas extraction; manufacturing (see note below); electricity, gas and water supply; construction; wholesale and retail trade, repairs, hotels and restaurants; transport, storage and communications; financial intermediation, real estate, renting and business activities; public administration, national defense and compulsory social security; education, health and social work; and other services, including sewage and refuse disposal. The manufacturing industry can be divided into manufacturing classes, which are food, beverages and tobacco products; textiles and leather products; wood and wood products; pulp, paper and products, printing and publishing; solid nuclear fuels, oil refining; chemicals and man-made fibers; rubber and plastic products; other non-metallic mineral products; basic metal and metal products; machinery and equipment; electrical and optical equipment; transport equipment; and other manufacturing.

7. Note that the following procedure is invalid in the presence of a unit root, $\rho = 1$. We shall therefore present a unit root test together with the results in Table 7.1, to show the validity of the estimation procedure.
8. The individual unemployment rate is higher than the national aggregate for the period in question. The difference is due to the measurement of intra-monthly unemployment spells, which are omitted in national aggregates, and the fact that national unemployment statistics have a different (and much stricter) definition of unemployment compared to claimant counts.
9. As the result is derived using maximum likelihood methods, we cannot give a coefficient of determination. The log likelihood is presented instead, but it only allows us to differentiate between different models, but does not reveal an overall goodness of fit.

8 On the Causality between Economic Growth and Unemployment

1. Note that this relation would hold in all three models presented here.

9 The Dynamics of Economic Growth and Unemployment

1. A more elaborate version can be found in chapter 6.
2. Note that the fact that both variables are integrated of order one rules out the possibility of explosive growth.

10 Conclusions and Policy Recommendations

1. The standard deviation of GDP is slightly above one per cent for most countries.
2. In the model of section 10.2, this is represented by the fact that productivity ϕn_t increases in knowledge. To give an illustrative example, note that it should be much easier to innovate a laptop computer with a given knowledge of desktops, rather than starting from scratch.

Bibliography

Acemoglu, D., Aghion, P., and Violante, G. (2000), Deunionization, Technical Change and Inequality, mimeo, Cambridge and London.

Agell, J. and Lommerud, K. E. (1993), Egalitarianism and Growth, *Scandinavian Journal of Economics*, vol. 95(3), 559–79.

Aghion, P. and Howitt, P. (1991), Unemployment: a Symptom of Stagnation or a Side-effect of Growth?, *European Economic Review*, vol. 35, 535–41.

Aghion, P. and Howitt, P. (1992), A Model of Growth through Creative Destruction, *Econometrica*, vol. 60, 323–51.

Aghion, P. and Howitt, P. (1994), Growth and Unemployment, *Review of Economic Studies*, vol. 61(3), 477–94.

Aghion, P. and Howitt, P. (1998), *Endogenous Growth Theory*, Cambridge, MA, MIT Press.

Agiakoglu, C. and Newbold, P. (1992), Empirical Evidence on Dickey–Fuller type Tests, *Journal of Time Series Analysis*, vol. 13, 471–83.

Akerlof, G. and Yellen, J. (1990), The Fair Wage-Effort Hypothesis and Unemployment, *Quarterly Journal of Economics*, vol. 105(2), 255–83.

Altissimo, F. and Violante, G. (1999), Nonlinear VAR: Some Theory and an Application to US GNP and Unemployment, *Temi di Discussione della Banca d'Italia*, no. 338.

Altissimo, F. and Violante, G. (2001), The Nonlinear Dynamics of Output and Unemployment in the US, *Journal of Applied Econometrics*, vol. 16(4), 461–86.

Ambler, S., and Cardia, E. (1998), The Cyclical Behavior of Wages and Profits under Imperfect Competition, *Canadian Journal of Economics*, vol. 31(1), 155–73.

Ambler, S., Cardia, E., and Farazli, J. (1999), Export Promotion, Learning by Doing and Growth, *Journal of Economic Dynamics and Control*, vol. 23(5–6), 747–72.

Angrist, J. D. and Kruger, A. B. (1999), Empirical Strategies in Labor Economics, in O. Ashenfelter and D. Card (eds), *Handbook of Labor Economics*, vol. 3A, Amsterdam, Elsevier, 1276–366.

Arellano, M. and Bond, S. (1991), Some Tests for Specification of Panel Data: Monte Carlo Evidence and an Application to Employment Equations, *Review of Economic Studies*, vol. 57(1), 127–34.

Attfield, C. L. F. and Silverstone, B. (1998), Okun's Law, Cointegration and Gap Variables, *Journal of Macroeconomics*, vol. 20(3), 625–37.

Bailey, M., Hulten, C., and Campbell, D. (1992), Productivity Dynamics in Manufacturing Plants, *Brookings Papers on Economic Activity: Microeconomics*, vol. 1, 187–267.

Ball, L. (1997), Disinflation and the NAIRU, in C. Romer and D. Romer (eds), *Reducing Inflation: Motivation and Strategy*, Chicago, University of Chicago Press.

Baltagi, B. H. (1995), *Econometrics of Panel Data*, Chichester, John Wiley and Sons.

Banerjee, A., and Hendry, D. (1992), Testing Integration and Cointegration, *Oxford Bulletin of Economics and Statistics*, vol. 54(3), 225–55.

Banerjee, A., Dolado, J., Galbraith, J. W., and Hendry, D. (1993), *Co-Integration, Error-Correction, and the Econometric Analysis of Non-Stationary Data*, Oxford, Oxford University Press.

Barro, R. J. (1990), Government Spending in a Simple Model of Endogenous Growth, *Journal of Political Economy*, vol. 98, S103–S125.

Barro, R. J. and Sala-i-Martin, X. (1992), Convergence, *Journal of Political Economy*, vol. 100, 223–51.

Barro, R. J. and Sala-i-Martin, X. (1995), *Economic Growth*, New York, McGraw-Hill.

Barth, E. and Zweimüller, J. (1995), Relative Wages under Decentralized and Corporatist Bargaining Systems, *Scandinavian Journal of Economics*, vol. 97(3), 369–84.

Baumol, W. J. (1967), *Welfare Economics and the Theory of the State*, London, Bell.

Bean, C. and Pissarides, C. (1993), Unemployment, Consumption and Growth, *European Economic Review*, vol. 37, 837–59.

Bentolila, S., and Dolado, J. (1994), Labour Flexibility and Wages, *Economic Policy*, vol. 24, 53–100.

Bertola, G. (1993), Factor Shares and Savings in Endogenous Growth Models, *American Economic Review,* vol. 83(5), 1184–98.

Bertola, G. (1994), Flexibility, Investment, and Growth, *Journal of Monetary Economics*, vol. 34(2), 215–38.

Beveridge W. (1942), *Social Insurance Allied Services*, Cmd 6404, London, HMSO.

Bishop, J. and Haveman, R. (1979), Selective Employment Subsidies: Can Okun's Law be Repealed?, *American Economic Review*, vol. 69(2), 124–30.

Blanchard, O. J. (1997), The Medium Run, *Brookings Papers on Economic Activity: Macroeconomics*, vol. 2, 89–157.

Blanchard, O. J. (1998a), Thinking about Unemployment, Paolo Baffi Lecture on Money and Finance, Rome.

Blanchard, O. J. (1998b), Revisiting European Unemployment: Unemployment, Capital and Factor Prices, *NBER Working Paper*, no. 6566.

Blanchard, O. J. (2000), The Economics of Unemployment. Shocks, Institutions, and Interactions, *The Lionel Robbins Memorial Lectures*, London School of Economics and Political Sciences.

Blanchard, O. J. and Fischer, S. (1992), *Lectures in Macroeconomics*, Cambridge, MA, MIT Press.

Blanchard, O. J. and Quah, D. (1989), The Dynamic Effects of Aggregate Demand and Supply Disturbances, *American Economic Review*, vol. 79(4), 655–73.

Blanchard, O. J. and Wolfers, J. (2000), Shocks and Institutions and the Rise of European Unemployment, *Economic Journal*, vol. 110(1), 1–33.

Böheim, R. and Taylor, M. (1999), Residential Mobility, Housing Tenure and the Labour Market in Britain, *ISER Working Paper*, no. 16, Colchester.

Boskin, M. J., Dulberger, E. R., Gordon, R. J., Eriliches, Z., and Jorgenson, D. W. (1997), The CPI Commission: Findings and Recommendations, *American Economic Review*, vol. 87(2), 78–83.

Bowles, S. (1985), The Production Process and in a Competitive Economy: Walrasian, Neo-Hobbesian and Marxian Models, *American Economic Review*, vol. 75(1), 16–36.

Brainard, W. and Tobin, J. (1968), Pitfalls in Financial Model-Building, *American Economic Review*, vol. 58(2), 99–122.

Bresnahan, T., and Trajtenberg, M. (1995), General Purpose Technologies: 'Engines of Growth', *Journal of Econometrics*, vol. 65, 83–108.

Bulli, S. (2000), Jobless Growth: an Empirical Analysis of the Effects of Technological Progress on Employment, *Summer School of the European Economic Association*, Barcelona.

Bunzel, H., Jensen, P., Westergård-Nielsen, N. (1993), *Panel Data and Labour Market Dynamics*, Amsterdam, North-Holland.

Caballero, R. J. and Hammour, M. L. (1996), On the Timing and Efficiency of Creative Destruction, *Quarterly Journal of Economics*, vol. 111(3), 805–52.

Caballero, R. J. and Hammour, M. L. (1997), Jobless Growth: Appropriability, Factor Stabilization, and Unemployment, *NBER Working Paper*, no. W6221.

Cahuc, P. and Michel, P. (1996), Minimum Wage Unemployment and Growth, *European Economic Review*, vol. 40, 1463–82.

Calmfors, L. and Driffill, J. (1988), Bargaining Structure, Corporatism, and Macroeconomic Performance, *Economic Policy*, vol. 6(1), 13–61.

Campbell, J. Y. and Mankiw, N. G. (1987), Are Output Fluctuations Persistent?, *Quarterly Journal of Economics*, vol. 102(4), 857–80.

Campbell, J. Y. and Mankiw, N. G. (1989), International Evidence on the Persistence of Economic Fluctuations, *Journal of Monetary Economics*, vol. 23(2), 319–33.

Candelon, B. and Hecq, A. (1998), Stability of Okun's Law in a Codependent System, *IRES Working Paper*, Université Catholique de Louvain.

Caves, R. E., and Barton, D. R. (1990), *Efficiency in U.S. Manufacturing Industries*, Cambridge, MA, MIT Press.

Chenery, H. B. (1960), Patterns of Industrial Growth, *American Economic Review*, vol. 50, 624–54.

Clark, C. (1957), *The Conditions of Economic Progress*, London, McGraw-Hill.

Cooley, T. F. and Smith, B. D. (1989), Dynamic Coalition Formation and Equilibrium Policy Selection, *Journal of Monetary Economics*, vol. 24(2), 211–33.

Courtney, H. (1991), The Beveridge Curve and Okun's Law: a Re-examination of Fundamental Macroeconomic Relationships in the United States, Massachusetts Institute of Technology, Cambridge, MA.

Daveri, F. and Tabellini, G. (2000), Unemployment, Growth and Taxation in Industrial Countries, *Economic Policy*, vol. 30, 47–104.

David, P. A. (1990), The Dynamo and the Computer: an Historical Perspective on the Modern Productivity Paradox, *American Economic Review*, vol. 80(2), 355–61.

Davis, S. J. and Haltiwanger, J. (1999), Gross Job Flows, in O. Ashenfelter and D. Card (eds), *Handbook of Labor Economics*, vol. 3B, Amsterdam, Elsevier, 2711–805.

Davis, S. J., Haltiwanger, J., and Schuh, S. (1998), *Job Creation and Destruction*, Cambridge, MA, MIT Press.

De Groot, H. (1996), The Struggle for Rents in a Schumpeterian Economy, *Discussion Paper*, no. 9651, Center for Economic Research, Tilburg University.

De Groot, H. (2000), *Growth, Unemployment, and Deindustrialization*, Cheltenham, Edward Elgar.

Diamond, P. A. (1982), Aggregate Demand Management in Search Equilibrium, *Journal of Political Economy*, vol. 90(2), 881–94.

Dickey, D. A. and Fuller, W. A. (1979), Distribution of the Estimators for Autoregressive Time Series with a Unit Root, *Journal of the American Statistical Association*, vol. 74(366), Theory and methods section, 427–31.

Dolado, J. J. and Jimeno, J. F. (1997), The Causes of Spanish Unemployment: a Structural VAR Approach, *European Economic Review*, vol. 41, 1281–307.

Echevarria, C. (1997), Changes in Sectoral Composition Associates with Economic Growth, *International Economic Review*, vol. 38(2), 431–52.

Erber, G. (2001), Okun's Law and the Employment Crisis, in H. Hagemann and S. Seiter (eds), *Growth Theory and Growth Policy*, London, Routledge.

European Commission (1993), *White Paper on Growth, Competitiveness, Employment: The Challenges and Ways Forward into the 21st Century*, COM(93) 700, Brussels.

European Commission (1995), *Green Paper on Innovation*, COM(95) 688, Brussels.

Evans, G. W. (1989), Output and Unemployment Dynamics in the United States: 1950–1985, *Journal of Applied Econometrics*, vol. 4, 213–37.

Flabbi, L. and Ichino, A. (1998), Productivity, Seniority, and Wages, *European University Institute Working Paper*, no. ECO 98/11.

Foster, L., Haltiwanger, J., and Krizan, C. J. (1998), Aggregate Productivity Growth: Lessons from Microeconomic Evidence, *NBER Working Paper*, no. 6803.

Gali, J. (1999), Technology, Employment, and the Business Cycle: Do Technology Shocks Explain Aggregate Fluctuations?, *American Economic Review*, vol. 89(1), 249–71.

Gordon, R. (1999), Has the 'New Economy' Rendered the Productivity Slowdown Obsolete?, mimeo, Northwestern University.

Granger, E. (1969), Investigating Causal Relationships by Econometric Models and Cross-spectral Methods, *Econometrica*, vol. 37, 424–38.

Granger, E. (1988), Some Recent Developments in a Concept of Causality, *Journal of Econometrics*, vol. 39, 199–211.

Greenspan, A. (1998), Question: Is there a New Economy, http://www.federalreserve.org//boarddocs/speeches/1998/19980904.htm

Griliches, Z. (1994), Productivity, R & D, and the Data Constraint, *American Economic Review*, vol. 84(1), 1–23.

Grossman, G. M. and Helpman, E. (1991a), *Innovation and Growth in the Global Economy*, Cambridge, MA and London, The MIT Press.

Grossman, G. M., and Helpman, E. (1991b), Quality Ladders in the Theory of Growth, *Review of Economic Studies*, vol. 58, 43–61.

Gujarati, D. N. (1995), *Basic Econometrics*, New York, McGraw-Hill.

Hage, J. (1998), An Endogenous Theory of Economic Growth from Innovation: Organizational and Institutional Determinants, Feedbacks, and Disequilibria, Presidential Address, Society for the Advancements of Socio-Economics, Vienna.

Hagemann, H. (1993), Technological Unemployment, in P. Arestis and M. Marshall (eds), *The Political Economy of Full Employment: Conservativism, Corporatism and Institutional Change*, Aldershot, Edward Elgar.

Harberger, A. C. (1998), A Vision of the Growth Process, *American Economic Review*, vol. 88(1), 1–33.

Hausmann, J. A. (1978), Specification Tests in Econometrics, *Econometrica*, vol. 46, 1251–71.

Heise, A. (2000), New Politics – Einige makroökonomisce Überlegungen zum Bündnis für Arbeit, *WSI-Mitteilungen*, no. 7, 444–52.
Helpman, E. (1998), *General Purpose Technologies and Economic Growth*, Cambridge, MA, MIT Press.
Holloway, T. M. (1989), An Updated Look at Okun's Law, *Social Science Quarterly*, vol. 70(2), 497–504.
Hoon, H. T. (1998), Capital Expansion, Endogenous Growth and Equilibrium Unemployment, *Australian Economic Papers*, vol. 37(3), 257–72.
Irmen, A. and Wigger, B. U. (2000), Trade Union Objectives and Economic Growth, *University of Canterbury Discussion Paper*, no. 2002, Christchurch.
Johansen, S. (1991), Estimation and Hypothesis Testing of Cointegration Vectors in Gaussian Vector Autoregressive Models, *Econometrica*, vol. 59, 1551–80.
Johansen, S. (1995), *Likelihood-Based Inference in Cointegrated Vector Autoregressive Models*, Oxford, Oxford University Press.
Jones, C. I. (1995), R&D-Based Models of Economic Growth, *Journal of Political Economy*, vol. 103(4), 759–84.
Jones, C. I. (1998), *Introduction to Economic Growth*, New York, W. W. Norton.
Jorgenson, D. W. and Stiroh, K. J. (2000), Raising the Speed Limit: U.S. Economic Growth in the Information Age, mimeo, Harvard University and Federal Reserve Bank of New York, paper presented at the XIIth Villa Mondragone International Economic Seminar.
Kaldor, N. (1961), *Essays on Economic Policy Stability and Growth*, London, Duckworth.
Kaldor, N. (1963), Capital Accumulation and Economic Growth, in F. A. Lutz and D. C. Hague (eds), *Proceedings of a Conference Held by the International Economics Association*, London, Macmillan.
Keuschnigg, C. (1997), Venture Capital: a Case for Investment Promotion, *Center for Economic Policy Research Discussion Paper*, no. 1887, London.
Keuschnigg, C. (1998), Investment Externality and a Corrective Subsidy, *International Tax and Public Finance*, vol. 5(4), 449–59.
Klausinger, H. (2000), Walras' Law and the IS–LM Model: a Tale of Progress and Regress, *Vienna University of Economics & B.A. Working Paper*, no. 69, Vienna.
Kongsamut, P., Rebelo, S., and Xie, D. (1997), Beyond Balanced Growth, *NBER Working Paper*, no. 6159.
Koput, K. W. and Powell, W. W. (2000), Science and Strategy: Organizational Evolution in a Knowledge-Intensive Field, mimeo, University of Arizona and Stanford University, paper presented at the Organization Science Winter Conference 2000.
Kuznets, S. (1957), Quantitative Aspects of the Economic Growth of Nations: II, *Economic Development and Change*, vol. 4(S), 3–111.
Lau, S. H. P. (1999), I(0) In, integration and cointegration out: Time Series Properties of Endogenous Growth Models, *Journal of Econometrics*, vol. 93(1), 1–24.
Lawlor, J. (1990), Monthly Unemployment Statistics: Maintaining a Consistent Series, *Employment Gazette*, 601–8.
Layard, R., Nickell, S., and Jackman R. (1991), *Unemployment: Macroeconomic Performance and the Labor Market*, Oxford and New York, Oxford University Press.
Leamer, E. (1983), Let's Take the Con out of Econometrics, *American Economic Review*, vol. 73(3), 31–43.

Lucas, R. E. (1988), On the Mechanics of Economic Development, *Journal of Monetary Economics*, vol. 26, 3–42.

MacKinnon, J. G. (1990) Critical Values for Integration, *Economics Discussion Paper*, no. 90-4, University of California at San Diego.

Maddala, G. S. (1993), *The Econometrics of Panel Data*, Volumes I and II, Aldershot, Edward Elgar.

Maddala, G. S. and Kim, I. M. (1998), *Unit Roots, Cointegration, and Structural Change*, Cambridge, Cambridge University Press.

Maier, G. (1999), Externalities, Growth, and Regional Stagnation, *Working Paper in Growth and Employment in Europe: Sustainability and Competitiveness*, no. 3, Vienna University of Economics and Business Administration.

Mankiw, N. G. (1985), Small Menu Costs and Large Business Cycles: a Macroeconomic Model, *Quarterly Journal of Economics*, vol. 100(2), 529–38.

Mankiw, N. G., Romer, D., and Weil, D. N. (1992), A Contribution to the Empirics of Economic Growth, *Quarterly Journal of Economics*, vol. 107, 407–37.

Marimon, R. and Zilibotti, F. (1998), Actual versus Virtual Employment in Europe: Is Spain Different?, *European Economic Review*, vol. 42(1), 123–54.

Matsuyama, K. (1995), Complementarities and Cumulative Processes in Models of Monopolistic Competition, *Journal of Economic Literature*, vol. 33, 701–29.

McDonald, I. and Solow, R. (1985), Wages and Employment in a Segmented Labor Market, *Quarterly Journal of Economics*, vol. 100(4), 1115–41.

Meidner, R., Rehn, G. et al. (1953), Trade Unions and Full Employment, Report to the LO Congress 1951, Stockholm, Landsorganisationen i Sverige.

Messina-Granovsky, J. (2000), The Role of Product Market Regulations in the Process of Structural Change, mimeo, Firenze.

Moffitt, R. A. (1999), New Developments in Econometric Methods for Labor Market Analysis, in O. Ashenfelter and D. Card (eds), *Handbook of Labor Economics*, vol. 3A, Amsterdam, Elsevier, 1367–97.

Mortensen, D. T. (1986), Job Search and Labor Market Analysis, in O. Ashenfelter and R. Layard (eds), *Handbook of Labor Economics*, vol. 2, Amsterdam, North-Holland, 849–919.

Mortensen, D. T. and Pissarides, C. A. (1999), New Developments in Models of Search in the Labor Market, in O. Ashenfelter and D. Card (eds), *Handbook of Labor Economics*, vol. 3B, Amsterdam, Elsevier, 2567–627.

Mühlberger, U. (1999), Explaining Atypical Employment, in D. Kantarelis (ed.), *Global Business and Economics Review – Anthology 1999*, Worcester, 281–292.

Mühlberger, U. (2000), *Neue Formen der Beschäftigung, Arbeitsflexibilisierung durch Atypische Beschäftigung in Österreich*, Wien, Braumüller.

Muysken, J. (1999), Job Growth and Social Harmony: a Dutch Miracle?, *GAPE Spring Meeting*, Hohenheim.

Nickell, S. and Kong, P. (1988) Investigation Into the Power of Insiders in Wage Determination, *Oxford Applied Economics Discussion Paper*, no. 49.

Nowotny, E. (1999), *Grundzüge der österreichischen Wirtschaftspolitik*, Wien, Manz.

Office of National Statistics (1997), Background Information on Juvos data provided to the ESRC data archive, mimeo, London, ONS.

Okun A. (1970), Potential GDP: Its Measurement and Significance, reprinted in A. Okun (ed.), *The Political Economy of Prosperity*, Washington, DC, Brookings Institution.

Osterwald-Lenum, M. (1992), A Note with Quantiles of the Asymptotic Distribution of the Maximum Likelihood Cointegration Rank Test Statistics, *Oxford Bulletin of Economics and Statistics*, vol. 54, 461–72.

Oum, T. H., and Yu, C. (1998), *Winning Airlines: Productivity and Cost Competitiveness of the World's Major Airlines*, Transportation Research, Economics and Policy, vol. 6, Dordrecht, Kluwer.

Palokangas, T. (1996), Endogenous Growth and Collective Bargaining, *Journal of Economic Dynamics and Control*, vol. 20, 925–44.

Pelloni, A. (1997), Nominal Shocks, Endogenous Growth, and the Business Cycle, *Economic Journal*, vol. 107, 467–74.

Peretto, P. F. (1998), Market Power, Growth and Unemployment, *Duke Economics Working Paper*, no. 98–16.

Piore, M. (1987), Historical Perspectives and the Interpretation of Unemployment, *Journal of Economic Literature*, vol. 25(4), 1834–50.

Pissarides, C. A. (1984), Short-Run Equilibrium Dynamics of Unemployment, Vacancies and Real Wages, *American Economic Review*, vol. 74, 676–90.

Pissarides, C. A. (1985), Job Search and the Functioning of Labour Markets, in D. Carline et al. (eds), *Labour Economics*, London, Longman, 159–85.

Pissarides, C. A. (1987), Search, Wage Bargains, and Cycles, *Review of Economic Studies*, vol. 54, 473–83.

Pissarides, C. A. (1990), *Equilibrium Unemployment Theory*, London, Basil Blackwell.

Prescott, E. C. and Boyd, J. H. (1986), Dynamic Coalitions, Growth, and the Firm, *Staff Report*, no. 100, Federal Reserve Bank of Minneapolis.

Ragacs, C. (2000), Minimum Wages, Employment, and Endogenous Growth, Dissertation, University of Vienna.

Ragacs, C., and Zagler, M. (2002), Persistence of Shocks to Output in Austria and Theories of Economic Growth, *Empirica*, vol. 29(4), 305–17.

Raj, B. and Baltagi, B. H. (1992), *Panel Data Analysis*, Heidelberg, Physica-Verlag.

Rebelo, S. (1991), Long-Run Policy against Long-Run Growth, *Journal of Political Economy*, vol. 99, 500–21.

Rehn, G. (1952), The Problem of Stability: an Analysis and Some Policy Proposals, in R. Turvey (ed.), *Wages Policy under Full Employment*, London, William Hodge and Company.

Romer, P. M. (1986), Increasing Returns and Long-Run Growth, *Journal of Political Economy*, vol. 94, 1002–35.

Romer, P. M. (1990), Endogenous Technological Change, *Journal of Political Economy*, vol. 98, S71–S102.

Romer, P. M. (1994), The Origins of Endogenous Growth, *Journal of Economic Perspectives*, vol. 8, 3–22.

Rowthorn, R. E. (1992), Centralisation, Employment and Wage Dispersion, *Economic Journal*, vol. 102(2), 506–23.

Rubinstein, A. (1982), Perfect Equilibrium in a Bargaining Model, *Econometrica*, vol. 50(1), 97–109.

Said, S. E. and Dickey, D. A. (1984), Testing for Unit Roots in Autoregressive-Moving Average Models of Unknown Order, *Biometrika*, vol. 71, 599–607.

Sala-i-Martin, X. (1997), I Just Ran Four Million Regressions, *NBER Working Paper*, no. 6252.

Salter, W. (1966), *Productivity and Technical Change*, Cambridge, Cambridge University Press.

Schaik, A. and de Groot, H. (1998), Unemployment and Endogenous Growth, *Labour*, vol. 12(2), 189–219.

Schwert, G. W. (1989), Test for Unit Roots: a Monte Carlo Investigation, *Journal of Business and Economic Statistics*, vol. 7, 147–59.

Shapiro, C. and Stiglitz, J. E. (1984), Equilibrium Unemployment as a Worker Discipline Device, *American Economic Review,* vol. 74, 433–44.

Solow, R. M. (1956), A Contribution to the Theory of Economic Growth, *Quarterly Journal of Economics,* vol. 71, 65–94.

Solow, R. M. (1988), Growth Theory and After, *American Economic Review,* vol. 78(3), 307–17.

Solow, R. M. (1994), Perspectives on Growth Theory, *Journal of Economic Perspectives*, vol. 8, 45–54.

Strozzi, C. (2000), Union Coordination and Product Market Integration, mimeo, Firenze.

Sudit, E. F. (1996), *Effectiveness, Quality and Efficiency*, Dordrecht, Kluwer.

Sweeney, K. (1996a), Occupational Characteristics of the Claimant Unemployed, *Labour Market Trends*, 143–52.

Sweeney, K. (1996b), Destination of Leavers from the Claimant Unemployment, *Labour Market Trends*, 443–52.

Tobin, J. (1993), Price Flexibility and Output Stability: an Old Keynesian View, *Journal of Economic Perspectives*, vol. 7(1), 45–65.

Topel, R. (1999), Labor Markets and Economic Growth, in O. Ashenfelter and D. Card (eds), *Handbook of Labor Economics*, vol. 3C, Amsterdam, Elsevier, 2943–84.

Uhlig, H. and Yanagawa, N. (1996), Increasing the Capital Income Taxation May Lead to Faster Growth, *European Economic Review*, vol. 40(8), 1521–40.

Unger, B. and Zagler, M. (2003), Institutional and Organizational Determinants of Product Innovations, *Innovation: The European Journal of Social Science Research*, vol. 16(3), 227–44.

Wadhwani, S. and Wall, M. (1990), The Effects of Profit-Sharing on Employment, Wages, Stock Returns and Productivity: Evidence from UK Micro-Data, *Economic Journal*, vol. 100, 1–17.

Walther H. (1999), Ökonomische Funktionen der österreichischen Abfertigungsregelung, in Lichte von Theorie und Empirie, *Working Papers in Growth and Employment in Europe: Sustainability and Competitiveness,* no. 2, Vienna University of Economics & B. A.

Ward, H. and Bird, D. (1995), The JUVOS Cohort: a Longitudinal Database of the Claimant Unemployed, *Employment Gazette*, 345–50.

Zagler, M. (1992), *Les Conséquences Monétaires du Président Mitterand,* Wien, Diplomarbeit, Wirtschaftsuniversität.

Zagler, M. (1995), *Contributions to the Theory of Endogenous Growth under Market Imperfections*, dissertation, Wien, Wirtschaftsuniversität.

Zagler, M. (1998), Economic Growth and Protection of Emerging Markets in Eastern Europe, *Journal of Economic Development*, vol. 23, 21–36.

Zagler, M. (1999a), *Endogenous Growth, Market Imperfections, and Economic Policy*, Basingstoke, Macmillan, and New York, St Martin's Press.

Zagler, M. (1999b), Langfristige Nichtneutralität von Geld in einem endogenen Wachstumsmodel, *Kredit und Kapital*, vol. 32(4), 520–46.

Zagler, M. (2000), Productivity and Economic Performance: On the Sources of Economic Growth in Austria, *International Advances in Economic Research*, vol. 6(2), 210–20.

Zagler, M. (2001), Efficiency, Innovation and Productivity: On the Impact of Unemployment on Endogenous Growth, in H. Hagemann and S. Seiter (eds), *Growth Theory and Growth Policy*, London, Routledge, 15–26.

Zagler, M. (2003), Producer Services, Innovation, and Outsourcing in the New Economy, in L. Paganetto (ed.), *Knowledge Economy, Information Technologies and Growth*, Aldershot, Ashgate.

Author Index

Subject Index